Serving the Mentally Ill Elderly

Contributors

Elinore E. Lurie, Ph.D.
Department of Social and Behavioral
    Sciences
Institute for Health & Aging
University of California, San Francisco

James H. Swan, Ph.D.
Department of Social and Behavioral
    Sciences
Institute for Health & Aging
University of California, San Francisco

Nancy Gourash Bliwise, Ph.D.
Human Development and Aging
    Program
University of California, San Francisco
Pacific Graduate School of Psychology
Menlo Park, California

James J. Callahan, Jr., Ph.D.
Policy Center on Aging
Brandeis University

Lenore E. Gerard, J.D.
Institute for Health & Aging
University of California, San Francisco

Cheryl A. Hall, M.A.
Department of Social and Behavioral
    Sciences
University of California, San Francisco

Barry Lebowitz, Ph.D.
Mental Disorders of the Aging
    Research Branch
Division of Clinical Research
National Institute of Mental Health

Enid Light, M.A.
Mental Disorders of the Aging
    Research Branch
Division of Clinical Research
National Institute of Mental Health

Maureen Linehan, M.P.A.
Institute for Health & Aging
University of California, San Francisco

Mary E. McCall, B.S.
Human Development and Aging
    Program
University of California, San Francisco

Ida VSW Red, M.A., M.S.L.S.
Institute for Health & Aging
University of California, San Francisco

Patricia Shane, M.S., M.P.H.
Prevention Research Center
Berkeley, California

Sandra J. Swan, M.P.H.
World Institute on Disability
Berkeley, California

Joel P. Weeden, B.S.
Institute for Health & Aging
University of California, San Francisco

Serving the Mentally Ill Elderly

Problems and Perspectives

Elinore E. Lurie
James H. Swan
and Associates

Nancy Gourash Bliwise
Jámes J. Callahan, Jr.
Lenore E. Gerard
Cheryl A. Hall
Morton A. Lieberman

Maureen Linehan
Mary E. McCall
Patricia Shane
Sandra J. Swan
Joel P. Weeden

Foreword by Enid Light and Barry Lebowitz
Ida VSW Red, Coordinating Editor

Lexington Books
D.C. Heath and Company/Lexington, Massachusetts/Toronto

Library of Congress Cataloging-in-Publication Data

Serving the mentally ill elderly.

   Includes bibliographies and index.
   1. Aged—Mental health services—United States. 2. Geriatric psychiatry. I. Lurie, Elinore
E. (Elinore Eisenson) II. Swan, James H. [DNLM: 1. Community Mental Health Services—in
old age—United States. 2. Health Policy—United States. 3. Mental Disorders—in old age.
WM 30 S492]
RC451.4.A5S46   1987   362.2'0880565   86-45732
ISBN 0-669-14113-5 (alk. paper)

Published simultaneously in Canada
Printed in the United States of America
International Standard Book Number: 0-669-14113-5
Library of Congress Catalog Card Number: 86-45732

The paper used in this publication meets the minimum requirements of American National
Standard for Information Sciences—Permanence of Paper for Printed Library Materials,
ANSI Z39.48-1984. ∞™

87 88 89 90 8 7 6 5 4 3 2 1

Contents

Foreword

Enid Light
Barry Lebowitz

I t is widely recognized that geriatric mental health services research is, in general, a field in its infancy. Specifically, services research that focuses on and is relevant to the needs of the public mental health sector is, with few exceptions, nonexistent. This book is one of those few exceptions. It focuses clearly on issues of importance to the mental health services sector and brings research knowledge to bear on these issues. Thus, it represents an important resource for both the policymaker seeking guidance from research and for the researcher seeking to learn more about the issues of vital importance to practitioners.

Much of the material in this volume is the direct outgrowth of ongoing efforts by the Mental Disorders of the Aging Research Branch, National Institute of Mental Health (NIMH) to stimulate services research and disseminate research findings. In 1984, the University of California, San Francisco (UCSF) received from NIMH a contract to develop a series of analysis and synthesis papers focusing on research issues of concern to the managers of mental health service delivery systems. Under this contract, provision was made for the staff of the UCSF Institute for Health and Aging to be assisted by a committee comprised of state and county service delivery managers, as well as of researchers from other settings. The members of this committee, because of their combined expertise and diverse backgrounds, brought a broad, national perspective to the selection and development of topics and issues. As is evidenced by this volume, the merging of the realistic concerns and experience of the practice community with the investigatory skills and scholarship of the research community has resulted in a balanced approach to the focal issues in the field of geriatric mental health services research.

Preface

James J. Callahan, Jr.

They can be found in the halls of academe, social laboratories, research departments of government, and think tanks. Their language is strange. They speak of experimental and controls, ANOVA, logit, chi square and hawthorne effects. An R2 of .45 fills them with delight. They take pride in exposing the error and weakness of each other's endeavors. They glory in a "finding of significance" independent of its import for everyday life. They sweat over having a research grant renewed, and they hope for the day when CBS will ask them to go live on the six o'clock news with their recent findings. They are the individuals who populate the world of research and analysis.

In addition to seeking truth unto its innermost parts, the researchers of the world hope that their efforts will improve the well-being of their friends and neighbors. The movers and shakers of the world, however, are the politicians and policymakers who themselves must be moved by the analysts' findings. The politician and policymaker must act frequently and immediately to solve problems or to respond to a political interest, often without benefit of the guidance from a matched control group with an N of 100.

Observers of this situation are quick to point out the disparate interests of the researcher/analyst and the politician/policymaker and to dismiss their mutuality of interests. They see two worlds very much apart.

Certainly the researcher/analyst and the politician/policymaker are not married to one another. They are neither engaged nor going steady, but they have occasional encounters and a relationship they want and need to maintain. The researcher will package results to make them more understandable and will seek out a sympathetic politician/policymaker or one whose career can be advanced by championing a finding. The politician/policymaker can use the data to support a position or attack an opponent. Most importantly, however, the results that flow from the researcher/analyst help the politician/policymaker assess the potential outcome of certain policies or political stands. The "purity" of truth enters into political calculus.

The translation from research to policy is relatively indirect. In some ways, it is like a tide that raises all boats. The change may seem imperceptible, but there is less danger of all running aground. Research finds its way into public hearings, legislative studies, and legal briefs. It shapes and influences the level and nature of public debate. Some items move from the debatable to the status of fact. New items arise for debate and generate additional research. And so goes the process.

This book represents the fruitful result of the interplay of researchers and policymakers convened under the auspices of the National Institute of Mental Health (NIMH) on behalf of older persons with mental health needs. Together in the same room, these two perspectives sometimes clashed and at other times generated mutual insights. Policymakers helped to direct analysis to real and pressing questions facing the polity—dementia, homelessness, organization of care, reimbursement. Researchers, using validated findings, blew apart popular stereotypes of older persons and their mental health needs—that dementia is irreversible, that older persons have a disproportionate amount of mental illness.

Readers will be able to judge the success of the approach that produced this work as they read each chapter. The researcher reader will be pleased to find so much significant research succinctly offered in one place and with such complete bibliographies. The policymaker will welcome the careful drawing of policy implications from the research. This book represents the state of the art today in research on the mental health needs of older persons. May it lead to an improvement in their well-being.

Introduction

Elinore E. Lurie
James H. Swan

Future mental health research and service delivery to the elderly should be solidly grounded in previous policy analysis and research of high quality. Much research has been conducted on elderly populations, but the question remains of how to assess its quality and its relevance to policymakers. This book attempts to synthesize and evaluate previous research and policy efforts in order to suggest directions for the future.

This book originated in a project entitled Analysis and Synthesis of Research on the Mentally Ill Elderly, supported by a contract from the National Institute of Mental Health (NIMH 278-84-0017 [SP]) with the Institute for Health & Aging at the University of California, San Francisco. Topics for analysis and synthesis were included in the project on the basis of their relevance for research and policy development purposes. Some were suggested by project staff, others by NIMH staff. The topics chosen for inclusion in the project by the study advisory panel are reflected in the chapters that follow, with the addition of chapters on the formal treatment system and on implications of the findings for policymakers.

The methods of analysis included computerized bibliographic searches of *Mental Health Abstracts, Psychological Abstracts,* and *Medline.* Searches were limited to English language articles published after 1978 and relating to the elderly or middle-aged, with keywords for selected psychiatric diagnoses and other selected topics. For each synthesis, the authors compiled a bibliography based on the computer searches, and project staff accessed the articles. The references in each article provided additional bibliographic entries. Additionally, journals were identified that were important for each topic area, and recent issues searched for the latest articles relevant to the synthesis, which also yielded additional references in their bibliographies.

Further bibliographic entries were identified through requests to NIMH for relevant reports; prior author knowledge of the topic areas; suggestions by the members of the advisory panel and other colleagues; published bibliographies; and entries in the 1984 programs of the annual meetings of the American Public Health Association, the Gerontological Society of America, and other conferences. Additional analysis was conducted of books that include earlier classic studies in epidemiology, later comprehensive community surveys, and relevant contemporary work in such areas as treatment effectiveness. The authors of each synthesis read and abstracted the articles and other bibliographic entries for each topic.

Literature syntheses included articles based on primary research, secondary research, literature and research reviews, and policy analyses and discussions. Several criteria were used in the selection of research reports: exclusion of case reports; judgment that sample sizes were sufficient; coverage of the elderly or of topics relevant to the elderly; judgment of adequacy of methodology (for example, use of standard diagnostic instruments); and judgment of substantive relevance to the topic area. Specific analyses employed additional criteria. The rigor of application of these standards necessarily varied by topic area.

This book additionally reports on primary research undertaken by the authors. Reference is made in chapter 4 to results of two studies that included samples of community mental health centers, including preliminary results from an ongoing study on the impact of diagnosis-related groups (DRGs) reimbursement on posthospital care. Much of the discussion in chapter 6 is informed by the author's own research on self-help groups. Chapter 7 is largely based on a survey of state units on aging. Some of the findings in chapter 8 are derived from a research project conducted among homeless and at-risk populations in San Francisco. Previously published research results are, of course, so cited.

We wish to thank NIMH project officer, Enid Light, and the director of the Center for Studies on the Aging, Barry Lebowitz, for their encouragement and guidance. We also acknowledge the support of Carroll L. Estes, director of the Institute for Health & Aging (IHA), and the IHA staff. The study advisory panel members were James Callahan, Sue Eisenberg, Jeffrey Foster, Robert Glover, Lorraine Kroetch, Noel Mazade, Marita McElvain, James Noble, Sue North, Thomas Romeo, and Jo Ruffin. We appreciate their choices of project topics, contributions to the conceptualization of this work, and major insights into the problems on which we have focused. The views expressed in this book are, however, those of the authors, and should not be attributed to NIMH, IHA, or the project advisory panel. We hope that the work presented here will stimulate research and policy development for the betterment of elders with mental health needs.

1

The Epidemiology of Mental Illness in Late Life

Nancy Gourash Bliwise
Mary E. McCall
Sandra J. Swan

Effective planning for mental health services for the elderly rests on solid understanding of the prevalence of specific psychiatric disorders and the risk factors for mental illness in late life. Many investigators in Europe and North America have studied the prevalence of mental disorders among community-resident elderly. Knowledge remains limited, however, because of major methodological differences that preclude direct comparison across studies.

Early epidemiological studies often used global measures of psychological symptoms rather than instruments that assess specific psychiatric disorder (Gurin, Veroff, & Feld, 1960; Srole, Langner, Michael, Opler, & Rennie, 1962). Other studies, especially those conducted in Europe, based assessments on clinical diagnosis of psychiatric disorders (Essen-Moller, Larsson, Uddenberg, & White, 1956; Kay, Beamish, & Roth, 1964; Nielsen, 1962; Parsons, 1965). Radical changes in psychiatric nosology (American Psychiatric Association, [APA], 1980), however, limit the conclusions that can be drawn from these early investigations.

This chapter reports findings from recent epidemiological studies of mental illness in community-resident elderly. Only studies that examine specific psychiatric disorders and use current psychiatric nomenclature are reviewed. The following criteria were used to select studies for review: (1) random sampling of men and women over age 60; (2) a sample size of at least 200; (3) explicit inclusion, exclusion, and diagnostic criteria; and (4) standardized rating scales and/or diagnostic procedures. The largest number of studies focused on prevalence rates and risk factors for late-life depressive illness; sizable literatures were also located for senile dementia and substance abuse. Studies of anxiety disorders, schizophrenia, and paranoia are also reviewed. Somatoform disorders were targeted for review, but only one study could be found applying current diagnostic criteria for these disorders to community-resident geriatric populations. Consequently, only studies of depression, senile dementia, substance abuse, anxiety disorders, and schizophrenia and paranoia are discussed in detail. Research recommendations and policy implications are presented.

Depression

Mental health professionals frequently disagree on the prevalence rates for depression in late life (Blazer, 1983). Because depression has long been recognized as a major psychiatric disorder in late life, it is essential for proper service planning to establish accurate rates for depressive illness. Responding to this need, mental health researchers focused on the development of valid and reliable assessment tools (Blazer, 1978; Radloff, 1977; Spitzer, Endicott, & Robins, 1978) that reflect a consistent approach to the diagnosis of psychiatric disorders (Feighner, Robins, Guze, Woodruff, & Winokur, 1972; Spitzer et al., 1978). Beginning in the late 1970s these newly developed instruments were used in large community surveys. These studies yielded more consistent rates for depression. In addition, correlates of depression—potential risk factors—were identified to help guide efforts at prevention. These more recent studies of the prevalence of unipolar depression in late life are summarized in the next section.

Prevalence

The availability of reliable diagnostic techniques makes it possible to obtain more accurate estimates of the prevalence of psychiatric disorders in the community. Ten studies of large community populations were found in which reliable measurement tools and specified diagnostic criteria were used to examine the prevalence of depressive illness in elderly men and women (see table 1–1). All studies used appropriate procedures to select large samples. Although measurement instruments and diagnostic criteria varied, the prevalence rates reported were fairly consistent across studies. The median prevalence rate for depressive disorder across studies was 3.75; the median for significant dysphoria was 14.75. Although a significant proportion of the elderly reported numerous symptoms of depression, only 4 to 5 percent met criteria for major depressive illness.

Of particular note are the low prevalence rates for depressive disorder among the elderly reported by George, Blazer, Winfield-Laird, Leaf, and Eischbach (1987). These findings were drawn from the Epidemiologic Catchment Area (ECA) program sponsored by the National Institute of Mental Health (Myers et al., 1984; Regier et al., 1984). The ECA program was designed to estimate the prevalence and incidence of specific psychiatric disorders as defined by current psychiatric nosology (that is, DSM-III criteria; APA, 1980), to estimate the proportions of treated and untreated psychiatric illness, and to identify risk factors for the development and maintenance of psychiatric illness. The emphasis on specific psychiatric disorders and operational criteria for diagnosis is a noteworthy feature of the ECA program and may account for the low prevalence rates. The Diagnostic Interview Schedule (DIS) was developed to reliably obtain information necessary to identify cases of psychiatric

Table 1-1
Quantitative Summary of Epidemiologic Studies of Depression in the Elderly

Authors	Sampling frame	N	Age range	Measurement instrument	Diagnostic criteria	Rates 65 +	
						Significant dysphoria	Depressive disorder[a]
Blazer & Williams (1980)	Stratified random (Durham, NC)	997	65+	OARS	DSM-III	14.7%	3.7%
Eaton & Kessler (1981)	Cluster probability (National)	2,867	25–74	CES-D(16+)	RDC	14.8%	—
Frerichs et al. (1981)	Cross-sectional probability (Los Angeles)	1,003	18+	CES-D(16+)	RDC	16.7%	—
George et al. (1987)	Area probability New Haven, CT Baltimore, MD St. Louis, MO Central NC	14,759	18+	DIS	DSM-III	—	3.4% 1.7% 1.6% 2.4%
Gurland et al. (1980)	Random (New York)	400	65+	CARE	DSM-II	12.5%	—
Murrel et al. (1983)	Area probability (Kentucky)	2,517	55+	CES-D(20+)	Feighner	15.8%[b]	
Romaniuk et al. (1983)	Area probability (Virginia)	2,146	60+	OARS	DSM-III	—	5.7%[c]
Uhlenhuth et al. (1983)	Cross-sectional probability (National)	2,552	18–80	HSCL	DSM-III	—	5.1%
Weissman & Myers (1979)	Stratified random (New Haven)	515	26+	SADS	RDC	8.1%	5.4%

[a]Depressive disorders include major depressive episode and dysthymia.
[b]Percentages reported for Ss age 55 +.
[c]Percentages reported for Ss age 60 +.

disorder according to DSM-III criteria, research diagnostic criteria (RDC), and Feighner criteria (Robins, Helzer, Croughan, & Ratcliff, 1981). In order to allow diagnosis across all three diagnostic systems, strict inclusion, exclusion, and diagnostic criteria were operationalized and applied to this instrument. It is, perhaps, the most stringent of all case-finding methods used in the community surveys reviewed and consequently yielded the lowest prevalence rates of depressive disorder.

The prevalence rates of depressive disorder among the elderly that emerged from the recent studies reviewed are substantially lower than previous estimates in either community (see reviews by Blazer, 1983; Kay & Bergmann, 1980) or psychiatric patient (see review by Redick & Taube, 1980) populations. This discrepancy is, in large part, due to significant methodological improvements in case-finding techniques. The possibility of cohort effects, however, must also be considered. Srole and Fischer (1980) noted cohort differences in psychiatric symptoms in a cross-sequential study of Manhattan adults. Later cohorts of middle-aged and elderly adults had significantly fewer psychiatric symptoms, even as they moved into late life. The higher estimates of depressive disorder reported in earlier cross-sectional studies of the elderly, therefore, may have reflected a life-long vulnerability to depression. Current cohorts of elderly enter old age with more education and better health than previous cohorts; these factors may provide some protection against depression.

Age Differences in Rates

Studies that compared rates of depression in the elderly to those of middle-aged and young adults found significantly less depression in older men and women (Eaton & Kessler, 1981; Frerichs, Aneshensel, & Clark, 1981; Myers et al., 1984; Uhlenhuth, Balter, Mellinger, Cisin, & Clinthorne, 1983; Weissman & Myers, 1979). The highest rates of depressive illness were consistently found among young adults, especially young women.

Mixed results were reported by investigators who provided detailed age breakdowns of depression within the over-65 population. Neither Blazer and Williams (1980) nor Romaniuk, McAuley, and Arling (1983) found age differences in their studies of elderly men and women residing in the Southeast. Their findings were supported by a recent summary of the results of four of the five ECA sites; no significant age differences were found for any of the functional disorders examined among respondents 65 years of age and older (George et al., 1987). In contrast, Murrel, Himmelfarb, and Wright (1983) found that depression significantly increased with age for men over 55 years of age; a curvilinear relationship was found for elderly women with rates highest in late middle age and old age. A similar curvilinear relationship with age was found by Gurland, Dean, Cross, and Golden (1980) for the elderly men studied; depression tended to decrease with age for women aged 65 and older.

Risk Factors

Gender, social class, marital status, and physical illness consistently predict depression in late life. Each will be discussed separately.

Higher rates of depression were reported for women at all ages in most studies reviewed (Blazer & Williams, 1980; Eaton & Kessler, 1981; Frerichs et al., 1981; Murrel et al., 1983; Myers et al., 1984; Romaniuk et al., 1983; Uhlenhuth et al., 1983). Indeed, Amenson and Lewinsohn (1981), statistically controlling for all other social background characteristics, found that gender differences in rates of depression remained. This was the most statistically sophisticated analysis of gender differences reviewed. The study was further enhanced for the purposes of this review by the oversampling of the elderly. Gurland et al. (1980), however, reported higher rates of pervasive depression in males over 80 compared to their female counterparts. Weissman and Myers (1979) found that the overall rates of depression were higher in women than men, but the observed gender difference disappeared after age 55. A close examination of age breakdowns by gender suggests that older women remain more vulnerable to depression than men well into late life, but that gender differences in the prevalence of depression are less striking in old age than in younger years (Frerichs et al., 1981; Gurland, 1976; Myers et al., 1984).

Whether defined by occupation, education, or income, there is strong evidence that rates of depression are significantly lower in people of higher social class (Comstock & Helsing, 1976; Steele, 1978; Warheit, Holzer, & Arey, 1975). This association holds into late life when the elderly with less education and low income are at greater risk for depression (Abrahams & Patterson, 1978–1979; Amenson & Lewinsohn, 1981; Eaton & Kessler, 1981; Frerichs et al., 1981; Murrel et al., 1983; Romaniuk et al., 1983.

In a review of the psychosocial risk factors for affective disorders, Hirschfeld and Cross (1982) concluded that marital status is significantly associated with depression and that separated and divorced persons are more vulnerable to depression than those who are currently married. Studies that included significant proportions of elderly men and women found that the widowed are also at risk for depression (Amenson & Lewinsohn, 1981; Frerichs et al., 1981; Murrel et al., 1983; Romaniuk et al., 1983). Indeed, prevalence rates for depression tended to be similar among those who were separated or divorced and those who were widowed.

The only factor that emerged from all studies as a significant predictor of depressive disorder was poor health (Abrahams & Patterson, 1978–1979; Blazer & Williams, 1980; Frerichs et al., 1981; Gurland et al., 1980; Murrel et al., 1983; Raymond, Michals, & Steer, 1980; Romaniuk et al., 1983). Poor health was associated with depression across all ages, but played a particularly significant role in late life. These findings are supported by studies of medical practice (see chapter 2). Psychiatric morbidity was greater in men and women attending general practice clinics than in the general population (Berndt, Berndt, & Byars, 1983; Hesbacher, Rickels, Morris, Newman, & Rosenfeld, 1980; Leeper, Badger, & Milo, 1985). High rates of depression were also found among elderly medical inpatients (Cavanaugh, 1983). The relationship between physical and mental illness is discussed in detail in chapter 2.

Prognosis

Major depressive episodes may be less prevalent but have greater consequences in late life. The probability of recovery is lower for older compared to younger patients, with the worst prognosis for elderly patients with recurring or chronic depression (Mann, Jenkins, & Belsey, 1981; Post, 1962, 1972; Watts, 1956; Zis & Goodwin, 1979). In contrast, Cole (1983) found no association between age and response to tricyclics, length of hospitalization, disposition at follow-up, or course of illness. These discrepant findings may be due, however, to the absence of physical illness in patients or the short follow-up period. Excessively high mortality rates have been found among older patients who have received diagnoses of affective disorder when compared to medical patients who have no diagnosed psychiatric illness (Schuckit, Miller, & Berman, 1980). In addition, patients with affective disorder are at high risk for institutionalization (Katona, Lowe, & Jack, 1983; Schuckit et al., 1980).

The poor prognosis for late-life depression may be due, in part, to the greater risk in old age for adverse reactions to psychotropic drugs (Davison, 1978; Salzman, 1985). The most common treatments for major depressive illness are pharmacotherapy alone (Bieleski & Friedel, 1976; Forde & Sbordone, 1980) and a combination of medication and psychotherapy (Orlean, George, Houpt, & Brodie, 1985). Given the reluctance of the elderly to seek specialized psychiatric care (Myers et al., 1984) and a similar reluctance among general practitioners to refer the elderly to mental health professionals (Mann et al., 1981; Richter, Barsky, & Happ, 1983), those who have adverse drug reactions and cannot continue drug therapy may not receive alternate treatments for their depression.

Special Features of Late-Life Depression

The majority of evidence suggests that there is no association between age and the nature of depressive symptoms (George et al., 1987; Winokur, Behar, & Schlesser, 1980; Zis & Goodwin, 1979). Researchers and clinicians, however, are beginning to note special features of late-life depression. Patients who met RDC criteria for primary unipolar depression with onset after age 60 were more likely to have delusions than depressed patients with early onset (Meyers, Kalayam, & Mei-Tal, 1984). Gurland (1976) noted an increase in anxiety, somatic concerns or hypochondriasis; loss of concentration; and memory problems in older depressed patients. A similar profile of more somatic symptoms and hypochondriasis was found among older clinic outpatients with unipolar endogenous depression compared to younger patients (Brown, Sweeney, Loutsch, Kocsis, & Frances, 1984). Although findings did not support a separate psychiatric syndrome, they suggested that elderly depressed patients may present a somewhat different clinical picture than younger patients.

Senile Dementia

As the absolute number and proportion of elderly in society increase, so do the actual number and proportion of the demented elderly. Diagnostic problems, however, make it difficult, if not impossible, to obtain accurate estimates of the prevalence and incidence of senile dementia. Diagnostic criteria have only recently been specified (APA, 1980; Eisdorfer & Cohen, 1980; McKhann et al., 1984); standardized case-finding techniques have not been developed. Despite these limitations, there is a small literature on the epidemiology of senile dementia. These studies and investigations of prognosis and family impact are presented below.

Prevalence

The majority of studies of senile dementia were conducted in Europe; North American investigators have only recently focused on the problem of senile dementia. Dementia associated with Alzheimer's disease and vascular or multiinfarct dementias are the most commonly observed dementias in late life (Mortimer, Schuman, & French, 1981). Other frequently observed dementias are dementia secondary to alcoholism and acute or "reversible" dementia. Despite recognized neuropathological differences associated with various senile dementias (Roth, 1971; Terry & Wisniewski, 1977; Tomlinson, Blessed, & Roth, 1970), only a few studies presented prevalence rates by cause of dementing illness (Akesson, 1969; Kaneko, 1969; Kay et al., 1964; Nielsen, 1962). The following review, therefore, considers prevalence rates by stated level of cognitive impairment rather than type of dementing illness.

Nine community studies were found in which both mild and moderate-to-severe dementia were examined (see table 1–2). Prevalence rates for mild cognitive impairment were quite variable; rates ranged from 2.6 percent to 23.3 percent with a median rate of 11.15 percent. This variability is not surprising given the difficulty in recognizing the early stages of dementia. Prevalence of severe cognitive impairment ranged from 1.3 percent to 6.5 percent with a median of 5.7 percent. Although variability remained, there was greater consistency across studies in assessments of severe cognitive impairment.

Table 1–2
Quantitative Summary of Epidemiologic Studies of Senile Dementia

Authors	Sampling frame	N	Age range	Diagnostic procedures	Rates 65 +	
					Mild	Severe
Akesson (1969)	Delimited area (Sweden)	2,979	60 +	Psychiatric interview	—	1.3[a]
Broe et al. (1976)	Random (Scotland)	808	65 +	Neurological examination	4.3	3.8
Cooper (1984)	Random registry (Germany)	343	65 +	Psychiatric interview	5.0	6.0
Essen-Moller et al. (1956)	Delimited area (Sweden)	443	60 +	Psychiatric interview	10.8[a]	5.0[a]
George et al. (1987)	Area probability New Haven, CT Baltimore, MD St. Louis, MO Central, NC	7,163	55 +	DIS— interview	11.5 14.7 15.0 23.3	2.7 4.9 2.2 6.5
Gurland et al. (1980)	Random (New York)	400	65 +	CARE— interview	—	5.8
Kay et al. (1964)	Random (England)	294	65 +	Psychiatric interview	5.7	5.6
Kay et al. (1970)	Random (England)	758	65 +	Psychiatric interview	2.6	6.2
Nielsen (1962)	Delimited area (Denmark)	994	65 +	Psychiatric interview	15.4	3.1

[a]Percentages reported for Ss age 60 + .

Most ratings of impairment were made on the basis of psychiatric interviews. Only George et al. (1987) and Gurland et al. (1980) based ratings of impairment on standardized mental status examinations. Given the large sample sizes, good sampling strategies, and use of reliable instruments to aid ratings, these studies provide the best estimates of cognitive impairment among community-resident elderly. It should be remembered, however, that these types of instruments are only screening tools to aid diagnosis. Definitive diagnosis can only be made upon autopsy (Department of Health and Human Services, 1984).

Prevalence rates based on studies of community-resident elderly are typically considered underestimates of the true prevalence of dementia (Mortimer et al., 1981). Although most of the elderly suffering from dementia remain in the community with their families (Larson, Reifler, Sumi, Canfield, & Chinn, 1985), those with severe cognitive impairment are at greatest risk for institutionalization (Brody, Lawton, & Liebowitz, 1984). Recent surveys indicated that 50 to 75 percent of nursing home patients had significant cognitive impairment (Rovner & Rabins, 1985). Epidemiological studies that include institutionalized elderly are currently under way (Regier et al., 1984). These studies should provide the most accurate estimates to date of the prevalence of intellectual impairment in the aged.

Age Differences in Rates

The dementias are primarily disorders of old age and are the only psychiatric disorders for which prevalence rates consistently increase over the life span (George et al., 1987; Roth, 1955). Senile dementia increases dramatically with age (see table 1–3). Prevalence rates exceeding 20 percent among persons aged 80 and older were found in several studies (Cooper, 1984; Essen-Moller et al., 1956; Kay et al., 1964). Again, estimates varied considerably across investigations, with studies employing the most stringent inclusion criteria yielding the lowest prevalence rates. Akesson (1969) based diagnosis on data gathered over a three-year period; only persons who were disoriented as to time and place at each measurement were considered demented. Point prevalence estimates were consistently the highest estimates (Cooper, 1984; Essen-Moller et al., 1956; Kay et al., 1964).

Prognosis

The specific course of varying forms of senile dementia is unknown. Most dementias, however, are progressive, irreversible, and directly associated with diminishing functional capacities, intellectual deterioration, and behavioral problems (Roth, 1971). Senile dementia is associated with significantly reduced life expectancy. Roth (1955) reported that 80 percent of patients with senile psychosis and 70 percent of patients with arteriosclerotic psychosis were dead

Table 1–3
Quantitative Summary of Epidemiologic Studies of Senile Dementia Age-Specific Prevalence

				Rates	
Authors	Country	N	60–69	70–79	80+
Akesson (1969)	Sweden	2,979	0.0	1.3	4.8
Cooper (1984)	Germany	343	5.0[a]	8.9	23.8
Essen-Moller (1956)	Sweden	443	0.9	5.1	21.8
Gurland et al. (1980)	New York	400	3.0[a]	4.0	11.0
Kaneko (1967)[b]	Japan	531	2.4	5.9	19.8
Kay et al. (1964)	England	294	4.0[a]	7.5	33.3
Nielsen (1962)	Denmark	994	0.0	1.8	12.6

[a]Percentages reported for Ss age 65 +.
[b]Cited in Post, 1972.

within two years of initial evaluation. Prognosis today remains poor (Bergmann, 1969; Kokmen & Schoenberg, 1980; Simon & Cahan, 1963); with better institutional care, however, current survival times are significantly longer (Blessed & Wilson, 1982; Duckworth, Kedward, & Bailey, 1979). Go, Todorov, and Elston (1978) estimated that the average survival time from diagnosis of senile dementia was 4 years for men and 6 years for women.

Dementia is rarely cited as the primary cause of death, even though some investigators have suggested that it may rank as the fourth or fifth most common cause of death in the United States (Katzman & Karasu, 1975). It is difficult to determine if the disease itself plays a direct role in shortening life, or whether the greater risk of mortality results from malnutrition, pneumonia, and other outcomes of poor self-care. If the mortality risk is secondary, comprehensive programs for the demented elderly and their families may improve prognosis.

Impact on the Family

Dementia is a serious disorder with malignant consequences not only for patients, but also for their entire support system. Most demented elderly are cared for in the home by family members (Johnson & Catalano, 1983; Moon,

1983) who often report feelings of stress and burden (Fengler & Goodrich, 1979; Sanford, 1975; Zarit, Reeuer, & Bach-Peterson, 1980). Heavy demands on family caregivers continue after institutionalization, often with no reduction of stress and strain (Brody, 1985). Family caregivers often experience depressive symptoms of sufficient severity and duration to meet diagnostic criteria for major depressive disorder (Cohen, Kennedy, & Eisdorfer, 1983; Steuer & Cohen, 1984).

Reversible Dementias

Senile dementia is not a unitary disorder with a single cause or set of causes. Thus, diagnosis is often quite difficult. Several studies have shown that many patients thought to have a primary dementing illness were found, upon careful reassessment in hospital, to have potentially treatable conditions (Cummings, Benson, & Loverma, 1980; Fox, Topel, & Huckman, 1975; Freemon, 1976; Freemon & Rudd, 1982; Hutton, 1981; Larson, Reifler, Featherstone, & English, 1984; Marsden & Harrison, 1972; Smith, Kiloh, Ratnavale, & Grant, 1976). The available data seem to indicate that 10 to 30 percent of patients evaluated for dementia had other disorders. Of particular note was the role of iatrogenesis in potentially reversible dementias. Medication side effects were the most common cause of reversible dementia, with psychotropic medications implicated more often than other classes of drugs.

Substance Abuse

Substance dependence and abuse are typically considered problems of young adults. There is a growing awareness, however, that drug and alcohol problems are experienced by significant proportions of the elderly population. There is more literature on alcohol than drug dependence and abuse in late life. Thus, the primary focus of this review is on investigations of late-life alcohol use and abuse, risk factors, and prognosis. The few studies of opiate and other drug dependence among the elderly are discussed briefly.

Prevalence of Alcohol Abuse and Dependence

Six large studies of community populations were found that used reliable measurement tools and/or specified diagnostic criteria to examine alcohol abuse and alcohol dependence in elderly men and women. Most investigators, though guided by current nomenclature, studied drinking patterns and associated social problems rather than attempting a specific diagnosis of alcoholism (see table 1–4). The prevalence rates were fairly consistent across studies, perhaps due to reliance on the Quantity-Frequency-Variability Index (QFV) developed and

Table 1–4
Quantitative Summary of Epidemiologic Studies of Alcohol Abuse

Study	Sampling frame	N	Age range	Measurement instrument	Diagnostic criteria	Heavy use			Abuse		
						M	F	Total	M	F	Total
Barnes (1979)	Stratified random (New York)	1,041	18+	QFV	—	16.0%	1.0%	7.0%	—	—	—
Cahalan (1970)	Area probability (National)	2,746	21+	QFV	DSM-II	—	—	—	8.0%	1.0%	5.0%
Cahalan & Cisin (1968)	Area probability (National)	2,746	21+	QFV	—	20.0%	2.0%	6.0%	—	—	—
George et al. (1987)	Area probability New Haven, CT Baltimore, MD St. Louis, MO Central NC	14,759	18+	DIS	DSM-III	— — — —	— — — —	— — — —	— — — —	— — — —	0.8% 1.4% 1.6% 0.4%
Myers et al. (1984)	Area probability (Boston)	5,314	18+	QFV	DSM-III	—	—	6.0%	—	—	4.0%
Room (1972)	Area probability (San Francisco)	1,268	18+	QFV	—	7.0%	0.0%	3.0%	—	—	—
Wechsler et al. (1978)	Area probability (Boston)	984	18+	QFV	—	19.0%	3.0%	9.0%	—	—	—

validated by Cahalan, Cisin, and Crossley (1969) for use in household surveys. The prevalence rates of heavy alcohol use among the elderly ranged from 3 to 9 percent with a median prevalence of 6 percent. Prevalence rates of alcohol abuse ranged from 1 to 5 percent with a median rate of 1.4 percent. Although many elderly men and women reported heavy alcohol consumption, only 1 to 2 percent met criteria for alcohol abuse or alcohol dependence.

Prevalence rates of alcoholism based on household surveys of elderly men and women are considered underestimates of the true prevalence of alcohol-related problems in old age. Elderly alcoholics are at risk for institutionalization either in hospital settings or nursing homes. Simon, Epstein, and Reynolds (1968) found that alcohol problems were implicated in admissions of 23 percent of the elderly patients seeking treatment at a psychiatric hospital. Older alcoholics are more likely than younger alcoholics to be admitted to medical rather than psychiatric hospitals (National Institute of Mental Health, 1970). Blose (1978) reported that 40 to 60 percent of white male patients residing in the nursing homes studied had alcohol-related problems.

Alcoholism in late life may also be underreported because the diagnostic criteria used are based on norms drawn from young patients. Current diagnostic criteria for alcohol abuse are based on the frequency and amount of alcohol consumed, physical impairments associated with alcohol use, and impaired performance in major social roles; alcohol dependence is diagnosed when there is evidence of physical tolerance to alcohol or alcohol withdrawal (DSM-III; APA, 1980). Age-related physiological and social changes, however, may reduce the applicability of these criteria to alcohol-related problems in late life. The elderly are affected by alcohol at lower doses than are the young; the same dose induces higher blood alcohol levels in older than in younger persons (Bosmann, 1984; Garver, 1984; Vestal et al., 1977). Because of this increased sensitivity to alcohol, the elderly tend to decrease the amount of alcohol consumed (Schuckit & Pastor, 1978). Given decreased consumption, withdrawal symptoms are less frequently observed in elderly alcoholics. In a study of 103 elderly patients admitted to either a geriatric or alcohol unit, Rosin and Glatt (1971) reported delirium tremens in only one patient. Role changes in late life tend to involve role exits (for example, retirement, widowhood) making significant impairments in role functioning less likely. By basing diagnosis on the frequency and amount of alcohol consumed, tolerance and withdrawal symptoms, and social role impairments, a large number of alcohol-related problems in late life may go unnoticed. New age-specific case-finding techniques may be needed for accurate assessment of the prevalence of alcohol abuse and alcohol dependence among the elderly.

Age Differences in Rates

All studies that compared rates of alcohol use and abuse in the elderly to middle-aged and young adults found significantly less heavy drinking and alcohol abuse in elderly men and women (Barnes, 1979; Cahalan, 1970; Cahalan & Cisin, 1968; Meyers, Hingson, Mucatel, & Goldman, 1982; Myers et al., 1984; Room, 1972; Wechsler, Demone, & Gottlieb, 1978). Peak rates for alcohol problems were consistently found among young adults, especially young men. When the elderly were divided into subgroups, the negative association between age and alcohol abuse/dependence was less clear. Two studies showed a continued decline of alcohol use and abuse well into late life (Meyers, Goldman, Hingson, Scotch, & Mangione, 1981–1982; Room, 1972). George et al. (1987) found no age differences among those 65 years of age and older who participated in the ECA studies. Clark and Midanik (1982) found that heavy drinking was more prevalent among men over 70 than men between the ages 61 and 70.

There is evidence from longitudinal studies of spontaneous remission of alcohol-related problems over long periods of time (Fillmore, Bacon, & Hyman, 1979; Fillmore & Midanik, 1984). This may account for the low prevalence of heavy drinking and alcohol abuse among the elderly found in cross-sectional studies. A more likely explanation, however, is that of cohort or generational effects (Mandolini, 1981). Present cohorts of the elderly experienced legal and social sanctions against alcohol use as young adults that may have produced life-long personal concerns about alcoholism. Indeed, Meyers et al. (1981–1982) found some evidence for such cohort effects. Among the elderly respondents studied, those who were young adults during Prohibition were more likely than younger respondents to express concerns about health risks associated with moderate drinking and to consume alcohol less frequently and in smaller quantities. Given the high rates of heavy drinking and alcohol abuse in current cohorts of young and middle-aged adults (Myers et al., 1984), much higher rates of alcohol-related problems may be anticipated in future cohorts of elderly men and women.

Risk Factors

Higher rates of heavy drinking and alcohol abuse were consistently reported for men compared to women at all ages (Barnes, 1979; Cahalan, 1970; Cahalan & Cisin, 1968; Myers et al., 1984; Room, 1972; Wechsler et al., 1978). The observed gender differences in prevalence rates increased with age with alcohol abuse almost nonexistent among older women (Cahalan, 1970; Myers et al., 1984). Men and women may also differ in the settings in which alcohol use occurs. Counte, Salloway, and Christman (1982) found that men were more likely to drink in social settings outside the home or in complete isolation; women, especially in midlife, tended to drink at home with one or two close friends.

Although epidemiological studies have found that abstinence from alcohol is most frequently observed in the lowest socioeconomic stratum (Cahalan,

1970; Room, 1972), few studies have examined social status and drinking patterns among the elderly. In a British sample of community-resident elderly, Smart and Liban (1981) found that heavy drinking was more prevalent among elderly with lower incomes. Siassi, Crocetti, and Spiro (1973) reported much higher prevalence rates for heavy drinking among elderly blue-collar workers and their spouses than typically found in community samples (men, 35 percent; women, 9 percent). Less stringent classification criteria for heavy drinking (6 or more alcoholic beverages per week), however, were used in this study.

The loss of a spouse is frequently cited as a stressor associated with alcohol abuse in late life (Finney & Moos, 1984; Glantz, 1981). Most household surveys show no relationship between marital status and heavy alcohol use or abuse (Guttman, 1978; Wechsler et al., 1978). These studies, however, failed to control for gender—an important factor, because older men are more likely than older women to be heavy drinkers and to be married. Barnes (1979) and Meyers et al. (1982) were the only investigators who considered the gender of respondents. Both found no differences in the prevalence of heavy drinking between elderly widows and widowers and their married peers. These investigators also found that alcohol use was unrelated to employment status in late life.

Special Late-Life Features

Two distinct groups of elderly alcoholics have been identified. One group consists of those with long-standing alcohol-related problems. The other group consists of elderly people who began drinking in late life, presumably in response to stress. Approximately one-third of the elderly alcoholics studied in clinical settings had a late onset of alcohol problems (see review by Finney & Moos, 1984); rates ranged from 0 to 71 percent. Samples, however, were unrepresentative of the larger population, and cutoffs of age of onset varied widely. Counte et al. (1982) found no differences in alcoholic symptomatology or drinking behavior between early- and late-onset alcoholics. Others have questioned the typology, suggesting that there are more than two types (Dunham, 1981) or that there are too few meaningful distinctions between early- and late-onset alcoholics (DiClemente & Gordon, 1984; Schuckit & Miller, 1976).

Several studies have directly examined the role of life stressors in triggering alcohol abuse in old age. Glatt (1978), Hubbard, Santos, and Santos (1979), Rosin and Glatt (1971), and Wattis (1981) all found that life events such as conjugal bereavement, job loss, and physical illness were more often implicated in the hospitalizations of late-onset alcoholics compared to elderly alcoholics who began drinking early in life. Schuckit, Atkinson, Miller, and Berman (1980), however, found that stressors were linked to both increased and decreased alcohol consumption in late life. No community studies directly examined the relationship between life stressors and age of onset of alcohol-related problems. As previously noted, investigations of community-resident elderly showed no relationship between current heavy drinking and either marital or employment status. Further research is needed to clarify the role of stress in late-life alcohol abuse. Finney and Moos (1984) outline a comprehensive causal model to guide such research.

Prognosis

Alcohol abuse is less prevalent but may have more serious consequences in late life. Low doses of alcohol may be toxic for the elderly (Flinn, Reisberg, & Ferris, 1984), especially in combination with nutritional deficiencies (Barboriak, Roomey, Leitschuk, & Anderson, 1978) or prescription medications (Kater, Roggin, Tobon, Zieve, & Iber, 1969; Rubin, Gang, Misra, & Lieber, 1970). Waller (1974) found evidence of prior alcohol use in 13 percent of emergency room patients over age 60 treated for injuries. This is consistent with an initial presentation of falls, injuries, and accidental hypothermia seen in many elderly alcoholics seeking treatment (Droller, 1964; Wattis, 1981). Alcohol abuse is also associated with neural damage (Cermak & Ryback, 1976; Jones, Moskowitz, & Butters, 1975) and early evidence of cognitive impairment (Korboot & Naylor, 1972; Williams, Ray, & Overall, 1973). Alcoholics have excess mortality for almost all causes of death (Black, Warrack, & Winokur, 1985a, 1985b; Brody & Mills, 1978; Costello, 1974). The peak death rate for cirrhosis of the liver is between 55 and 64 years of age (National Center for Health Statistics, 1979). Heavy drinking and alcohol abuse are associated with greater risk for suicide, homicide, and accidental death (see review by Blum and Braunstein, 1967). Alcoholics may be particularly at risk for suicide in late life (Ripley, 1973).

Elderly men and women with alcohol-related problems typically do not seek treatment until associated medical problems become physically debilitating (Rosin & Glatt, 1971; Schuckit & Miller, 1976). When treatment is sought, physicians often fail to make the appropriate diagnosis. Schuckit, Miller, and Hahlabohm (1975) found that admitting physicians failed to diagnose alcohol abuse in 12 percent of 50 elderly patients admitted to acute medical and surgical wards in a general hospital. In a similar study, McCusker, Cherubin, and Zimberg (1971) found that alcohol-related problems went unrecognized in approximately half of the alcoholics treated in an acute care facility.

There is some evidence that, when treated, the probability for recovery is greater in older compared to younger patients (Bateman & Peterson, 1971; Blaney, Radford, & MacKenzie, 1975; Glatt, 1978; Linn, 1978). In contrast, Janik and Dunham (1983) found no age differences in treatment outcome across 550 alcohol treatment programs. Prognosis is poor for elderly alcoholics who are homeless, live in single-room occupancy hotels (Myerson & Mayer, 1966), or have an associated dementing illness (Gaitz & Baer, 1971; Roth, 1955; Simon, Epstein, & Reynolds, 1968).

Prevalence of Drug Abuse

The literature on drug abuse in late life is sparse. Typically, studies focus on drug misuse, especially misuse of prescription medications, rather than drug dependence. All studies specifically examining drug abuse and dependence found very low prevalence rates in late life. Ball and Chambers (1970) found that only 4 percent of the admissions for addictions to Public Health Service hospitals in Lexington, Kentucky, and Forth Worth, Texas, during 1963 were for men and women aged 60 or older. Studies of methadone maintenance programs in large cities revealed prevalence figures of 5 percent for patients aged 45 and over (Capel & Stewart, 1971) and 2 percent for patients aged 60 and over (Pascarelli & Fischer, 1974).

Only one study of drug abuse among community-resident elderly was located. Reporting data from the ECA studies, Myers et al. (1984) found that drug abuse among men and women aged 65 was almost nonexistent. A prevalence rate of 0.2 percent was found among elderly women residing in St. Louis, Missouri; prevalence rates were 0.0 for all other sites. These figures are extremely low, especially because the criteria for drug abuse that were applied included dependence, withdrawal symptoms, and delusions associated with use across nine categories of legal and illegal drugs (barbiturates, opioids, cocaine, amphetamines, PCP, hallucinogens, cannabis, tobacco, and caffeine).

Elderly drug abusers may be underrepresented in treatment programs because of early mortality associated with opioid addiction (Capel, Goldsmith, Waddell, & Stewart, 1972; O'Donnell, 1969). Longitudinal studies suggest that older addicts who continue to use opioids change their lifestyle to avoid contact with legal and social service agencies (Capel et al., 1972; Capel & Pepper, 1978; Maddix & Desmond, 1980; Pottieger & Inciardi, 1981). Other elderly drug abusers switch from heroin to other drugs, decrease daily consumption, or substitute alcohol, barbiturates, or antidepressants for opioids (Capel et al., 1972; Pascarelli, 1979). Opioid dependence is less prevalent in older compared to younger substance abusers (Ball & Chambers, 1970; Capel & Stewart, 1971), but may be increasing. Capel and Pepper (1978) found that the proportion of clients over age 60 in New York City methadone maintenance programs doubled from 0.5 percent in 1974 to 1.1 percent in 1980.

Elderly men and women are the largest consumers of prescription drugs. Although the elderly constituted only 10 percent of the population, they received approximately 25 percent of all prescriptions written in 1967 (Task Force on Prescription Drugs, 1968). The most frequently prescribed drugs were cardiovascular medications (22 percent); tranquilizers (10 percent); diuretics (9 percent); and sedative-hypnotics (9 percent) (Guttman, 1978). The elderly, especially elderly women, also are more likely than younger adults to be regular users of psychotropic medications (Chambers, 1971; Stephens, Haney, & Underwood, 1981; Warheit, Arey, & Swanson, 1976). Many analysts have suggested that the disproportionately high use of prescription medications among the elderly places them at an increased risk of drug misuse (Pascarelli & Fischer, 1974; Petersen & Thomas, 1975). Indeed, several investigators have found that medication compliance was lower among the elderly than any other age group (Brand, Smith, & Brand, 1977; Neely & Patrick, 1968; Schwartz, Wang, Zeitz, & Goss, 1962). The elderly were also more likely to hoard and share drugs (Doyle, 1976; James, 1979). The rate of medication misuse in late life, however, is unknown. Studies of elderly patients seeking medical treatment for drug reactions report that 5 to 9 percent of patients are aged 50 and over (Heller & Wynne, 1974; Petersen & Thomas, 1975; Schernitski, Bootman, Byers, Likes, & Hughes, 1980), with only 2.6 percent aged 60 or older (Inciardi, McBride, Russe, & Wells, 1978). Chien, Townsend, and Townsend (1978) studied medication misuse among 242 elderly participants of senior programs in New York state. Medication misuse was defined as use of drugs for reasons not indicated in standard medical manuals. Misuse was greatest for anti-Parkinson medications and dental preparations (50 percent), followed by anti-histamines (33.3 percent); antidepressants (16.7 percent); minerals and electrolytes (12.5 percent); and antipsychotics (10 percent). Of particular note is the low rate of misuse reported for anxiolytics (4 percent), hypnotics (0 percent), and cardiovascular medications (0 percent). Further research on a large, representative sample is needed, however, to provide more accurate estimates of the prevalence of medication misuse in the elderly.

Anxiety Disorders

Traditionally, anxiety disorders have received little attention in the study of mental health problems in late life. Recent studies suggest that the elderly, more than any other age group, are likely to take anxiolytic medication; such studies have focused attention on anxiety disorders in old age. In order to understand the high rates of anxiolytic use by the elderly, it is essential to have accurate prevalence rates of anxiety disorders and knowledge of the risk factors for late-life anxiety.

Prevalence

Current psychiatric nomenclature (APA, 1980) distinguishes between generalized anxiety, phobias (both simple phobia and agoraphobia), and panic reactions. One of the best-designed studies (Uhlenhuth et al., 1983) reported prevalence rates for generalized anxiety of 7.1 percent of respondents aged 65–79. For this age group, the same study reported rates for agoraphobia of 1.7 percent, and for panic disorders, 1.4 percent. Similar rates were reported in the ECA studies (Myers et al., 1984). For men and women aged 60 or older, prevalence rates for agoraphobia ranged from 1.0 to 5.5 percent across study sites, simple phobias from 0.7 to 12.5 percent, and panic disorders from 0.1 to 0.4 percent.

Age Differences in Prevalence Rates

Comparisons across age groups in large epidemiological studies have revealed that those over the age of 65 are less likely than young and middle-aged adults to suffer from anxiety disorders (Myers et al., 1984; Uhlenhuth et al., 1983). These findings, however, should not lead us to disregard anxiety disorders as a major mental health problem of the elderly. These same studies found that rates for anxiety disorders far outweigh rates for depressive disorders in the elderly. In addition, anxiety in late life may be manifested in ways that deserve special attention by mental health researchers and practitioners.

Gender Differences in Prevalence Rates

In general, most findings suggest that women have higher rates of anxiety disorders than men (Himmelfarb & Murrel, 1984; Myers et al., 1984; Uhlenhuth et al., 1983). However, the manifestations seem to differ with men displaying more physical symptoms and having higher mortality than women. Women, on the other hand, tend to report more psychological symptoms and show more personality dysfunction than men (Kay & Bergmann, 1980). Such findings suggest that treatments for anxiety may need to differ by symptom presentation.

Diagnostic Issues

There are numerous discussions in the literature on the difficulty of diagnosing anxiety in the elderly (Gurland & Cross, 1982; Kay & Bergmann, 1980; Simon, 1980). Factors such as adverse social conditions, loneliness, widowhood, family problems, and previous psychiatric problems can all contribute to the disguise or exacerbation of symptoms of anxiety in the elderly. The major complicating variable, however, is physical illness. Both acute and chronic illnesses can produce the same physical signs (for example, cold sweats, heart palpitations) that are symptoms of anxiety. The inextricable relationship between the physical and mental health of the elderly has been clearly established (see chapter 2). Thus, accurate diagnosis is difficult and the coexistence of physical illness and anxiety disorder often goes unrecognized.

Researchers generally agree that late onset of anxiety disorders is uncommon (Pasaminick, Roberts, Lemkau, & Krueger, 1975; Robins et al., 1984; Thyer, Parrish, Curtis, Nesse, & Cameron, 1985), but that anxiety disturbances appear in late life (Kay & Bergmann, 1980; Simon, 1980). These disturbances tend to be expressed in a wide range of symptoms and are thus more likely to be detected by symptom checklists than by stricter DSM-III diagnosis. The range of possible expressions of anxiety contributes to the difficulty of diagnosing anxiety disorders in late life and calls into question the suitability of DSM-III criteria for the elderly (Kay & Bergmann, 1980; Simon, 1980).

Prognosis

No investigations of the nature and course of anxiety disorders in late life were found. Systematic studies of the probability of recovery for older compared to younger patients with anxiety disorders could not be located. The typical treatment for any late-life anxiety disorder is drug prescription (Shader & Greenblatt, 1983). Two investigators, however, found that antianxiety medications were prescribed by family physicians at equal rates for elderly patients with primary diagnoses of physical illness and for elderly patients with primary diagnoses of mental health problems (Mellinger, Balter, Parry, Manheimer, & Cisin, 1984; Uhlenhuth et al., 1983).

Uhlenhuth et al. (1983) also found that somatic health—rather than age, gender, level of emotional distress, or life crisis—was the determining factor that distinguished those who did and did not use anxiolytic medications on a regular basis. Most long-term (daily use for over one year) users of anxiolytic medication were 50 years of age or older. The association between age and use of anxiolytics could be explained by physical health. Without making any definitive statements about prognosis for elderly men and women suffering from anxiety disorders, these studies suggest that the treatment and course of anxiety disorders are inextricably tied to the course of physical illness.

Schizophrenia and Paranoid Disorders

Schizophrenia and paranoia in late life are typified by serious disturbances in thinking and behavior. Current nomenclature describes schizophrenia and paranoia as distinct disorders (APA, 1980). Many clinicians and researchers, however, have adopted the European term *paraphrenia* to describe elderly patients with a schizophrenic-like syndrome that includes paranoid delusions and that arises in late life (Bridge & Wyatt, 1980; Gurland & Cross, 1982; Raskind, Alvarez, & Herlin, 1979; Spira, Dysken, Lazarus, Davis, & Salzman, 1984). For the purposes of the present review, empirical investigations of schizophrenia, paranoia, and paraphrenia are reported together.

Prevalence

Most studies of schizophrenia and paranoid disorders in late life were conducted in Europe. Although these studies used appropriate sampling techniques to obtain large representative samples, investigators relied exclusively on psychiatric interviews without always specifying diagnostic criteria to identify cases (see table 1–5). Prevalence rates for schizophrenia ranged from 0.0 to 1.1 with a median of 0.15; rates reported for paraphrenia and paranoia ranged from 0.0 to 1.8 percent with a median of 0.6. The only U.S. figures were reported by George et al. (1987) as part of the ECA studies. Prevalence rates for schizophrenia in old age were consistent with European studies, suggesting a prevalence of less than 1 percent in the geriatric population. No study conducted in the United States specifically examined late-onset schizophrenia or paranoid disorders. Two studies of paranoid symptoms among community-resident elderly were located. Lowenthal et al. (1967) found that 17 percent of elderly men and women who reported significant psychological symptoms had symptoms of suspiciousness; 13 percent reported paranoid delusions. Christenson and Blazer (1984) found a 4 percent prevalence of generalized persecutory ideation in a community-resident geriatric population.

Risk Factors

Schizophrenia is typically acquired before the age of 35 with hereditary factors implicated in the etiology of the disorder (see review by Bridge & Wyatt, 1980). Patients admitted to mental hospitals with late-onset disorders were less likely to have a family history of schizophrenia than were younger schizophrenic patients, but were more likely than community-resident elderly to have such a family history (Funding, 1961; Kay, 1963). Studies of geropsychiatric hospital admissions also revealed that women were more likely to have late-onset disorders than were men (Kay & Roth, 1961; Raskind et al., 1979). High rates of hearing impairment were also found among elderly patients with paranoid disorders (Cooper, Garside, & Kay, 1976; Kay & Roth, 1961; Post, 1966). Christenson and Blazer (1984) found significant associations between visual and hearing impairment and paranoid ideation among community-resident elderly.

Special Late-Life Features

Studies that followed schizophrenic patients into old age revealed declines in affective expression, diminished severity of psychotic symptoms, and increased sociability (Bleuler, 1974; Ciompi, 1985; Wenger, 1958). Chronic schizophrenics also tended to remain single and have unstable employment histories (Astrup, Essum, & Holmboe, 1962). Cognitive impairment was frequently observed as chronic schizophrenics aged; rates of cognitive impairment were similar to or only slightly higher than among community-resident elderly (Ciompi, 1985; Muller, 1971; Roth, 1955).

Table 1-5
Quantitative Summary of Epidemiologic Studies of Schizophrenia and Paranoid Disorder

Authors	Sampling frame	N	Age range	Diagnostic procedures	Rates 65 +	
					Schizophrenia	Paranoia/ paraphrenia
Bollerup (1975)	Delimited area (Denmark)	588	70	Psychiatric interview	0.3%	—
Cooper (1984)	Random registry (Germany)	343	65 +	Psychiatric interview	0.0%	—
George et al. (1987)	Area probability New Haven, CT Baltimore, MD St. Louis, MO Central NC	14,759	18 +	DIS— interview	0.2% 0.9% 0.0% 0.0%	—
Kay et al. (1964)	Random (England)	294	65 +	Psychiatric interview	1.1%	0.0%
Nielsen (1962)	Delimited area (Denmark)	994	65 +	Psychiatric interview	0.3%	0.6%
Parsons (Swansea) (1965)	Random (Swansea)	271	65 +	Psychiatric interview	—	1.8%
Weissman & Myers (1979)	Stratified random (Connecticut)	515	26 +	SADS— interview	0.0%	—

Elderly patients with late-onset disorders tend to present with paranoid symptoms (Chacko, Molinari, Marmion, Adams, & Moffic, 1984; Larson & Nyman, 1970; Pfeiffer, 1976); only about one-half also experience hallucinations and bizarre delusions (Chacko et al., 1984; Molinari & Chacko, 1983). In the remaining elderly patients, the delusional idea is usually focused on one theme and often occurs in the presence of normal daily functioning and an otherwise intact sensorium (Raskind, 1982; Tarter & Perley, 1975). Further research is needed to determine whether late-onset schizophrenia and paranoid disorders are distinct disorders with symptomatology unique to old age.

Prognosis

The prognosis of schizophrenia is poor. Schizophrenics are at greater risk for mortality, primarily due to more frequent suicides, than are their age-matched peers (Black, Warrack, & Winokur, 1985a, 1985b; Christie, 1982; Haugland, Craig, Goodman & Siegel, 1985; Marinow, 1972; Martin, Cloninger, Guze, & Clayton, 1985; Tsuang & Woolson, 1977). Recent studies suggest that prognosis is improving with the widespread use of neuroleptic medications (Beck, 1968; Duckworth et al., 1979; Katona et al., 1983). Despite these improvements, schizophrenics are at risk for institutionalization. Release from psychiatric hospitals often means reinstitutionalization in nursing homes (Beck, 1968; Muller, 1971). Elderly patients with late-onset paranoid disorders have a relatively favorable outcome compared to patients with chronic schizophrenia and dementing illnesses (Blessed & Wilson, 1982; Kay & Roth, 1961; Roth, 1955). In addition, Duckworth et al. (1979) found that current patients diagnosed with a paranoid disorder are more than three times as likely to be discharged from the hospital than their counterparts 20 years ago.

Conclusions and Research Recommendations

Depression

Depressive illness is less prevalent in late life but remains a significant problem. Approximately 15 percent of community-resident elderly experience significant dysphoria and 4 to 5 percent suffer from major depressive disorder. Identified risk factors for late-life depression are not unique to the elderly, but are significant correlates of depression throughout life. The fact that low education, low income, being female, divorced, separated, or widowed, and in poor health predict depressive disorder at all ages suggests that the etiology of depression is the same throughout the life course. Symptom presentation, however, may change in late life. The elderly are more likely than younger patients to have delusional depressions or to have somatic complaints or hypochondriasis along with more typical depressive symptoms. The prognosis for depression in late life is worse than in younger years. Elderly patients with recurrent or chronic depression are at greater risk both for institutionalization and death.

More research is needed in a number of areas. Accurate estimates of the prevalence of depression in institutional populations is needed; little is known about the mental health needs of the elderly living in nursing homes and board and care facilities. More research is needed on chronic depressive illness in late life. With the poor prognosis for elderly with chronic depression, research that focuses on the chronic patient may point the way toward new, more effective treatment strategies. Although the link between physical illness and depression is clear, prospective studies that target the incidence and sequencing of both physical and psychiatric illness may lead to better prevention and early identification and treatment of psychiatric disorders (see chapter 2).

Senile Dementia

The rates for senile dementia increase dramatically with age and are in excess of 20 percent for people aged 80 or older. Estimates of the prevalence of severe cognitive impairment are more consistent than prevalence estimates for mild dementia and indicate that approximately 6 percent of those over the age of 65 suffer from serious intellectual impairment. Dementia of the Alzheimer's type and multi-infarct dementia are the most common forms of dementia. Potentially reversible dementias, however, are found in 10 to 30 percent of those evaluated, highlighting the need for careful diagnosis. The prognosis of senile dementia is poor; the risks of institutionalization and mortality are higher for the demented elderly than for their nondemented peers. The social, financial, and emotional impact of dementia on the family is great, with family caregivers at risk themselves for major depressive disorder.

There are far-reaching gaps in the literature on senile dementia. Research diagnostic criteria that allow differential diagnosis must be developed before accurate prevalence rates can be established. Studies must also include the institutionalized elderly; very little is known about the prevalence of senile dementia among the institutionalized elderly and efforts to provide treatment within institutional settings. Prospective studies that allow risk factors to be identified are needed. Finally, careful studies that chart the intellectual, functional, and behavioral declines associated with senile dementia and the impact of such declines on the family are needed in order to identify potential points for intervention.

Alcohol Abuse and Dependence

Alcohol abuse and dependence are less prevalent in late life but remain a significant problem, especially for elderly men. Approximately 6 percent of community-resident elderly report heavy drinking. Only 1.4 percent suffer from alcohol abuse or dependence. Men are at greater risk for alcohol-related problems than are women. No other risk factors consistently emerged from the literature. Elderly alcoholics are often grouped as early- or late-onset alcoholics. Clear differences between the two groups with regard to symptomatology, drinking patterns or treatment outcome have not been found. Elderly alcoholics are at high risk for institutionalization and death. Treatment is often delayed until physical complications are severe. Physicians frequently fail to diagnose alcohol-related problems in the elderly. When treated, success occurs at a rate equal to or higher than in younger alcoholic patients.

Systematic studies of symptomatology, premorbid characteristics, and course of illness will confirm or refute proposed differences between early- and late-onset alcoholics. The role of stressors as potential triggers of alcohol consumption in old age requires further study. Finney and Moos (1984) have proposed a comprehensive causal model to guide future research on stress and drinking patterns in late life. Finally, research that compares various diagnostic criteria is needed to determine whether age-specific criteria are needed to accurately diagnose alcoholism in geriatric populations.

Drug Abuse and Dependence

Drug abuse and dependence is almost nonexistent among community-resident elderly. Elderly patients with opiate dependence are found in drug treatment programs, but at rates much lower than in younger patients. Opiate dependence among the elderly is increasing rapidly, however, as younger addicts age. Elderly men and women are the largest consumers of prescription drugs, with the elderly more likely than younger adults to regularly take psychotropic medications. Medication compliance is less likely among the elderly than other age groups, but the actual prevalence of medication misuse is unknown.

Drug abuse in old age is understudied. Although prevalence data from the ECA studies suggest that drug abuse and dependence among community-resident elderly is almost nonexistent, there may be significant medication misuse in this population. Elderly men and women are the highest consumers of psychotropic medications despite a lower prevalence in old age for almost all psychiatric disorders. Patterns of consumption, types of misuse, and risk factors for misuse need further study.

Anxiety Disorders

Anxiety disorders are less prevalent in old age than in young adulthood or middle age but are among the more prevalent psychiatric disorders in late life. Generalized anxiety is most frequently diagnosed in the elderly followed by simple phobias, agoraphobia, and panic disorders. Because late onset of anxiety disorders is uncommon, late-life anxiety disorders are typically chronic. Women are at greater risk for anxiety disorders in late life than are men. In addition, the manifestations of anxiety disorders differ between men and women; men display more physicial symptoms whereas women express anxiety with more psychological symptoms and personality dysfunction. The elderly are typically treated for anxiety disorders with anxiolytic agents prescribed by family physicians. Somatic health complaints are primary predictors of anxiolytic medications in late life.

More research on nonpharmacologic treatments for the elderly with anxiety disorders is needed. This is particularly important because the elderly are more likely to use multiple psychotropic agents and are at greater risk of complications due to polypharmacy. If effective nonpharmacologic treatments are found, a wider range of treatment options would be available for the elderly who suffer from anxiety disorders. Research on high-risk groups is also needed. It has been suggested that local registers of older people could be used to generate data for prospective studies of high-risk groups within elderly populations (Kay & Bergmann, 1980). Such studies could provide not only accurate prevalence data, but also facilitate investigations of those multiply at risk for anxiety disorders in late life.

Schizophrenia and Paranoid Disorders

Schizophrenia and paranoid disorders are quite rare in community-resident elderly. Household surveys suggest that the prevalence of these disorders is less than 1 percent. Controversy about diagnostic criteria, however, limits confidence in these prevalence estimates. Genetic factors play a primary role in the acquisition of schizophrenia, which typically occurs before age 35. Elderly women and those with hearing impairments are at risk for late-onset disorders. Paraphrenia may also have a genetic component but with a different mechanism than that observed for schizophrenia. Symptom patterns and course of illness may differ for early- and late-onset schizophrenia and paranoid disorders. Systematic research in community-resident and institutional populations is needed to verify clinical reports. Prognosis for schizophrenia is poor, but has improved with the development of neuroleptic medications. Prognosis is more favorable for late-onset disorders.

Very little is known about schizophrenia and paranoid disorders in late life. A comprehensive research program is needed to determine the prevalence of and risk factors for these disorders. Research that considers age of onset is needed to determine whether a separate diagnostic category is needed for late-onset schizophrenia accompanied by paranoid delusions.

Policy Recommendations

Education

Educational efforts directed toward medical and mental health professionals can help ensure accurate diagnosis of senile dementia, alcohol and substance abuse, and anxiety disorders. Awareness of the many possible clinical presentations of these problems can only help to reduce diagnostic error. Educational efforts directed to elderly medical patients can increase awareness of the dangers of polypharmacy and boost medication compliance.

Screening and Referral Services

Screening and referral services in which mental health professionals work directly with the elderly in medical services would reach a group at highest risk for depression and anxiety disorders. Geriatric nurse practitioners could work with psychologists and psychiatrists to add mental health evaluation to comprehensive medical screening offered in specialized geriatric health clinics (see chapter 4).

Community Outreach Programs

Community outreach programs are needed to target those at risk for psychiatric disorders and either bring direct treatment to elderly patients or encourage their involvement in prevention programs (see chapters 4 and 8). Programs for the newly widowed currently operate on such a model and could be expanded to include others at risk for various psychiatric disorders. Outreach programs in the community may lead to early diagnosis and treatment of potentially reversible dementias. Early detection and treatment may also lead to improved care by the family and prevent institutionalization later in the course of the disease. Outreach programs are also needed to identify and treat those elderly with substance abuse problems who are at greatest risk for institutionalization and death. Comprehensive and aggressive treatments that include nutrition education, family therapy, stress reduction, and individual psychotherapy need to be brought into the community.

Prevention Programs

Programs designed for community-resident elderly and focusing on more transient psychological symptoms or specific risk factors may help to prevent major psychiatric illness. One prototype is the kind of class offered by the Menlo Park and Palo Alto Veterans Administration hospitals in California. Behavioral therapy techniques are used to teach older class members to monitor depressing symptoms and alter mood by increasing pleasant activities.

Programs designed for community-resident elderly with hearing impairments may help to prevent or slow down the development of paranoid symptoms in old age. A self-help model may be least threatening and could provide support for the use of hearing aids, concerns about losses associated with aging, and coping strategies.

Comprehensive Home-Based Services

Comprehensive home-based services may help to maintain the elderly suffering from schizophrenia and paranoia in the community. Chronic schizophrenics and patients with paranoid disorders have been successfully discharged into the community. Patients with few family resources may require assistance with medications and social service needs. Comprehensive home-based programs are also needed to assist family caregivers and elderly persons with senile dementia. Because many demented persons eventually need institutionalization, program planning could be based on a continuum of services that includes direct community services to the patient, supportive services to family caregivers, and services brought into institutions after placement.

References

Abrahams, R.B., & Patterson, R.D. (1978–1979). Psychological distress among the community elderly: Prevalence, characteristics and implications for service. *International Journal of Aging and Human Development, 9,* 1–18.

Akesson, H.O. (1969). A population study of senile and arteriosclerotic psychoses. *Human Heredity, 19,* 546–566.

Amenson, C.S., & Lewinsohn, P.M. (1981). An investigation into the observed sex difference in prevalence of unipolar depression. *Journal of Abnormal Psychology, 90,* 1–13.

American Psychiatric Association. (1980). *Diagnostic and statistical manual of mental disorders* (3rd ed.). Washington, DC: Author.

Astrup, C., Essum, P., & Holmboe, R. (1962). *Prognosis in functional psychosis.* Springfield, IL: C.C. Thomas.

Ball, J.C., & Chambers, C.D. (1970). *The epidemiology of opiate addiction in the United States.* Springfield, IL: C.C. Thomas.

Barboriak, J.L., Roomey, C.B., Leitschuk, T.H., & Anderson, A.J. (1978). Alcohol and nutrient intake of elderly men. *Journal of the American Dietetic Association, 72,* 493–495.

Barnes, G.M. (1979). Alcohol use among older persons: Findings from a Western New York State general population survey. *Journal of the American Geriatrics Society, 27,* 244–250.

Bateman, N.I., & Peterson, D.M. (1971). Variables related to outcome of treatment for hospitalized alcoholics. *International Journal of Addiction, 6,* 215–224.

Beck, M.N. (1968). Twenty-five and thirty-five-year follow up of first admissions to mental hospitals. *Canadian Journal of Psychiatry, 13,* 219–229.

Bergmann, K. (1969). The epidemiology of senile dementia. *British Journal of Hospital Medicine, 44,* 727–732.

Berndt, S.M., Berndt, D.J., & Byars, W.D. (1983). A multi-institutional study of depression in family practice. *The Journal of Family Practice, 16,* 83–87.

Bieleski, R.J., & Friedel, R.O. (1976). Prediction of tricyclic antidepressant response: A critical review. *Archives of General Psychiatry, 26,* 57–63.

Black, D.W., Warrack, G., & Winokur, G. (1985a). The Iowa record-linkage study: Pt. 1. Suicides and accidental deaths among psychiatric patients. *Archives of General Psychiatry, 42,* 71–75.

Black, D.W., Warrack, G., & Winokur, G. (1985b). The Iowa record-linkage study: Pt. 3. Excess mortality among patients with "functional" disorders. *Archives of General Psychiatry, 42,* 82–88.

Blaney, R., Radford, I.S., & MacKenzie, G., (1975). A Belfast study of outcome in the treatment of alcoholism. *British Journal of Addiction, 70,* 40–50.

Blazer, D.G. (1978). *Multidimensional functional assessment: The OARS methodology* (2nd ed.). Durham, NC: Duke University Center for the Study of Aging and Human Development.

Blazer, D.G. (1983). The epidemiology of psychiatric disorder in the elderly population. In L. Grinspoon (Ed.), *Psychiatry update: The American Psychiatric Association annual review* (Vol. 2, pp. 247–261). Washington, DC: American Psychiatric Press.

Blazer, D.G., & Williams, C.D. (1980). Epidemiology of dysphoria and depression in an elderly population. *American Journal of Psychiatry, 137,* 439–444.

Blessed, G., & Wilson, I.D. (1982). The contemporary history of mental disorder in old age. *British Journal of Psychiatry, 141,* 59–67.

Bleuler, M. (1974). The long-term course of the schizophrenic psychoses. *Psychological Medicine, 4,* 244–254.

Blose, I.L. (1978). The relationship of alcohol and the elderly. *Alcoholism, 2,* 17–21.

Blum, R.H., & Braunstein, L. (1967). Mind-altering drugs and dangerous behavior. In President's Commission on Law Enforcement and Administration of Justice Task Force, *Report: Drunkenness.* Washington, DC: Government Printing Office.

Bosmann, H.B. (1984). Pharmacology of alcoholism and aging. In J.T. Hartford & T. Samorajski (Eds.), *Alcoholism in the elderly: Social and biomedical issues* (pp. 161–174). New York: Raven.

Brand, F.N., Smith, R.T., & Brand, P.A. (1977). Effect of economic barriers to medical care on patients' noncompliance. *Public Health Reports, 92,* 72–78.

Bridge, P.T., & Wyatt, R.J. (1980). Paraphrenia: Paranoid states of late life: Pt. 2. American research. *Journal of the American Geriatrics Society, 28,* 201–205.

Brody, E.M. (1985). Parent care as a normative family stress. *Gerontologist, 25,* 19–29.

Brody, E.M., Lawton, M.P., & Liebowitz, B. (1984). Senile dementia: Public policy and adequate institutional care. *American Journal of Public Health, 74,* 1381–1383.

Brody, J.A., & Mills, G.S. (1978). On considering alcohol as a risk factor in specific diseases. *American Journal of Epidemiology, 107,* 462–466.

Broe, G.A., Akhtav, A.J., Andrews, G.R., Caird, F.I., Gilmore, A.J.J., & McLennan, W.J. (1976). Neurological disorders in the elderly at home. *Journal of Neurology, Neurosurgery, & Psychiatry, 39,* 362–366.

Brown, R.P. Sweeney, J., Loutsch, E., Kocsis, J., & Frances, A. (1984). Involutional melancholia revisited. *American Journal of Psychiatry, 141,* 24–28.

Cahalan, D. (1970). *Problem drinkers.* San Francisco, CA: Jossey-Bass.

Cahalan, D., & Cisin, I.H. (1968). American drinking practices: Summary of findings from a national probability sample: Pt. 1. Extent of drinking by population subgroups. *Quarterly Journal of Studies on Alcohol, 29,* 130–151.

Cahalan, D., Cisin, I.H., & Crossley, H.M. (1969). *American drinking practices.* New Brunswick, NJ: Rutgers University Press.

Capel, W., Goldsmith, B., Waddell, K., & Stewart, G. (1972). The aging narcotic addict: An increasing problem for the next decades. *Journal of Gerontology, 27,* 102–106.

Capel, W.C., & Pepper, L.G. (1978). The aging addict: A longitudinal study of known abusers. *Addictive Diseases, 3,* 389–403.

Capel, W.C., & Stewart, G.T. (1971). The management of drug abuse in aging populations: New Orleans findings. *Journal of Drug Issues, 1,* 114–120.

Cavanaugh, S.V.A. (1983). The prevalence of emotional and cognitive dysfunction in a general medical population: Using the MMSE, GHQ, and BDI. *General Hospital Psychiatry, 5,* 15–24.

Cermak, L.S., & Ryback, R.S. (1976). Recovery of verbal short-term memory in alcoholics. *Journal of Studies on Alcohol, 37,* 46–52.

Chacko, R.C., Molinari, V., Marmion, J., Adams, G.L., & Moffic, S. (1984). DSM-III diagnosis in the geropsychiatric patient. *Clinical Gerontologist, 2,* 3–15.

Chambers, C.D. (1971). *An assessment of drug use in the general population.* New York: New York State Narcotics Addiction Control Commission.

Chien, C., Townsend, E.J., & Townsend, A. (1978). Substance use and abuse among the community elderly: The medical aspect. *Addictive Diseases, 3,* 357–372.

Christenson, R., & Blazer, D. (1984). Epidemiology of persecutory ideation in an elderly population in the community. *American Journal of Psychiatry, 141,* 1088–1091.

Christie, A.B. (1982). Changing patterns in mental illness in the elderly. *British Journal of Psychiatry, 140,* 154–159.

Ciompi, L. (1985). Aging and schizophrenic psychosis. *Acta Psychiatrica Scandinavica, 17*(Suppl. 319), 93–105.

Clark, W.B., & Midanik, L. (1982). Alcohol use and alcohol problems among U.S. adults: Results of the 1979 national survey. In National Institute on Alcohol Abuse and Alcoholism, *Alcohol consumption and related problems* (Alcohol and Health, Monograph No. 1, pp. 3–54). Washington, DC: Government Printing Office.

Cohen, B., Kennedy, G., & Eisdorfer, C. (1983). *Clinical reality of the family caring for a relative with Alzheimer's disease and family management.* Paper presented at the annual meeting of the Gerontological Society, San Francisco, CA.

Cole, M.G. (1983). Age, age of onset and course of primary depressive illness in the elderly. *Canadian Journal of Psychiatry, 28,* 102–104.

Comstock, G.W., & Helsing, K.J. (1976). Symptoms of depression in two communities. *Psychological Medicine, 6,* 551–563.

Cooper, A.F., Garside, R.F., & Kay, D.W.K. (1976). A comparison of deaf and non-deaf patients with paranoid and affective psychoses. *British Journal of Psychiatry, 129,* 297–303.

Cooper, B. (1984). Home and away: The disposition of mentally ill old people in an urban population. *Social Psychiatry, 19,* 187–196.

Costello, R.M. (1974). Mortality in an alcoholic cohort. *International Journal of Addiction, 9,* 355–363.

Counte, M.A., Salloway, J.C., & Christman, L. (1982). Age and sex related drinking patterns in alcoholics. In W.G. Wood & M.F. Elias (Eds.), *Alcoholism and aging: Advances in research* (pp. 17–27). Boca Raton, FL: CRC Press.

Cummings, J., Benson, D.F., & Loverma, S. (1980). Reversible dementia: Illustrative cases, definition and review. *Journal of the American Medical Association, 243,* 2434–2439.

Davison, W. (1978). Neurological and mental disturbances due to drugs. *Age and Ageing, 7*(Suppl.), 119–126.

Department of Health and Human Services. (1984). *Alzheimer's disease: Report of the Secretary's Task Force on Alzheimer's Disease* (DHHS Publication No. [ADM] 84–1323). Washington, DC: Government Printing Office.

DiClemente, C.C., & Gordon, J.R. (1984). Aging, alcoholism and addictive behavior change: Diagnostic treatment models. In J.T. Hartford & T. Samorajski (Eds.), *Alcoholism in the elderly: Social and biomedical issues* (pp. 263–275). New York: Raven.

Doyle, J. (1976). *Medication use and misuse study among older persons.* Jacksonville, FL: Cathedral Foundation.

Droller, H. (1964). Some aspects of alcoholism in the elderly. *Lancet, 2,* 137–139.

Duckworth, G.S., Kedward, H.B., & Bailey, W.F. (1979). Prognosis of mental illness in old age: A four-year follow-up study. *Canadian Journal of Psychiatry, 24,* 674–682.

Dunham, R.G. (1981). Aging and changing patterns of alcohol use. *Journal of Psychoactive Drugs, 13,* 143–151.

Eaton, W.W., & Kessler, L.G. (1981). Rates of symptoms of depression in a national sample. *American Journal of Epidemiology, 114,* 528–538.

Eisdorfer, C., & Cohen, D. (1980). Diagnostic criteria for primary neuronal degeneration of the Alzheimer's type. *The Journal of Family Practice, 11,* 553–557.

Essen-Moller, E., Larsson, H., Uddenberg, C., & White, G. (1956). Individual traits and morbidity in a Swedish rural population. *Acta Psychiatrica Scandinavica* (Suppl. 100).

Feighner, J.P., Robins, E., Guze, S.B., Woodruff, R.A., & Winokur, G. (1972). Diagnostic criteria for use in psychiatric research. *Archives of General Psychiatry, 26,* 57–63.

Fengler, A., & Goodrich, N. (1979). Wives of elderly disabled men: The hidden patients. *Gerontologist, 19,* 175–185.

Fillmore, K.M., Bacon, S.D., & Hyman, M. (1979). *The 27-year longitudinal panel study of drinking by students in college, 1949–1976* (Report No. PB 300–302). Springfield, VA: National Technical Information Service.

Fillmore, K.M., & Midanik, L. (1984). Chronicity of drinking problems among men: A longitudinal study. *Journal of Studies on Alcohol, 45,* 228–236.

Finney, J.W., & Moos, R.H. (1984). Life stressors and problem drinking among older adults. *Recent Developments in Alcoholism, 2,* 267–288.

Flinn, G.A., Reisberg, B., & Ferris, S.H. (1984). Neuropsychological models of cerebral dysfunction in chronic alcoholics. In J.T. Hartford & T. Samorajski (Eds.), *Alcohlism in the elderly: Social and biomedical issues* (pp. 175–191). New York: Raven.

Forde, C.V., & Sbordone, R.J. (1980). Attitudes of psychiatrists toward elderly patients. *American Journal of Psychiatry, 137,* 571–575.

Fox, J.H., Topel, J.L., & Huckman, M.S. (1975). Dementia in the elderly—a search for treatable illness. *Journal of Gerontology, 34,* 557–564.

Freemon, F.R. (1976). Evaluation of patients with progressive intellectual deterioration. *Archives of Neurology, 37,* 658–659.

Freemon, F.R., & Rudd, S.M. (1982). Clinical features that predict potentially reversible progressive intellectual deterioration. *Journal of the American Geriatrics Society, 30,* 449–451.

Frerichs, R.R., Aneshensel, C.S., & Clark, V.A. (1981). Prevalence of depression in Los Angeles County. *American Journal of Epidemiology, 113,* 691–699.

Funding, T. (1961). Genetics of paranoid psychoses of later life. *Acta Psychiatrica Scandinavica, 37,* 267–271.

Gaitz, C.M., & Baer, P.E. (1971). Characteristics of elderly patients with alcoholism. *Archives of General Psychiatry, 24,* 372–378.

Garver, D.L. (1984). Age effects on alcohol metabolism. In J.T. Hartford & T. Samorajski (Eds.), *Alcoholism in the elderly: Social and biomedical issues* (pp. 153–159). New York: Raven.

George, L.K., Blazer, D.G., Winfield-Laird, I., Leaf, P.J., & Eischbach, R. (1987). Psychiatric disorders and mental health service use in later life: Evidence from the Epidemiologic Catchment Area program. In J. Brody & G. Maddox (Eds.), *Epidemiology in late life* (pp. 13–27). New York: Springer.

Glantz, M. (1981). Predictions of elderly drug abuse. *Journal of Psychoactive Drugs, 13,* 117–126.

Glatt, N.M. (1978). Experiences with elderly alcoholics in England. *Alcoholism: Clinical and Experimental Research, 2,* 23–26.

Go, R.C.P., Todorov, A.B., & Elston, R.C. (1978). The malignancy of dementias. *Annals of Neurology, 3,* 559–561.

Gurin, G., Veroff, J., & Feld, S. (1960). *Americans view their mental health.* New York: Basic Books.

Gurland, B.J. (1976). The comparative frequency of depression in various adult age groups. *Journal of Gerontology, 31,* 283–292.

Gurland, B.J. & Cross, P.S. (1982). Epidemiology of psychopathology in old age. *Psychiatric Clinics of North America, 5,* 11–26.

Gurland, B.J., Dean, L., Cross, P., & Golden, R. (1980). The epidemiology of depression and dementia in the elderly: The use of multiple indicators of these conditions. In J.O. Cole & J.E. Barrett (Eds.), *Psychopathology in the aged* (pp. 37–60). New York: Raven.

Guttman, D. (1978). Patterns of legal drug use by older Americans. *Addictive Diseases, 3,* 337–356.

Haugland, G., Craig, T.J., Goodman, A.B., & Siegel, C. (1983). Mortality in the era of deinstitutionalization. *American Journal of Psychiatry, 140,* 848–852.

Heller, F., & Wynne, R. (1974). Drug misuse by the elderly: Indications and treatment suggestions. In E. Senay, V. Shorty, & H. Alksne (Eds.), *Developments in the field of drug abuse* (pp. 945–955). Cambridge, MA: Schenkman.

Hesbacher, P.T., Rickels, K., Morris, R.J., Newman, H., & Rosenfeld, H. (1980). Psychiatric illness in family practice. *Journal of Clinical Psychiatry, 41,* 6–10.

Himmelfarb, S., & Murrel, S.A. (1984). The prevalence and correlates of anxiety symptoms in older adults. *The Journal of Psychology, 116,* 159–167.

Hirschfeld, R.M.A., & Cross, C.K. (1982). Epidemiology of affective disorders: Psychosocial risk factors. *Archives of General Psychiatry, 39,* 35–46.

Hubbard, R.W., Santos, J.F., & Santos, M.A. (1979). Alcohol and older adults: Overt and covert influences. *Social Casework, 60,* 166–170.

Hutton, J.T. (1981). Results of clinical assessment for dementia: Implications for epidemiologic studies. In J.A. Mortimer & L.M. Schulman (Eds.), *The epidemiology of dementia* (pp. 62–69). New York: Oxford University Press.

Inciardi, J., McBride, D., Russe, B., & Wells, K. (1978). Acute drug reactions among the aged: A research note. *Addictive Diseases, 3,* 383–388.

James, M. (1979). *Substance abuse among Michigan's senior citizens: Patterns of use and provider perspectives.* Lansing, MI: Michigan Office of Service to the Aging and Michigan Office of Substance Abuse Services.

Janik, S.W., & Dunham, R.G. (1983). A nationwide examination of the need for specific alcoholism treatment programs for the elderly. *Journal of Studies on Alcohol, 44,* 307–317.

Johnson, C.L., & Catalano, D.J. (1983). A longitudinal study of family supports to impaired elderly. *Gerontologist, 23,* 612–618.

Jones, B.P., Moskowitz, H.R., & Butters, N. (1975). Olfactory discrimination in alcoholic Korsakoff patients. *Neuropsychologia, 13,* 173–179.

Kaneko, Z. (1969). Epidemiological studies on mental disorders of the aged in Japan. In *Proceedings of the 8th International Congress of Gerontology: Vol. 1. Abstracts of symposia & lectures* (pp. 284–287). Washington, DC: International Association of Gerontology.

Kater, R.M.H., Roggin, G., Tobon, F., Zieve, P., & Iber, F.L. (1969). Increased route of clearance of drugs from the circulation of alcoholics. *American Journal of Medical Science, 258,* 35–39.

Katona, C.L.E., Lowe, D., & Jack, R.L. (1983). *Acta Psychiatrica Scandinavica, 67,* 297–306.

Katzman, R., & Karasu, T.B. (1975). Differential diagnosis of dementia. In W. Fields (Ed.), *Neurological and sensory disorders in the elderly* (pp. 103–134). New York: Stratton Intercontinental Medical Book Corp.

Kay, D. (1963). Late paraphrenia and its bearing on the aetiology of schizophrenia. *Acta Psychiatrica Scandinavica, 39,* 159–163.

Kay, D.W.K., Beamish, P., & Roth, M. (1964). Old age and mental disorders in Newcastle-upon-Tyne. *British Journal of Psychiatry, 110,* 668–682.

Kay, D.W.K., & Bergmann, K. (1980). Epidemiology of mental disorders among the aged in the community. In J.E. Birren & R.B. Sloane (Eds.), *Handbook of mental health and aging* (pp. 34–55). Englewood Cliffs, NJ: Prentice-Hall.

Kay, D.W.K., Bergmann, K., Foster, E., McKechnie, A.H., & Roth, M. (1970). Mental illness and hospital usage in the elderly: A random sample followed up. *Comprehensive Psychiatry, 11,* 26–35.

Kay, D.W.K., & Roth, M. (1961). Environmental and hereditary factors in the schizophrenia of old age (late paraphrenia) and their bearing on the general problem of causation in schizophrenia. *Journal of Mental Science, 107,* 649–686.

Kokmen, E., & Schoenberg, B.S. (1980). Epidemiological patterns and clinical features of dementia in a defined U.S. population (Abstract). *Annals of Neurology, 8,* 116.

Korboot, P., & Naylor, G.F.K. (1972). Patterns of WAIS and MIA in alcoholic dementia. *Australian Journal of Psychology, 24,* 227–234.

Larson, C., & Nyman, G. (1970). Age of onset in schizophrenia. *Human Heredity, 20,* 241.

Larson, E.B., Reifler, B.V., Featherstone, H.J., & English, D.R. (1984). Dementia in elderly outpatients: A prospective study. *Annals of Internal Medicine, 100,* 417–423.

Larson, E.B., Reifler, B.V., Sumi, S.M., Canfield, C.G., & Chinn, N.M. (1985). Diagnostic evaluation of 200 elderly outpatients with suspected dementia. *Journal of Gerontology, 40,* 536–543.

Leeper, J.D., Badger, L.W., & Milo, T. (1985). Mental disorders among physical disability determination patients. *American Journal of Public Health, 75,* 78–79.

Linn, M.W. (1978). Attrition of older alcoholics from treatment. *Addictive Disease, 3,* 437–447.

Lowenthal, M.F., Berkman, P.L., Brissette, G.C., Buehler, J.A., Pierce, R.C., Robinson, B.C., & Trier, M.L. (1967). *Aging and mental disorder in San Francisco: A social psychiatric study.* San Francisco, CA: Jossey-Bass.

Maddix, J.F., & Desmond, D.P. (1980). New light on the maturing out hypothesis in opioid dependence. *Bulletin on Narcotics, 32,* 15–25.

Mandolini, A. (1981). The social contexts of aging and drug use: Theoretical and methodological insights. *Journal of Psychoactive Drugs, 13,* 135–142.

Mann, A.H., Jenkins, R., & Belsey, E. (1981). The twelve-month outcome of patients with neurotic illness in general practice. *Psychological Medicine, 11,* 535–550.

Marinow, A. (1972). Suicide among schizophrenics. *Vita, 82,* 1–16.

Marsden, C.D., & Harrison, M.J.G. (1972). Outcome of investigations in patients with presenile dementia. *British Medical Journal, 2,* 249–252.

Martin, R.L., Cloninger, R., Guze, S.B., & Clayton, P.J. (1985). Mortality in a follow-up of 500 psychiatric outpatients: Pt. 2. Cause-specific mortality. *Archives of General Psychiatry, 42,* 58–66.

McCusker, J., Cherubin, C.F. & Zimberg, S. (1971). Prevalence of alcoholism in a general municipal hospital population. *New York State Journal of Medicine, 71,* 751–754.

McKhann, G., Drachman, D., Folstein, M., Katzman, R., Price, D., & Stadlan, E.M. (1984). Clinical diagnosis of Alzheimer's disease: Report of the NINCDS–ADRDA work group under the auspices of Department of Health and Human Services Task Force on Alzheimer's Disease. *Neurology, 34,* 939–944.

Mellinger, G.D., Balter, M.B., Parry, H.J., Manheimer, D.I., & Cisin, I.H. (1984). An overview of psychotherapeutic drug use in the United States. In E. Josephson & E.E. Carroll (Eds.), *Drug use: Epidemiological and sociological approaches* (pp. 333–366). New York: Hemisphere.

Meyers, A.R., Goldman, E., Hingson, R., Scotch, N., & Mangione, T. (1981–1982). Evidence for cohort or generational differences in the drinking behavior of older adults. *International Journal of Aging and Human Development, 14,* 31–44.

Meyers, A.R., Hingson, R., Mucatel, M., & Goldman, E. (1982). Social and psychological correlates of problem drinking in old age. *Journal of the American Geriatrics Society, 30,* 452–456.

Meyers, B.S., Kalayam, B., & Mei-Tal, V. (1984). Late-onset delusional depression: A distinct clinical entity? *Journal of Clinical Psychiatry, 45,* 347–349.

Molinari, V., & Chacko, R. (1983). The classification of paranoid disorders in the elderly: A clinical problem. *Clinical Gerontologist, 1*(4), 31–37.

Moon, M. (1983). The role of the family in the economic well-being of the elderly. *Gerontologist, 23,* 45–50.

Mortimer, J.A., Schuman, L.M., & French, L.R. (1981). Epidemiology of dementing illness. In J.A. Mortimer & L.M. Schuman (Eds.), *The epidemiology of dementia* (p. 3). New York: Oxford University Press.

Muller, C. (1971). Schizophrenia in advanced senescence. *British Journal of Psychiatry, 118,* 347–348.

Murrel, S.A., Himmelfarb, S., & Wright, K. (1983). Prevalence of depression and its correlates in older adults. *American Journal of Epidemiology, 117,* 173–185.

Myers, J.K., Weissman, M.M., Tischler, G.L., Holzer, C.E., Leaf, P.J., Orvaschel, H., Anthony, J.C., Boyd, J.H., Burke, J.D., Kramer, M., & Stoltzman, R. (1984). Six-month prevalence of psychiatric disorders in three communities. *Archives of General Psychiatry, 41,* 959–970.

Myerson, D.J., & Mayer, J. (1966). Origins, treatment and destiny of skid-row alcoholic men. *New England Journal of Medicine, 275,* 419–426.

National Center for Health Statistics. (1979). Advance report: Final mortality statistics, 1977. *Monthly Vital Statistics Report, 28,* 1–11.

National Institute of Mental Health. (1970). *Statistical note* (No. 31). Washington, DC: Government Printing Office.

Neely, E., & Patrick, M.L. (1968). Problems of aged persons taking medications at home. *Nursing Research, 17,* 52–55.

Nielsen, J. (1962). Geronto-psychiatric period-prevalence investigation in a geographically delimited population. *Acta Psychiatrica Scandinavica, 38,* 307–330.

O'Donnell, J.A. (1969). *Narcotic addicts in Kentucky* (Public Health Service Publication No. 1881). Washington, DC: Government Printing Office.

Orlean, C.T., George, L.K., Houpt, J.L., & Brodie, H.K.H. (1985). How primary care physicians treat psychiatric disorders: A national survey of family practitioners. *American Journal of Psychiatry, 142,* 52–57.

Parsons, P.L. (1965). Mental health of Swansea's old folk. *British Journal of Preventive and Social Medicine, 19,* 43–47.

Pasaminick, B., Roberts, D.W., Lemkau, P.V., & Krueger, D.E. (1975). A survey of mental disease in an urban population. *American Journal of Public Health, 47,* 923–929.

Pascarelli, E.F. (1979). An update on drug dependence in the elderly. *Journal of Drug Issues, 9,* 47–54.

Pascarelli, E.F., & Fischer, W. (1974). Drug dependence in the elderly. *International Journal of Aging and Human Development, 5,* 347–356.

Petersen, D., & Thomas, C. (1975). Acute drug reactions among the elderly. *Journal of Gerontology, 30,* 552–556.

Pfeiffer, E. (1976). Psychopathology and social pathology. In S.E. Birren & K.W. Schaie (Eds.), *Handbook of the psychology of aging.* New York: Van Nostrand.

Post, F. (1962). *The significance of affective symptoms in old age: A follow-up study of one hundred patients.* London: Oxford University Press.

Post, F. (1966). *Persistent persecutory states of the elderly.* Oxford: Pergamon.

Post, F. (1972). The management and nature of depressive illnesses in late life: A follow-through study. *British Journal of Psychiatry, 121,* 393–404.

Pottieger, A.E., & Inciardi, J.A. (1981). Aging on the street: Drug use and crime among older men. *Journal of Psychoactive Drugs, 13,* 199–211.

Radloff, L.S. (1977). The CES-D Scale: A self-report depressive scale for research in the general population. *Journal of Applied Psychological Measurement, 1,* 385–401.

Raskind, M.A. (1982). Paranoid syndromes in the elderly. In C. Eisdorfer & W.E. Fann (Eds.), *Treatment of psychopathology in the aging* (pp. 184–191). New York: Springer.

Raskind, M.A., Alvarez, C., & Herlin, S. (1979). Fluphenazine enanthate in the outpatient treatment of late paraphrenia. *Journal of the American Geriatrics Society, 27,* 459–463.

Raymond, E.F., Michals, T.J., & Steer, R.A. (1980). Prevalence and correlates of depression in elderly persons. *Psychological Reports, 47,* 1055–1061.

Redick, R.W., & Taube, C.A. (1980). Demography and mental health care of the aged. In J.E. Birren & R.B. Sloane (Eds.), *Handbook of mental health and aging* (pp. 57–71). Englewood Cliffs, NJ: Prentice-Hall.

Regier, D.A., Myers, J.K. Kramer, M., Robins, L.N., Blazer, D.G., Hough, R.L., Eaton, W.W., & Locke, B.Z. (1984). The NIMH Epidemiologic Catchment Area studies: An overview. *Archives of General Psychiatry, 41,* 934–941.

Richter, J.M., Barsky, A.J., & Happ, J.A. (1983). The treatment of depression in elderly patients. *The Journal of Family Practice, 17,* 43–47.

Ripley, H.S. (1973). Suicidal behavior in Edinburgh and Seattle. *American Journal of Psychiatry, 130,* 995–1001.

Robins, L.N., Helzer, J.E., Croughan, J., & Ratcliff, K.S. (1981). National Institute of Mental Health Diagnostic Interview Schedule: Its history, characteristics, and validity. *Archives of General Psychiatry, 38,* 381–389.

Robins, L.N., Helzer, J.E., Weissman, M.M., Orvaschel, H., Gruenberg, E., Burke, J.D., & Regier, D.A. (1984). Life-time prevalence of specific psychiatric disorders in three sites. *Archives of General Psychiatry, 41,* 949–958.

Romaniuk, M., McAuley, W.J., & Arling, G. (1983). An examination of the prevalence of mental disorders among the elderly in the community. *Journal of Abnormal Psychology, 92,* 458–467.

Room, R. (1972). Drinking patterns in large U.S. cities: A comparison of San Francisco and national samples. *Quarterly Journal of Studies on Alcohol*(Suppl. 6), 28–57.

Rosin, A.J., & Glatt, M.M. (1971). Alcohol excess in the elderly. *Quarterly Journal of Studies on Alcohol, 32,* 53–59.

Roth, M. (1955). The natural history of mental disorder in old age. *Journal of Mental Science, 101,* 281–301.

Roth, M. (1971). Classification and aetiology in mental disorders of old age: Some recent developments. In D.W.K. Kay & A. Walk (Eds.), *Recent developments in psychogeriatrics* (pp. 87–89). Ashford, UK: Healey Bros.

Rovner, B.W., & Rabins, P.V. (1985). Mental illness among nursing home patients. *Hospital and Community Psychiatry, 36,* 119–128.

Rubin, E., Gang, H., Misra, P.S., & Lieber, C.S. (1970). Inhibition of drug metabolism by acute ethanol intoxication. *American Journal of Medicine, 49,* 801–806.

Salzman, C. (1985). Geriatric psychopharmacology. *Annual Review of Medicine, 36,* 217–218.

Sanford, R.A. (1975). Tolerance of debility in elderly dependents by supporters at home. *British Medical Journal, 3,* 471–473.

Schernitski, P., Bootman, J.L., Byers, J., Likes, K., & Hughes, J.H. (1980). Demographic characteristics of elderly drug overdose patients admitted to a hospital emergency department. *Journal of the American Geriatrics Society, 28,* 544–546.

Schuckit, M.A., Atkinson, J.H., Miller, P.L. & Berman, J. (1980). A three-year follow-up of elderly alcoholics. *Journal of Clinical Psychiatry, 41,* 412–416.

Schuckit, M.A., & Miller, P.L. (1976). Alcoholism in elderly men: A survey of a general medical ward. *Annals of the New York Academy of Science, 273,* 558–571.

Schuckit, M.A., Miller, P.L., & Berman, J. (1980). The three-year course of psychiatric problems in a geriatric population. *Journal of Clinical Psychiatry, 41,* 27–32.

Schuckit, M.A., Miller, P.L. & Hahlabohm, D. (1975). Unrecognized psychiatric illness in elderly medical–surgical patients. *Journal of Gerontology, 30,* 655–659.

Schuckit, M.A., & Pastor, P.A. (1978). Alcohol-related psychopathology in the aged. *University of Washington Alcohol and Drug Abuse Institute Technical Report, 10,* 78.

Schwartz, D., Wang, M., Zeitz, L., & Goss, M.E.W. (1962). Medication errors made by elderly chronically ill patients. *American Journal of Public Health, 52,* 2018–2029.

Shader, R.I., & Greenblatt, D.J. (1983). Some current treatment options for symptoms of anxiety. *Journal of Clinical Psychiatry, 44,* 21–29.

Siassi, I., Crocetti, G., & Spiro, H.R. (1973). Drinking patterns and alcoholism in a blue-collar population. *Quarterly Journal of Studies on Alcohol, 34,* 917–926.

Simon, A. (1980). The neuroses, personality disorders, alcoholism, drug use and misuse, and crime in the aged. In J.E. Birren & R.B. Sloane (Eds.), *Handbook of mental health and aging* (pp. 653–670). Englewood Cliffs, NJ: Prentice-Hall.

Simon, A., & Cahan, R.B. (1963). The acute brain syndrome in geriatric patients. *Psychiatric Research Reports, 16,* 8–21.

Simon, A., Epstein, L.J., & Reynolds, L. (1968). Alcoholism in the geriatrically ill. *Geriatrics, 23,* 125–131.

Smart, R.G., & Liban, C.B. (1981). Predictors of problem drinking among elderly, middle-aged and youthful drinkers. *Journal of Psychoactive Drugs, 13,* 153–163.

Smith, S.J., Kiloh, L.G., Ratnavale, G.S., & Grant, D.A. (1976). The investigation of dementia: The results in 100 consecutive admissions. *The Medical Journal of Australia, 2,* 403–405.

Spira, H., Dysken, M.W., Lazarus, L.W., Davis, J.M., & Salzman, C. (1984). Treatment of agitation and psychosis. In C. Salzman (Ed.), *Clinical geriatric psychopharmacology* (pp. 49–76). New York: McGraw-Hill.

Spitzer, R.D., Endicott, J., & Robins, E. (1978). Research diagnostic criteria. *Archives of General Psychiatry, 35,* 773–782.

Srole, L., & Fischer, A.K. (1980). The mid-town Manhattan longitudinal study vs. "the mental paradise lost" doctrine. *Archives of General Psychiatry, 37,* 209–221.

Srole, L., Langner, T.S., Michael, S.T., Opler, M.K., & Rennie, T.A.C. (1962). *Mental health in metropolis.* New York: McGraw-Hill.

Steele, R.E. (1978). Relationship of race, sex, social class, and social mobility to depression in normal adults. *Journal of Social Psychology, 104,* 37–47.

Stephens, R.C., Haney, C.A., & Underwood, S. (1981). Psychoactive drug use and potential misuse among persons aged 55 years and older. *Journal of Psychoactive Drugs, 13,* 185–193.

Steuer, J.L. & Cohen, A. (1984). *Depression in spouses of patients with Alzheimer's disease.* Paper presented at the annual meeting of the American Psychological Association, Toronto.

Tarter, R.F., & Perley, R.N. (1975). Clinical and perceptual characteristics of paranoids and paranoid schizophrenics. *Journal of Clinical Psychology, 31,* 42–48.

Task Force on Prescription Drugs. (1968). *The drug users.* Washington, DC: Department of Health, Education, and Welfare.

Terry, R.D., & Wisniewski, H.M. (1977). Structural aspects of aging and the brain. In C. Eisdorfer & R.O. Friedel (Eds.), *Cognitive and emotional disturbance in the elderly* (pp. 3–9). Chicago, IL: Year Book Medical Publishers.

Thyer, B.A., Parrish, R.T., Curtis, G.C., Nesse, R.M., & Cameron, O.G. (1985). Ages of onset of DSM-III anxiety disorders. *Comprehensive Psychiatry, 26,* 113–122.

Tomlinson, B., Blessed, G., & Roth, M. (1970). Observations on the brains of demented old people. *Journal of Neurological Sciences, 11,* 205.

Tsuang, M.I., & Woolson, R.F. (1977). Mortality in patients with schizophrenia, mania and depression and surgical conditions. *British Journal of Psychiatry, 130,* 162–166.

Uhlenhuth, E.H., Balter, M.B., Mellinger, G.D., Cisin, I.H., & Clinthorne, J. (1983). Symptom checklist syndromes in the general population: Correlations with psychotherapeutic drug use. *Archives of General Psychiatry, 40,* 1167–1178.

Vestal, R.E., McGuire, E.A., Tobin, J.D., Andres, R., Norris, A.H., & Mezey, R. (1977). Aging and ethanol metabolism in man. *Clinical Pharmacology and Therapeutics, 21,* 343–354.

Waller, J.A. (1974). Injury in aged. *New York State Journal of Medicine, 74,* 2200–2208.

Warheit, G., Arey, S., & Swanson, E. (1976). Patterns of drug use: An epidemiological overview. *Journal of Drug Issues, 6,* 223–237.

Warheit, G.J., Holzer, E.E., & Arey, S.A. (1975). Race and mental illness: An epidemiologic update. *Journal of Health and Social Behavior, 16,* 243–256.

Wattis, J.P. (1981). Alcohol problems in the elderly. *Journal of the American Geriatrics Society, 29,* 131–134.

Watts, C.A.H. (1956). The incidence and prognosis of endogenous depression. *British Medical Journal, 1,* 1392–1397.

Wechsler, H., Demone, H.W., & Gottlieb, N. (1978). Drinking patterns of Greater Boston adults: Subgroup differences on the QFV Index. *Journal of Studies on Alcohol, 39,* 1158–1165.

Weissman, M.M., & Myers, J.K. (1979). Depression in the elderly: Research directions in psychopathology, epidemiology, and treatment. *Journal of Geriatric Psychiatry, 12,* 187–201.

Wenger, P.A. (1958). A comparative study of the aging process in groups of schizophrenics and mentally well veterans. *Geriatrics, 13,* 367–370.

Williams, J.D., Ray, C.G., & Overall, J.E. (1973). Mental aging and organicity in an alcoholic population. *Journal of Consulting and Clinical Psychology, 41,* 392–396.

Winokur, G., Behar, D., & Schlesser, M. (1980). Clinical and biological aspects of depression in the elderly. In J.O. Cole & J.E. Barrett (Eds.), *Psychopathology in the aged* (pp. 145–153). New York: Raven.

Zarit, S., Reeuer, K., & Bach-Peterson, J. (1980). Relatives of impaired elderly: Correlates of feelings of burden. *Gerontologist, 6,* 649–655.

Zis, A.P., & Goodwin, F.K. (1979). Major affective disorder as a recurrent illness. *Archives of General Psychiatry, 36,* 835–839.

2

The Interrelationship of Physical and Mental Illness in the Elderly

Elinore E. Lurie

The interaction of physical and mental illness in the elderly is an area of particular importance, affecting service design, delivery, and utilization. Effective prevention and intervention require the identification of those groups at joint risk of physical and mental illness. In recent years, increased attention has been paid to what Blazer (1982) calls the integration of the "biological substrate of mental illness with social stresses" and with other psychosocial factors. Foremost among these is low socioeconomic status (SES), itself a risk factor for morbidity and such subsumed conditions as poor nutrition and vitamin deficiency states that predispose towards morbidity (see, for example, Gershell, 1981).

In general, the association of physical and mental disease and causal relationships between them, both across the life span and in the aged, has been of interest to researchers and clinicians since the early 1950s. It has been addressed in community and epidemiological studies, studies of practices (including both office ambulatory care practices and populations of inpatients), and clinical studies. This chapter reviews community and practice studies and examines review articles for research and policy implications.

Some empirical generalizations found in the literature about the association of mental with physical illness in the elderly are true for other age groups as well. These include the effects of SES; traumatic events such as disfiguring disease or operations; life crises such as loss of a spouse or child; and such physiological sequelae as delirium states after cardiac surgery. These factors have known impact across all ages; however, their frequency of occurrence increases directly with age.

Other generalizations are age specific. Blazer (1982) suggests, for example, that the genetic contribution to depression is weaker in late life than in earlier life. Certain reactions to disease processes, symptom presentation, and interactions are specific to elderly rather than younger people. These age-specific generalizations may, in turn, represent the results either of normal age-associated changes or of age-associated pathology. For example, Foster and Reisberg (1984) discuss how age per se affects psychiatric disorder that began earlier in life. Minaker and Rowe (1981) discuss normal changes in elderly renal function—changes that are themselves risk factors, versus abnormal changes or renal disease.

Many authors have noted the symptomatology and presentation of mental illness in the aged as symptoms of physical disease. Others have noted a number of pathological states in which physical causes present as symptoms usually associated with mental illness or psychological ill health. These symptoms and states underscore the need for careful differential diagnosis, especially for the elderly. Although it is beyond the scope of this chapter to discuss service delivery systems, some authors (for example, Brown, 1986; Schulberg, McClelland, Coulehan, Block, & Werner, 1986) have noted that the primary care physician, the "front line" caregiver usually consulted by the aged, is biased towards perceiving symptomatology as reflecting physical illness.

The literature also demonstrates the methodological problems of measuring prevalence of both physical and mental illness, especially in the elderly. Methods and measuring instruments need to differentiate symptoms of mental and physical disorder; must capture symptoms of those states of psychological ill-health or lack of well-being that do not meet accepted, defined criteria for diagnosed mental illness (Gurland et al., 1983; Rodin & Voshart, 1986); should measure "caseness" with validity and reliability; and so on. This chapter will not directly address methodological issues, but rather will note how these affect findings.

Physical Illness in Early Life as Associated with Mental Illness and Pathological Behavior in Old Age

Community, epidemiological, and practice studies have long sought to trace the antecedents of late-life mental disorder. For greater detail on epidemiological and practice studies, see chapters 1 and 3.

Community and Epidemiological Studies and Their Implications for Elderly Populations

The interrelationship of physical and mental illness in the elderly may result from events occurring earlier in the life span as well as in old age. Comprehensive research in this area should begin with studies of genetic predisposition, preferably longitudinal studies such as the classic studies of schizophrenia in twins by Kallman and Sander (1949) and follow-up studies by Jarvik, Ruth, and Matsuyama (1980), or the types of studies employed in risk-factor research as summarized by Regier and Allen (1983). Consideration of such studies is, however, beyond the scope of this chapter.

The coexistence of mental with physical illnesses and their increasing association with age were confirmed by the first studies of Lundby, Sweden, by Essen-Moller, Larsson, Uddenberg, and White (1956). The restudy of Lundby by Hagnell (1966 as discussed in Schwab & Schwab, 1978) showed that the presence of reported psychosomatic symptomatology in the early 1950s led to a higher incidence of mental disorder in 1966 than would have occurred by chance. Further, earlier circulatory disorders in men and infectious or endocrine diseases in women were predictive of mental disorder ten years later. These effects peaked in subjects aged 50 and under. Likewise, in Srole's Midtown Manhattan restudy (Srole, 1975), age was not associated with a marked increase in mental disorder; those who exhibited psychosomatic symptoms or mental pathology in the earlier period were as likely in the later period to improve as to remain the same or worsen. By contrast, effects associated with old age were seen for both sexes, but particularly for women, in an urban area in "Stirling County" (Leighton et al., 1971; also summarized in Schwab & Schwab, 1978). It is not clear whether the association is stronger in old age.

Another classic epidemiological study of mental illness in the aged, conducted in the English city of Newcastle-upon-Tyne, is reported in Kay, Beamish, and Roth (1964) and in Garside, Kay, and Roth (1965). This study sampled 309 subjects aged 65 and over, randomly chosen from the electoral register in five wards, thus underrepresenting those who are not registered to vote, who live in wards different in socioeconomic status and other characteristics, and who are in institutions. The sample size was not large, and no measures of statistical significance were used, thus preventing generalization. Nevertheless, this study offers findings confirmed by later, larger studies: high prevalence of organic brain disorders (using the psychiatric terminology of the period) and high prevalence of physical health problems in this population.

Methodological Considerations of Early Studies

Essen-Moller et al. (1956), Hagnell (1966, in Schwab & Schwab, 1978), Srole (1975), and Leighton et al. (1971) belong to a "second generation" of epidemiological studies. Rather than follow the first generation in focusing on such cases of identified pathology as residents of state hospitals, these newer studies addressed the prevalence of pathology among community residents. Essen-Moller and Hagnell assigned clinical diagnoses through direct interviews and case reviews by clinicians. Srole and Leighton used lay interviewers to collect data, in part through structured standardized instruments, about which judgments were then made by clinicians. Srole and Leighton were interested in a continuum of pathology from wellness to illness in community-resident populations rather than the assignment of clinical diagnoses. Leighton was unique in focusing on the impact of social conditions on mental health. Hagnell, Srole, and Leighton restudied populations previously studied, Leighton comparing

Leighton's Canadian and Hagnell's Swedish populations. None of these studies, however, focused specifically on the aged.

The Leighton study suffers from attrition of respondents over time (inevitable in a panel study). Because the communities were not comparable, the joint study was weighted to represent the Swedish community. "Caseness" was determined by a four-point (ridit) scale based on symptomatology. No age-specific effects were found. Results differed between communities in the extent to which sex, education, occupation, and class were associated with psychiatric impairment.

The Srole restudy of Midtown Manhattan also suffered from considerable attrition. Only 42 percent of the original sample could be reinterviewed. The loss of nonlocatables (32 percent) occurred primarily among women who were young to middle-aged, and nonmarried in the first wave. Judgments of impairment were based on symptom checklists and interview protocols; 82 items from the original study were repeated. Those impaired earlier were as likely to improve as to remain impaired at the later period. No particular attention is given to the old in either study period. However, the great contribution of the Midtown Manhattan restudy is its follow-up of a single cohort over almost one generation. A "regression to the mean" of normalcy was displayed, rather than a picture of continued pathology over time. Thus, transient situational factors cannot be discounted in cross-sectional population studies of pathology.

Both the original Lundby study (Essen-Moller et al., 1956) and its follow-up (Hagnell, 1966, in Schwab & Schwab, 1978) are almost faultless as state-of-the-art epidemiology of their generation. These two studies of the same self-contained, almost homogeneous community are, however, insufficient to support in full an empirical generalization that physical illness in earlier life is predictive of mental illness in later life. General psychiatric epidemiological caveats must apply, regarding the lack of replication in large heterogeneous communities; shifts in diagnostic entities (for example, "asthenia") and in criteria and methods of assessing "caseness"; absence of an institutionalized subpopulation; and lack of other confirming longitudinal data. The deficits of these and other community studies call for more longitudinal and cohort-sequential studies of the incidence in given populations of physical and mental health conditions over the life span. Nevertheless, the suggestion that physical illness may be a precursor or at least an associate of mental illness is present in these early studies.

Recent Community Studies

Aneshensel, Frerichs, and Huba (1984) conducted a four-wave study over a one-year period of adults over 18 from the Los Angeles Metropolitan Area Study ($N = 744$). The middle-aged and elderly were grouped together into a single 45-and-over category. For all age groups, physical illness had a large contemporaneous effect of increasing depressive symptomatology over previous levels; depressive symptomatology had a smaller four-month lagged effect on increasing levels of physical illness. There were age-specific effects, with the one-year lagged coefficients maximal for those 45 and older, minimal for the youngest adults. Thus, effects of physical and mental ill health were interactive over the life span but increased in intensity with age.

Gurland et al. (1983) conducted community studies of the aged in New York City and London. Measurement was based on the Comprehensive Assessment and Referral Evaluation (CARE), an instrument of proven reliability and validity. Systematic assessment of health and social needs employed semistructured interview techniques, with scripted questions for all subjects and with each of the relevant responses defined. The interviews lasted from 1 to 3 hours, potentially eliciting over 1,500 bits of itemized information, an extensive set of global evaluations, and a systematic narrative summary. The discrete bits of information were then collapsed into scaled scores. The assessment rating inventories allowed the assignment of a score for psychopathology over a wide range of severity. A follow-up assessment was conducted at one year, using a modified version of the CARE schedule.

The New York City study was based on a probability sample first used for a state-wide study of the elderly in 1972. Selected dwelling units were located in 66 clusters throughout the five boroughs. A replicated design was used, with the whole sample divided into five randomly selected, stratified, interpenetrating subsamples, in which each New York City household had a known probability of selection. To ensure that final samples were not composed of easy-to-complete interviews, each subsample was put into the field separately, and maximum efforts made to complete it before moving on to the next. Each subsample provides an estimate of all characteristics of the sampling frame. To update the enumeration, records were divided into two strata: dwelling units that in 1972 contributed an interview of someone aged 65 or older; and dwelling units with no 1972 residents aged 65 or older, where someone 65 or older lived but was not interviewed, or where there was no contact.

The London sample employed an enumeration of all those aged 65 or older who were listed as patients of general practitioners. A replicated subsample design was used. Whether the sample was randomly selected is not reported.

Gurland et al. (1983) stress the importance of measuring aspects of ill health not meeting standard diagnostic criteria for mental illness. Depression was measured on scales that capture transient signs of lowered mood or affect, as well as symptoms comprising diagnosable criteria of clinical depression in frequency and duration. The pervasively depressed used more medical services, took more psychotropic medications, more often received multiple drugs, saw their doctors more often, received more "special investigations," and were admitted to hospitals more frequently. Contacts of these elderly with the medical care system did not, however, result in treatment specific to mental health problems:

Nevertheless, little in the way of specific treatment for depressions is seen in London and even less in New York. There is clearly more than sufficient contact with the medical services, but opportunities for more vigorous treatment of depression are probably being missed, especially in New York [Gurland et al., 1983, p. 159].

Depression was not associated with environment, economics, heterogeneity of neighborhood, or language difficulties; it was associated with physical illness, disability, and dependence, which had similar frequencies in the two cities. Those dependent on others were somewhat more depressed in New York than in London.

George, Blazer, Winfield-Laird, Leaf, and Eischbach (in press) summarize findings to date of the National Institute of Mental Health Epidemiologic Catchment Area (ECA) studies, represented here by Blazer, George, and Landerman (1986), Myers et al. (1984), Regier et al. (1984), Robins et al. (1984), and Shapiro et al. (1984). These investigators present current, state-of-the-art studies in which a standard instrument, the Diagnostic Interview Schedule (DIS), is used by lay interviewers. The DIS generates selected computer-based DSM-III diagnoses. Symptoms must meet minimum DSM-III criteria of frequency and duration. Because the DIS is an interview schedule, it does not count the prevalence of such specific behaviors as suicide among older men.

Each ECA site used multistage probability sampling to generate stratified random samples of approximately 3,000 community and 500 institutional residents from their defined populations. The sites vary in their representation of rural residence, level of education, and ethnic group membership, so that generalizations from the findings to groups defined by such criteria may be limited. For example, more New Haven residents than Baltimore residents were college-educated. Hispanics, as diverse a group as "English speakers" or "English surnames" would be, are represented by one site dominated by a single major Hispanic subgroup. No attention is given to Asians, one of the largest and most rapidly growing population groups, itself ethnically diverse. Despite these limitations and the fact that ECA samples constitute neither a nationwide sample nor census, they are nevertheless exemplary in their representation of all age groups and their inclusion of the institutionalized as well as the community resident. Three sites oversampled older, noninstitutionalized adults, with high response rates beween 76 and 80 percent. Findings from these subsamples may be generalized with confidence.

In all four sites, lifetime and six-month prevalence of cognitive impairment is greater in the elderly than in any other age group. The prevalence is lower in the aged for other specific disorders—substance abuse, schizophrenia, major depression and dysthymia, and anxiety and somatoform disorders.

The ECA studies may also underestimate the prevalence of mental illness in the elderly. Because of the use of the DIS, symptoms that do not meet minimum criteria for frequency and duration may be present but not counted toward DSM-III diagnoses. Thus, existent depressive symptoms may be insufficient in number or duration for a diagnosis of major depression. The presence of uncounted symptomatology must be noted in assessing the results of these studies and their implications for the elderly, because symptoms rather than clinically undiagnosed illness may be related to normal life changes and losses associated with aging. Further, the present cohort of elderly may be seen as survivors of disorders such as schizophrenia and substance abuse characterized by higher risk of mortality at earlier ages. Finally, the methodology of the study excludes suicide, a behavior with high prevalence among older men.

In the ECA sites, persons with diagnosed disorders were more likely to have used mental health services and to have seen providers of all types. As has been reported in many other studies, however, the aged (whatever their problems, including cognitive disorders) were least likely to have seen mental health specialists; were more likely to have used inpatient services for physical health problems; and to have seen other health providers for physical problems.

Over all age groups, ECA respondents with DIS/DSM-III disorders were more likely to have seen a physician in the six months prior to their first diagnostic interviews; to be currently receiving medical care (Kessler et al., 1987); and to have been hospitalized for physical health conditions in the previous year (George et al., in press; Myers et al., 1984; Robins et al., 1984; Shapiro et al., 1984). Thus, physical illness, symptomatology, and use of physical health facilities may precede and serve as a risk indicator for the appearance of mental illness or symptomatology; and appear to predict increased likelihood of mental disorders at a later time.

Studies of Practices

Widmer and Cadoret (1978) used the case records of a physician in a small stable town in the Midwestern United States to examine physical symptomatology and health services utilization at two time periods. The sample consisted of 154 patients who were later diagnosed as depressed, and of two groups of controls, one at each time period, never so diagnosed. It is unclear how depression was diagnosed—apparently a symptoms checklist used in scoring the Feighner/RDC was employed, but this instrument is never mentioned. At each time period, the two groups were compared, using chi square as the statistical test. At both periods, those later diagnosed as depressed had more illnesses, had more functional complaints, manifested more anxiety, and visited the family practitioner more often. Women and older patients were higher on functional complaints, whether or not they were later diagnosed as depressed.

This study focuses on longitudinal examination, is ingenious in attempts to identify predictors of depression, and is one of the few studies to use control groups. However, it does not specifically address the mental health of the aged, having dichotomized at age 41; and, because the study community is ethnically homogeneous, the results are qualified in their generalizability to other ethnic groups. Nevertheless, Widmer and Cadoret (1978) found, as reported in other studies, an association between physical and mental impairment. The attempt to identify causative direction and persons at risk for mental impairment is commendable and intriguing.

Post (1962) followed a geriatric sample of 100 patients admitted between 1949 and 1951 to a geriatric unit at Bethlem Royal Hospital who manifested affective symptomatology. More severe and sustained physical ill health prior to first admission was related to poor physical health at time of admission. Thus, physical illness at an earlier period preceded associated physical and mental illness at a later period.

Identified Cases

Identifying cases already diagnosed and disposed is analogous to the "first generation" studies of cohorts of patients already institutionalized for mental illness. Studies of suicides constitute an important example. Case studies show that suicides of all ages tend to have seen physicians and to have been hospitalized for physical illness prior to committing suicide (Bourque, Cosand, & Kraus, 1983a, 1983b; Farberow, 1981; Hagnell & Rorsman, 1980; Marshall, Burnett, & Brasure, 1983). Again, physical illness precedes an act, which may reflect mental illness.

Special Considerations in the Association of Physical Disease in Early Life with Mental Illness in Late Life

Both normal and abnormal aging processes affect psychiatric disorders that may have begun earlier in life, changing their presentation and symptomatology. Underlying physical illness interacts with preexisting as well as late-life mental disorders (Foster & Reisberg, 1984; Minaker & Rowe, 1981). Minaker and Rowe note that normal age-related changes in renal function place the aged at risk of physical complications that may manifest themselves in disordered mental states (for example, confusion or agitation). The incidence of renal disease also increases with age, interacting with other disease states to place the elderly at greater risk, with greater likelihood of disordered mental states.

Physical Illness in Late Life as Associated with Mental Illness and Pathological Behavior in Old Age

There is considerable evidence from studies using a variety of methods that mental and physical illness are associated with each other at any given stage in the life span. This is especially true in old age.

Epidemiological and Community Studies

Blazer and Williams (1980) analyzed a population of 997 community residents aged 65 and older, urban and rural, black and white. They found symptoms of dysphoria and depression, as measured on the Older American Resources and Services (OARS) Depressive Scale (ODS), to be associated with physical ill health in 44 percent of cases. Numerous studies of general populations have found similar associations (Frerichs, Aneshensel, Yokopenic, & Clark, 1982; Neff, Husaini, & McCorkel, 1980; Schwab, Bell, Warheit, Schwab, & Traven, 1978–1979; Schwab, Fennell, & Warheit, 1974; Schwab & Traven, 1979).

Sinott (1984–1985) found relatively few symptoms in a community study of 364 older adults, using Langner mental health symptomatology screening scores. She did, however, find physical health symptoms related to independent reports of nervousness and depression, especially for women, and more symptomatology for women. She partially replicated these findings for 100 community-resident elderly volunteers in Baltimore. Sinott questions the applicability of Holmes and Rahe stress scores to female populations, noting that this scale was standardized for men and that men seem more specifically sensitive than do women to physical illness as a primary associate of depression. The findings of both of Sinott's studies are based, however, on secondary analyses of data gathered for other purposes (that is, for sex roles or over-the-counter drug use).

Blazer et al. (1986) report on a substudy of the ECA community residents of the Piedmont Health Survey. They note that older adults with depressive symptomatology reported more somatic symptoms, such as abdominal pain, back pain, and sleep difficulties, than did their middle-aged depressed counterparts; but when controls with no DSM-III diagnoses were compared, only constipation and sleep difficulties were reported more often among the elderly. Older depressed adults were more likely to report psychological symptoms, particularly a subjective sense of current depression, thoughts about death, and death wishes. There was thus no support for the widely held belief in the existence of "masked" depression among the elderly (for example, Evans, 1982, among many). On the other hand, the members of this sample were not in practice studies—that is, they were not "captured" through examination of the case records of general, internal medicine, or psychiatric physicians.

These findings suggest that results of community studies will always differ from those of case studies and practices. Differences in pathology rates may reflect the presentation of symptoms by the aged who have self-selected themselves, or been selected by others, as needing medical or psychiatric care. Thus, the symptomatology presented may be tailored to the care system chosen for the assumed cause.

Case and Practice Studies

Numerous case and practice studies confirm the association of mental and physical illness

> among identified physical health cases, especially in studies of practices, as discussed in the preceding section;

> for the elderly alone;

> across the life span; and

> among identified mental health cases.

Elderly Populations. Classic studies of the association of physical and mental illness in the elderly include those of Bellin and Hardt (1958); Kay et al. (1964); Lowenthal (1964); Lowenthal et al. (1967); New York State Department of Mental Hygiene (1961); Roth and Kay (1956); and Simon and Talley (1969). Aged patients with identified psychiatric problems are likely to have physical health problems—in some cases causative, in others merely associated with their mental health problems. These problems are likely to be unrecognized by both patients and mental health professionals unless specific physical health screening is provided. The classic study of elderly mental health patients in the United States confirming these findings is reported by Lowenthal (1964) and Lowenthal et al. (1967).

Luke, Norton, and Denbigh (1981) studied 200 "old-old" people (aged 80 and over) in two Canadian cities—a sample of identified cases known to social agencies, then a snowball of other aged known to the cases. The usual cautions apply about generalization from a nonrandom sample that began with identified problem cases and excluded the institutionalized. Measures were of self-reported well-being (the Affect Balance Scale, the Rosow and Breslau Functional Scale) rather than of clinical diagnosis of depression. Psychotropic medication usage was employed as an indicator of poor psychological health, thereby confounding this factor with physician prescribing patterns. Other mental health indices included depressive symptomatology, periods of inability to function, and problems with alcohol. Poor psychological health was associated with poor self-rated health (which were possibly confounded, because later studies appear to show a common perceptual base for both measures), with impaired mobility and hearing, and with accidents. In spite of the many caveats related to the methodology of this study, its finding of association between poor mental and physical well-being in the elderly is supported in many other types of studies.

For example, Blazer and various colleagues in several studies found poor physical health and disability associated with depression in the elderly (Blazer & Houpt, 1979; Blazer & Maddox, 1982; Blazer & Williams, 1980). Low SES has sometimes been found to be a major predictor of both impaired physical and mental health (Blazer & Houpt, 1979; Blazer & Maddox, 1982; Johnston & Ware, 1976; Schwab, Traven, & Warheit, 1978). Other predictors in some studies have included gender and level of marital satisfaction (Weiss & Aved, 1978). However, the findings have not been universally confirmed (Hankin & Locke, 1982; Leighton et al., 1971) and need further study.

Studies across the Life Span. The association of physical and mental illness across the life span is quite evident when identified physical health cases are examined for mental health symptomatology, as in studies of practices (Brennan & Noce, 1981; Freedman, Bucci, & Elkowitz, 1982; Goldberg, Kay, & Thompson, 1976; Hankin & Locke, 1982; Johnston & Ware, 1976; Leeper, Badger, & Milo, 1985; Turner, Noh, & Levin, 1985; Widmer & Cadoret, 1978). Studies across age ranges of rates of mental disorders in primary care settings, as summarized by Hankin and Oktay (1979) and Hankin (1985), as well as the more recent studies by Brennan and Noce (1981) and others (Widmer and Cadoret, 1978, and the studies summarized therein) confirm this finding. The association of physical and mental illness thus does *not* appear to be age specific. The elderly are more likely than other age groups to have physical illnesses, and the rate of associated mental illness may appear lower than for other age groups. Nevertheless, physical illness is still a risk or predisposing factor for mental illness.

Brennan and Noce (1981) studied 188 randomly selected case records from a family practice in a working-class area of a small Canadian city, which underrepresented the elderly (age range, 3–76). They found physical health to be associated with "psychosocial" and "interpersonal" problems.

Cameron (1985) reviewed literature to date, noting that the prevalence of anxiety states meeting DSM-III criteria for panic, or generalized anxiety, disorder has been estimated at 2.0 to 4.7 percent in the general population, at 10 to 14 percent in patients with cardiovascular symptoms, and at 27 percent in general medical practice patients with psychiatric symptoms. Cavanaugh (1983) administered the Mini-Mental Status Exam, General Health Questionnaire–30 (GHQ), and Beck Depression Inventory to 335 randomly selected hospital medical patients aged 17 to 88 (mean age, 57; males, 47 percent; white, 57 percent; heterogeneous in SES on the Hollingshead class scale). She found 27 percent with evidence of cognitive dysfunction measured on the

Mini; 61 percent with emotional dysfunction measured on the GHQ; and 36 percent with depression measured on the Beck. Medical-resident diagnoses, however, did not show high concordance with these mental-state measurements. The measured level of dysfunction was higher than in other studies, perhaps because the subjects were hospital inpatients well postadmission. Age was not associated with dysfunction.

Casper et al. (1985) matched 80 controls to 132 patients with major mental disorder diagnoses (aged 21 to 76; average age, 46), administering the National Institute of Mental Health (NIMH), Clinical Research Branch Schedule of Affective Disorders and Schizophrenia (SADS) interview and assigning RDC diagnoses and subtypes. "Classic" signs of depression were more common among the aged; "atypical" symptoms less so.

Popkin, Callies, and Mackenzie (1985) reviewed 1,649 psychiatric consultations from seven time periods between March 1976 and December 1982 in a major Midwestern teaching hospital. These yielded 78 medical or surgical cases meeting DSM-III criteria for major depression. A controlled study of psychotropic medication of these patients failed to show positive results. The sample was too small, however, for adequate analysis of the number of variables examined by the authors (age, sex, preexistence of affective or of primary medical disorder).

Rodin and Voshart (1986), in an excellent review article, note numerous methodological problems in the diagnosis of depression in the medically ill. These include lack of clarity regarding the definition of a case; the absence of assessment measures that have been standardized in medically ill cases and that exclude symptomatology reflective of both medical and physical illness; selection bias, in that the depressed with medical illnesses may be more likely to seek health care facilities (as suggested by Blazer et al., 1986); the heterogeneity of medically ill subject cases and disease states; the absence of appropriate controls; problems with self-report measures of depression; the nonspecific diagnostic significance of depressive symptoms; and false negative diagnoses of depression due to the presence of pain or to somatic symptoms not caused by the somatic illness. These methodological problems characterize studies of mental illness among medical populations of all ages.

Studies of Identified Cases Seeking or Receiving Mental Health Care. Studies of identified mental health cases are similar to the first rather than to the current generation of epidemiological studies. They underrepresent the institutionalized and healthy community residents who do not consult physicians, but overrepresent lower SES and populations outside the United States.

Babigian and Odoroff (1969) used 1,966 case records for all patients who came in contact with the public mental health system in Monroe County, New York, thereby accessing records for 39,475 cases from childhood through age 99 for a population that is both urban and rural, varies in social class, and includes nonwhites as well as whites. Koranyi (1979) studied a lower- and lower-middle-class, predominantly French Canadian, mental health clinic population, not representative of the Canadian population at large.

Anderson and Davidson (1975) reviewed studies through 1971 of the physical status of psychiatric patients. These studies usually represent consecutive admissions to psychiatric units in the United Kingdom or Australia, but include some studies from the United States, such as Simon and Talley (1969). Studies covering all age groups were contrasted to those of patients aged 60 and over. In both were found many physical illnesses and disease conditions, some concomitant, some either contributing to the physical condition or resulting from it. For example, cerebrovascular disease and sensory deficits (hearing loss in particular) were clearly associated with paranoid states and late paraphrenia. In one study, visual loss was also so associated. In community studies, one-third of the aged seen at home in psychiatric consultations had physical illness severe enough to justify admission to psychogeriatric units. The reviewers also note physical causes of mental confusion in the aged *not* found in earlier life—for example, fecal impaction and urinary retention; disease states; vitamin deficiency; acute infection; small cerebrovascular accidents; over-the-counter drug and laxative use; and the side effects of prescription drugs. In these studies, stroke is often associated with depression.

For "identified" psychiatric patients, there is clear evidence across the life span for high rates of morbidity and mortality attributable to physical illness among the mentally ill (Babigian & Odoroff, 1969; Eastwood & Trevelyan, 1972; Karasu, Waltzman, Lindenmayer, & Buckley, 1980; Koranyi, 1979). Barnes, Mason, Greer, and Ray (1983) found in physical and laboratory evaluations of 144 chronic psychiatric Veterans Administration hospital inpatients that 26 percent had medical illnesses, and 13 percent had illnesses undetected prior to the researchers' chart review. Cameron (1985) notes that at minimum 2 percent of psychiatric outpatients and inpatients have been found to have medical disorders that present with anxiety syndromes. Cardiovascular and respiratory diseases, endocrine, neurologic, and drug-related syndromes are most common. Because onset of anxiety disorders is usually early in life, older patients with this disorder are probably chronically mentally ill, and are thus more likely to have cardiovascular and respiratory disease.

Other work supporting these findings includes that of Davies (1965), who examined 36 consecutive cases referred to a psychiatrist in a psychiatric clinic in England. Although his was a small and unrepresentative sample, findings are confirmed by studies of larger psychiatric populations (Herridge, 1960; Hilkevitch, 1965; Hoenig & Hamilton, 1966; Johnson, 1968; Karasu et al., 1980; Koran, 1984; Koranyi, 1979; Maguire & Granville-Grossman, 1968; Marshall, 1949). Much of this work is not North American—Davies, Johnson, Herridge, Hoenig and Hamilton, Maguire and Granville-Grossman are all British. Thus, the findings can be generalized cross-culturally.

Koran (1984) studied public mental health system patients from five California counties, with a mix in ages, ethnicity, and urban–rural residence. Almost half had an active important physical disease, one-sixth having such a disease that exacerbated or caused the mental disorder. Community mental health programs tended to be unaware of exacerbating disease. Although aware of causative physical diseases, neither they nor physical health providers were likely to be treating them.

Schulberg et al. (1985) administered the NIMH, Center for Epidemiologic Studies Depressive Symptomatology Scale (CES-D) and DIS to all new outpatients seeking care at three primary medical care (PMC) and three community mental health center (CMHC) clinics in Pittsburgh and its suburbs, between July 1981 and December 1982, obtaining a sample of 1,554 (50 percent) PMC and 869 (58 percent) CMHC patients. Of the PMC patients, 47 percent were at the 16+ cutoff on the CES-D, higher than the 21 percent found by Hankin and Locke (1982) and 29 percent by Hough, Landsverk, Stone, Jacobsen, and McGranahan (1983). Lower rates were found for DIS depression scores, and even lower rates for diagnoses by clinicians, for PMC patients (9 percent DIS and 4 percent clinical diagnosis) than for CMHC patients (28 percent DIS and 45 percent clinical diagnosis). These disparities in clinical and standardized diagnosis recall Cavanaugh (1983). Patients with higher CES-D scores were younger, but the difference was not statistically significant. Variations in findings are attributed to the use of different instruments and different diagnostic systems. Primary care physicians used ICD code hierarchies, but CMHC clinicians used either DSM-III hierarchies or reimbursable diagnostic categories. The study was not controlled; patients were neither blind-assigned nor assigned to neutral clinicians not associated with a given site. Although depression clearly exists among the physically ill, this study demonstrates the difficulties of accurately measuring its extent in patients with known illnesses.

Psychiatric Symptoms as Manifestations of Physical Illness

A complete review of the association of mental and physical illness would take note of the many physical illnesses presenting as apparent mental health symptomatology. It is beyond the scope of this chapter to do so, but excellent detailed reviews may be found in Blazer (1982), Cameron (1985), Howells (1975), Kay and Burrows (1984), Levenson and Hall (1981), Levy and Post (1982), and Restak (1986).

The significance of these reviews lies in their underscoring of the need for careful differential diagnoses both across the life span and for the aged, for whom there is even greater symptom overlap. There is often a bias in cases of symptom overlap toward diagnosing physical illness.

Issues Raised by the Concurrence of Mental and Physical Illness in the Elderly

The association of mental and physical illness in the elderly presents special issues. These include non–mental health treatment patterns, questions of diagnosis and symptomatology, and the location of elderly persons in need of mental health treatment.

Non–Mental Health Treatment

The elderly are likely to seek care for mental disorders from non–mental health professionals, who are less well-trained to recognize these conditions and apparently more likely to use psychotropic medication without other therapeutic modes. Numerous studies of utilization of health care have shown that those with mental disorders (however measured) are high users of physical health care services, both inpatient and outpatient. The ECA studies show that, though younger persons are likely to receive mental health care from mental health professionals, the aged and those suffering from the more common disorders associated with age (for example, cognitive impairment) are less likely to see a mental health specialist. The bias toward diagnosis of physical illness only may result in undertreatment of mental illness among the elderly.

Diagnosis and Symptomatology

Symptoms of many physical health problems of the aged present as symptoms of mental disorder, necessitating careful differential diagnosis. Conversely, symptoms of mental disorder may present as unexplained but persistent somatic symptoms. Because the aged express mental disorder in physical symptoms, the presence of psychosomatic symptomatology in elderly populations is especially troubling from the perspective of differentiating and appropriately treating physical and mental illness. Further, given the higher proportion of the aged in the population and the increasing life expectancy for younger cohorts, the prevalence of psychosomatic symptomatology, along with organic brain syndromes and the physical chronic diseases characteristic of the elderly, can be expected to increase.

Location

The locations of noncommunity-resident elderly, especially in long-term care facilities, may be cause for concern regarding adequate physical and mental health treatment. Many elderly nursing home residents have both mental and physical disorders. The mentally disordered are less likely to be diagnosed on the record, and are more likely to receive psychotropic medications rather than other forms of psychotherapeutic intervention—for reasons related to reimbursement, Medicaid certification, and perhaps staff ignorance.

Nonetheless, Bliwise (chapter 3) and Swan and McCall (chapter 4), reviewing the literature on nursing homes, note that many elderly nursing home residents have mental health diagnoses. The aged with mental health problems are especially likely to be found in skilled nursing facilities, even though Medicare and Medicaid reimbursement practices and licensing requirements, as well as state licensing regulations, have reinforced the tendency of nursing homes to limit numbers or avoid admissions of residents with primary mental health diagnoses, or to admit with physical health diagnoses. Consequently, mental illness may be much higher among the aged in nursing homes than is reflected in official records, and many aged persons with mental disorders may be given physical health diagnoses for admission and reimbursement purposes. (Medicaid nursing home reimbursement provides a disincentive to diagnosis and recording of mental illness in residents, because skilled nursing facilities that have 50 percent or more of their patients with primary psychiatric diagnoses are considered institutions for mental disease, limiting the types of patients they may serve, and often preventing Medicaid reimbursement altogether.)

Policy Implications

All these findings suggest the desirability of integrating the physical health, mental health, and long-term care systems. This ideal integration would include both public and private providers. Service integration would further earlier and more appropriate intervention for both physical and mental health problems. However, structural and financial barriers to service integration cannot be minimized (see chapter 7). The call for integration of services to the elderly is not new: It was heard in the 1960s. Indeed, studies of the last 20 years in both Britain and the United States have demonstrated that people of all ages with mental disorders are more likely to see primary care physicians than mental health specialists; and that "the case for a closer integration of the general medical and the mental health services would therefore seem to be self-evident" (Shepherd, 1987, p. 13; also see chapter 3). It appears to have been achieved only in countries with national health services, however. In the United States, as discussed later in this book, competing constituencies have led to various service and reimbursement systems.

In the absence of intersystem integration, the mental health system might assume the lead in targeting high-risk populations among the aged. These include those with histories of mental or of physical illness in early life; those who consult physicians for persistent symptomatology not attributable to physical disorder after differential diagnosis; those who have recently suffered bereavement or other social or economic losses; those with chronic or serious physical illness in late life; and residents of nursing homes and other long term care institutions.

Mental health systems may need to provide more preventive and educational modes to avoid higher costs in the future. Outreach by mental health care providers is in order to primary care physicians who treat the aged, to the elderly themselves, and to their caregivers. Such outreach might deal with the meaning of psychosomatic and psychopathological symptomatology and with risk factors for depression and suicide. These efforts may prevent excessive utilization of the physical and mental health care systems, and effect lower rates of psychosomatic symptomatology, depression, and suicide in the aged.

More liaison psychiatry and other mental health services to nursing homes might lead to more appropriate therapeutic interventions with nursing home patients. Ombudspersons or geriatric nurse practitioners might be used for these purposes as well. Such services can sometimes be provided without insistence upon a primary psychiatric diagnosis for patients, which would jeopardize the status and funding of many nursing homes. Finally, community mental health service providers might develop treatment programs for geriatric patients in nursing homes.

Research Implications

Future studies should include prospective longitudinal research on heterogeneous populations across the life span to capture the incidence, sequencing, and etiology of physical and mental illness. Ambiguous symptomatology and bodily changes such as menopause and impairment (events that may predispose towards mental illness) need to be researched. Studies of the nature and sequence of physical and mental disorder across the life span would serve to establish the direction of causality, to identify cases at risk of mental health impairment, and to encourage earlier and more effective intervention. Risk factors that should be studied include the cumulative nature of physical health problems; the life-threatening nature, or progressive deterioration, characteristic of various conditions; and any of these in combination with such predisposing conditions as low SES, recent bereavement, or disorganization of the social environment.

Standard criteria should be developed for epidemiological methodology in mental health and aging. These might include sampling strategies; minimum sample number; age range and oversampling of the aged; geographic area studied; inclusion or exclusion of the institutionalized; threats to validity sampling, and methods of statistical analysis employed; diagnostic criteria and means of assessment employed; sources of data; clarity of independent and dependent variables; "caseness"; and measures neither weighted to mental or physical symptomatology nor containing symptoms representing both types of pathology. Epidemiological studies should include upper- and middle-income respondents to permit generalization to a broad range of age and population groups. (Past studies from the United States have overstudied low-income public-sector patients, who are often easier to access. Upper-income patients served are often protected by private practitioners. This is not true of the more comprehensive British and Canadian health care systems and studies based on them.)

More risk indicators and more effective modes of service delivery need to be developed to prevent, identify, and effectively treat mental illness among the elderly. This calls for more targeted research, and more efforts, on all levels, from systemwide to individual providers, to recognize the association of physical and mental illness and the need for integrated services and interventions.

References

Anderson, W.F., & Davidson, R. (1975). Concomitant physical states. In J. G. Howells (Ed.), *Modern perspectives in the psychiatry of old age* (pp. 84–106). Edinburgh: Churchill Livingstone.

Aneshensel, C.S., Frerichs, R.R.R., & Huba, G.J. (1984). Depression and physical illness: A multiwave, nonrecursive causal model. *Journal of Health and Social Behavior, 25,* 350–371.

Babigian, H.M., & Odoroff, C.L. (1969). The mortality experience of a population with psychiatric illness. *American Journal of Psychiatry, 126,* 470–480.

Barnes, R.F., Mason, J.C., Greer, C., & Ray, F.T. (1983). Medical illness in chronic psychiatric outpatients. *General Hospital Psychiatry, 5,* 191–195.

Bellin, S., & Hardt, R. (1958). Marital status and mental disorders among the aged. *American Sociological Review, 23,* 155–162.

Blazer, D.G. (1982). *Depression in late life.* St. Louis, MO: C.V. Mosby.

Blazer, D.G., George, L., & Landerman, R. (1986). The phenomenology of late life depression. In P.E. Babbington & R. Jacoby (Eds.), *Psychiatric disorders in the elderly.* London: Mental Health Foundation, 92–101.

Blazer, D.G., & Houpt, J. (1979). Perception of poor health in the health of older adults. *Journal of the American Geriatrics Society, 27,* 330–334.

Blazer, D.G., & Maddox, G. (1982). Using epidemiological survey data to plan geriatric mental health services. *Hospital and Community Psychiatry, 33,* 42–45.

Blazer, D.G., & Williams, C.D. (1980). Epidemiology of dysphoria and depression in an elderly population. *American Journal of Psychiatry, 137,* 439–444.

Bourque, L.B., Cosand, B.J., & Kraus, J.F. (1983a). Attributes of suicide in females. *Suicide and Life-Threatening Behavior, 13,* 123–138.

Bourque, L.B., Cosand, B.J., & Kraus, J.F. (1983b). Comparison of male and female suicides in a defined community. *Journal of Community Health, 9,* 7–17.

Brennan, M., & Noce, A. (1981). A study of patients with psychosocial problems in a family practice. *The Journal of Family Practice, 13,* 837–843.

Brown, G. (1986). Mental illness. In L. Aiken & D. Mechanic (Eds.), *Applications of social science to clinical medicine and health policy* (pp. 175–203). New Brunswick, NJ: Rutgers University Press.

Cameron, O. (1985). The differential diagnosis of anxiety: Psychiatric and medical disorders. *Psychiatric Clinics of North America, 8,* 3–24.

Casper, R., Redmond, E., Katz, M., Schaffer, C.B., Davis, J.M., & Koslow, S.H. (1985). Somatic symptoms in primary affective disorder: Presence and relationship to the classification of depression. *Archives of General Psychiatry, 42,* 1098–1104.

Cavanaugh, S.A. (1983). The prevalence of emotional and cognitive dysfunction in a general medical population: Using the MMSE, GHQ, and BDI. *General Hospital Psychiatry, 5,* 15–24.

Davies, D.W. (1965). Physical illness in psychiatric outpatients. *British Journal of Psychiatry, 3,* 27–33.

Eastwood, M.R., & Trevelyan, M.H. (1972). Relationship between physical and psychiatric disorder. *Psychological Medicine, 2,* 363–372.

Essen-Moller, E., Larsson, H., Uddenberg, C.E., & White, G. (1956). Individual traits and morbidity in a Swedish rural population [Special issue]. *Acta Psychiatrica et Neurologica Scandinavica* (Suppl. 100).

Evans, J.G. (1982). The psychiatric aspects of physical disease. In R. Levy & F. Post (Eds.), *The psychiatry of late life* (pp. 114–142). Oxford: Blackwell Scientific.

Farberow, N.L. (1981). Suicide prevention in the hospital. *Hospital and Community Psychiatry, 32,* 99–104.

Foster, J.R., & Reisberg, B. (1984). Effects of ageing on psychiatric disorders beginning earlier in life. In D.W.K. Kay & G.D. Burrows (Eds.), *Handbook of studies on psychiatry and old age* (pp. 265–276). Amsterdam: Elsevier.

Freedman, N., Bucci, W., & Elkowitz, E. (1982). Depression in a family practice elderly population. *Journal of the American Geriatrics Society, 30*(6), 372–377.

Frerichs, R.R., Aneshensel, C.S., Yokopenic, P.A., & Clark, V.A. (1982). Physical health and depression: An epidemiological study. *Preventive Medicine, 11,* 639–642.

Garside, R.F., Kay, D.W.K., & Roth, M. (1965). Old age mental disorders in Newcastle-upon-Tyne: Part 3. A factoral study of medical, psychiatric and social characteristics. *British Journal of Psychiatry, 3,* 939–946.

George, L.K., Blazer, D.G., Winfield-Laird, I., Leaf, P.J., & Eischbach, R. (in press). Psychiatric disorders and mental health service use in later life: Evidence from the epidemiologic catchment area program. In J. Brody & G. Maddox (Eds.), *Epidemiology in late life.* New York: Springer.

Gershell, W.J. (1981). Psychiatric manifestations and nutritional deficiencies in the elderly. In A.J. Levenson & R.C. Hall (Eds.), *Neuropsychiatric manifestations of physical disease in the elderly* (pp. 119–132). New York: Raven.

Goldberg, D., Kay, C., & Thompson, L. (1976). Psychiatric morbidity in general practice and the community. *Psychological Medicine, 6,* 565–569.

Gurland, B., Copeland, J., Kuriansky, J., Kelleher, M., Sharpe, L., Dean, L. (1983). *The mind and mood of aging: Mental health problems of the community elderly in New York and London.* New York: Haworth.

Hagnell, O., & Rorsman, B. (1980). Suicide in the Lundby study: A controlled prospective investigation of stressful life events. *Neuropsychobiology, 6,* 319–332.

Hankin, J.R. (1985). *Patterns of medical and psychiatric morbidity in a prepaid health plan population* (Personal Services Contract Purchase Order No. 84 MO5 86190 ID). Rockville, MD: U.S. National Institute of Mental Health.

Hankin, J.R., & Locke, B.Z. (1982). The persistence of depressive symptomatology among prepaid group practice enrollees: An exploratory study. *American Journal of Public Health, 72,* 1000–1007.

Hankin, J.R., & Oktay, J. (1979). *Mental disorder and primary medical care: An analytical review of the literature* (National Institute of Mental Health, Series D, No. 5, DHEW Publication No. [ADM] 78–661). Washington, DC: Government Printing Office.

Herridge, C.F. (1960). Physical disorders in psychiatric illness: A study of 209 consecutive admissions. *The Lancet, 2,* 949–981.

Hilkevitch, A. (1965). Psychiatric disturbances in outpatients of a general medical outpatient clinic. *International Journal of Neuropsychiatry, 1,* 371–375.

Hoenig, J., & Hamilton, M.W. (1966). Mortality and psychiatric patients. *Acta Psychiatrica Scandinavica, 42,* 349–361.

Hough, R., Landsverk, J., Stone, J., Jacobsen, G., & McGranahan, C. (1983). *Comparison of psychiatric screening questionnaires for primary care patients: Report on contract 278-81-0036 (DB).* Bethesda, MD: National Institute of Mental Health.

Howells, J.G. (Ed.). (1975). *Modern perspectives in the psychiatry of old age.* Edinburgh: Churchill Livingstone.

Jarvik, L.F., Ruth, V., & Matsuyama, S.S. (1980). Organic brain syndromes and aging. *Archives of General Psychiatry, 37,* 280–286.

Johnson, D.A.W. (1968). The evaluation of routine physical examination in psychiatric cases. *The Practitioner, 200,* 686–691.

Johnston, S.A., & Ware, J.E. (1976). Income group differences in relationship among survey measures of physical and mental health. *Health Services Research, 11,* 416–429.

Kallman, F.J., & Sander, G. (1949). Twin studies of senescence. *American Journal of Psychiatry, 106,* 29–36.

Karasu, T.B., Waltzman, S.A., Lindenmayer, J., & Buckley, P.J. (1980). The medical care of patients with psychiatric illness. *Hospital and Community Psychiatry, 31,* 463–472.

Kay, D.W.K., Beamish, P., & Roth, M. (1964). Old age mental disorders in Newcastle-upon-Tyne. *British Journal of Psychiatry, 110,* 146–158, 668–682.

Kay, D.W.K., & Burrows, G.D. (Eds.). (1984). *Handbook of studies on psychiatry and old age.* Amsterdam: Elsevier.

Kessler, L.G., Burns, B.J., Shapiro, S., Tischler, G.L., George, L.K., Hough, R.L., Bodison, D., & Miller, R.H. (1987). Psychiatric diagnoses of medical service users: evidence from the Epidemiologic Catchment Area Program. *American Journal of Public Health, 77,* 18–24.

Koran, L. (1984). Senate Bill 929 Final Report: A Medical Evaluation Study of Mental Health Service Clients (State Contract 82-73099). Sacramento, CA: California Legislature.

Koranyi, E.K. (1979). Morbidity and rate of undiagnosed physical illnesses in a psychiatric clinic population. *Archives of General Psychiatry, 36,* 414–419.

Leeper, J.D., Badger, L.W., & Milo, T. (1985). Mental disorders among physical disability determination patients. *American Journal of Public Health, 75,* 78–79.

Leighton, D.C., Hagnell, O., Leighton, A.H., Harding, J.S., Keller, S.R., & Danley, R.A. (1971). Psychiatric disorder in a Swedish and a Canadian community: An exploratory study. *Social Science and Medicine, 5,* 189–209.

Levenson, A.J., & Hall, R.C.W. (1981). *Neuropsychiatric manifestations of physical disease in the elderly.* New York: Raven.

Levy, R., & Post, F. (1982). *The psychiatry of late life.* Oxford: Blackwell Scientific.

Lowenthal (Fiske), M. (1964). *Lives in distress: The paths of the elderly to the psychiatric ward.* New York: Basic Books.

Lowenthal (Fiske), M., Berkman, P.L., Brissette, G.C., Buehler, J.A., Pierce, R.C., Robinson, B.C., & Trier, M.L. (1967). *Aging and mental disorder in San Francisco: A social psychiatric study.* San Francisco, CA: Jossey-Bass.

Luke, E., Norton, W., & Denbigh, K. (1981). Medical and social factors associated with psychological distress in a sample of community aged. *Canadian Journal of Psychiatry, 26,* 244–250.

Maguire, G.P., & Granville-Grossman, K.L. (1968). Physical illness in psychiatric patients. *British Journal of Psychiatry, 115,* 1365–1369.

Marshall, H.E.S. (1949). Incidence of physical disorders among psychiatric in-patients. *British Medical Journal, 1,* 468–470.

Marshall, J.R., Burnett, W., & Brasure, J. (1983). On precipitating factors: Cancer as a cause of suicide. *Suicide and Life-Threatening Behavior, 13,* 15–27.

Minaker, K.L., & Rowe, J.W. (1981). Behavioral manifestations of renal disease in the elderly. In A.J. Levenson, & R.C. W. Hall (Eds.), *Neuropsychiatric manifestations of physical disease in the elderly* (pp. 93–102). New York: Raven.

Myers, J.K., Weissman, M.M., Tischler, B.L., Holzer, L.E., Leaf, P.J., Orvaschel, H., Anthony, J.C., Boyd, J.M., Burke, J.D., Kramer, M., & Stoltzman, R. (1984). Six-month prevalence of psychiatric disorders in three communities. *Archives of General Psychiatry, 41,* 959–970.

Neff, J.A., Husaini, B., & McCorkel, J. (1980). Psychiatric and medical problems in rural communities. *Social Science and Medicine, 14A,* 331–336.

New York State Department of Mental Hygiene. (1961). *Mental health survey of older people.* New York: State Hospital Press.

Popkin, M.K., Callies, A.L., & Mackenzie, T.B. (1985). The outcome of antidepressant use in the medically ill. *Archives of General Psychiatry, 42,* 1160–1163.

Post, F. (1962). *The significance of affective symptoms in old age: A follow-up study of one hundred patients.* London: Oxford University Press.

Regier, D.A., & Allen, G. (1983). Risk factor research in the major mental disorders (U.S. National Institute of Mental Health, DHHS Pub. No. [ADM] 83-1068). Washington, DC: Government Printing Office.

Regier, D.A., Myers, J.K., Kramer, M., Robins, L.N., Blazer, D.G., Hough, R.L., Eaton, W.W., & Locke, B.Z. (1984). The NIMH Epidemiologic Catchment Area Program. *Archives of General Psychiatry, 41,* 934–941.

Restak, R.M. (Ed.). (1986). Neuropsychiatry [Special issue]. *The Psychiatric Clinics of North America, 9.*

Robins, L.N., Helzer, J.E., Weissman, M.M., Orvaschel, H., Gruenberg, E., Burke, J.D., & Regier, D.A. (1984). Life-time prevalence of specific psychiatric disorders in three sites. *Archives of General Psychiatry, 41,* 949–958.

Rodin, G., & Voshart, K. (1986). Depression in the medically ill: An overview. *American Journal of Psychiatry, 143,* 696–705.

Roth, M., & Kay, D.W.K. (1956). Affective disorders arising in the senium: Pt. 2. Physical disability as an aetiological factor. *Journal of Mental Science, 102,* 141–150.

Schulberg, H.C., McClelland, M., Coulehan, J.L., Block, M., & Werner, G. (1986). Psychiatric decision making in family practice: Future research directions. *General Hospital Psychiatry, 8,* 1–6.

Schulberg, H.C., Saul, M., McClelland, M., Ganguli, M., Christy, W., & Frank, R. (1985). Assessing depression in primary medical and psychiatric practices. *Archives of General Psychiatry, 42,* 1164–1170.

Schwab, J.J., Bell, R.A., Warheit, G.J., Schwab, R.B., & Traven, N.D. (1978–1979). Some epidemiologic aspects of psychosomatic medicine. *International Journal of Psychiatry in Medicine, 9,* 147–158.

Schwab, J.J., Fennell, E.B., & Warheit, G.J. (1974). The epidemiology of psychosomatic disorders. *Psychosomatics, 15,* 88–93.

Schwab, J.J., & Schwab, M.E. (1978). *Sociocultural roots of mental illness: An epidemiological survey.* New York: Plenum Medical Book Company.

Schwab, J.J., & Traven, N.D. (1979). Factors related to the incidence of psychiatric illness. *Psychosomatics, 20,* 307–315.

Schwab, J.J., Traven, N.D., & Warheit, G.J. (1978). Relationship between physical and mental illness. *Psychosomatics, 19,* 458–663.

Shapiro, S., Skinner, E.A., Kessler, L.G., Von Korff, M., German, P.S., Tischler, G.L., Leaf, P.J., Benham, L., Cottler, L., & Regier, D.A. (1984). Utilization of health and mental health services: Three epidemiologic catchment area sites. *Archives of General Psychiatry, 41,* 971–978.

Shepherd, M. (1987). Mental illness and primary care. *American Journal of Public Health, 77,* 12–13.

Simon, A., & Talley, J. (1969). The role of physical illness in geriatric mental disorders. In *Psychiatric disorders in the aged: Report on the symposium held by the World Psychiatric Association at the Royal College of Physicians, London, 1965* (pp. 154–170). Manchester, UK: World Psychiatric Association.

Sinott, J.D. (1984–1985). Stress, health and mental health symptoms of older women and men. *International Journal of Aging and Human Development, 20,* 123–132.

Srole, L. (1975). Measurement and classification in sociopsychiatric epidemiology: Midtown Manhattan study (1954) and Midtown Manhattan restudy (1974). *Journal of Health and Social Behavior, 16,* 347–364.

Turner, R.J., Noh, S., & Levin, D. (1985). Depression across the life course: The significance of psychosocial factors among the physically disabled. In A. Dean (Ed.), *Depression in multidisciplinary perspective.* New York: Brunner-Mazel, 32–59.

Weiss, R.L., & Aved, B.M. (1978). Marital satisfaction and depression as predictors of physical health status. *Journal of Consulting and Clinical Psychology, 46,* 1379–1384.

Widmer, R.B., & Cadoret, R.J. (1978). Depression in primary care: Changes in patterns of patient visits and complaints during a developing depression. *The Journal of Family Practice, 7,* 293–302.

3

The Psychotherapeutic Effectiveness of Treatments for Psychiatric Illness in Late Life

Nancy Gourash Bliwise

The diagnosis and appropriate treatment of mental disorders in late life have received new attention in recent years. As greater proportions of the population have survived into their seventh and eighth decades, there has been a related increase in attempts to establish reliable estimates of the need for mental health services (Blazer, 1983; Gaitz, 1985) and to provide a wide range of treatment options (Foster, 1980; Goodstein, 1982; Ingebretsen, 1977; Kahana, 1979; Muslim & Epstein, 1980; Williamson & Ascione, 1983; Woods & Britton, 1977; Zevon, Karuza, & Brickman, 1982). Despite the interest in effective treatment strategies for older persons with mental health problems, there are few controlled treatment outcome studies. This chapter will evaluate the current literature on psychotherapeutic treatments for the elderly and outline some of the major problems that require further research.

There have been many changes in approaches to treating psychiatric disorders among patients of all ages since the late 1950s. Total institutional care is no longer the only option for treating major psychiatric disorders. The advent of neuroleptic and other psychotropic medications has allowed many psychiatric patients to be treated for emotional problems while remaining in the community (see chapter 4). There is a new need for community-based treatment programs to serve the elderly and for careful evaluations of such programs. This chapter summarizes the current literature on the effectiveness of various treatments for elderly patients with emotional problems.

In his classic review of the status of psychotherapy with elderly geriatric patients, Rechtschaffen (1959) noted the lack of controlled outcome studies and called for more systematic research. Little has changed in the years since the publication of this early review; the relevant literature is characterized by anecdotal descriptions of interventions, case reports, and uncontrolled studies. More recent reviews still call for systematic research using appropriate controls and well-specified measures of outcome (Eisdorfer & Stotsky, 1977; Ingebretsen, 1977; Mintz, Steurer, & Jarvik, 1981; Steuer & Clark, 1982).

Standards for psychotherapy outcome research have been recommended by Bergin and Garfield (1971), and others who have been working in the field for many years. Valid assessments of treatment effectiveness require

1. a specified treatment population;
2. a sample that has been reliably diagnosed by mental health professionals;
3. specification of the intervention;
4. description of the training and experience of those conducting the intervention;
5. an appropriate control/comparison group or control period in single case designs;
6. random assignment to treatment groups where appropriate;
7. specified criteria for successful outcome;
8. reliable and valid instruments or observation techniques for measuring change; and
9. appropriate data analysis techniques for assessing intra- and interindividual change.

Ideally these outcome studies should be directed toward identifying what treatment, by whom, is most effective for a particular individual with a specific problem or set of problems. Only a handful of studies met all of these criteria. Studies meeting all or a large percentage of the design criteria outlined above are weighted more heavily than studies with design flaws. In spite of study limitations, important questions can still be addressed, although definitive conclusions may be impossible to provide in most areas.

This chapter is divided into two main sections. The first offers a critical review of the literature in the following areas: affective disorders; senile dementia; anxiety disorders; alcohol abuse; schizophrenia and paranoid disorders; and prevention programs. Following this section is one that touches on general considerations, specific research recommendations, and policy recommendations.

Three questions guide the literature review summarized in this chapter: (1) Which interventions have proven to be most effective for treating the major psychiatric disorders of late life? (2) Is there evidence that interventions need to be revised for maximum effectiveness with elderly patients? (3) Are there specific problems typical of late life that, when effectively addressed, will prevent either the development of significant mental health problems or further declines among men and women who already experience emotional distress?

Affective Disorders

Findings from the most recent large-scale epidemiological surveys suggest that the actual rate of depressive disorders in the elderly may be somewhat lower than previous estimates (see chapter 2). However, depression is second only to cognitive disorders as the mental health problem for which the elderly are most likely to be treated (Ban, 1978; Redick, Kramer, & Taube, 1973; Redick & Taube, 1980; Sadavoy, 1981). The treatment settings and interventions for depression in late life are quite varied. Outcome studies conducted in inpatient settings rarely allow a discussion of the differential effectiveness of the multiple interventions provided. Thus, discussions of outcome are more global for these institutional settings. The review of single interventions is based on outpatient programs. Classic studies of the prognosis of late-life affective illness conducted in Europe are included. Attempts are made, wherever possible, to link European studies to similar investigations conducted in the United States.

Inpatient Hospitalization

Prior to the widespread availability and use of psychotropic medications, inpatient hospitalization was the primary treatment setting for the elderly with depressive disorders. Inpatient treatment largely consisted of support, occupational therapy, and social work, with some patients also receiving electroconvulsive therapy (Post, 1962; Roth, 1955). In one of the earliest follow-up studies of mental disorder in a geriatric population, Roth (1955) reported a good prognosis for patients diagnosed as having affective psychosis. Over half of the 318 patients studied in 1948 and 1949 were diagnosed with either a depressive or manic presentation of psychotic symptoms. Of these, a little over 60 percent had sufficient symptom remission to be discharged from the psychiatric hospital two years after admission; 17 percent remained hospitalized; 4 percent could not be located; and 19 percent were dead at follow-up. The diagnostic classification used did not allow a separate examination of patients with unipolar depression, nor does the diagnosis of affective psychosis correspond with current psychiatric nosology.

Post (1962) found less reason to be optimistic in his six-year follow-up of 81 elderly depressive patients discharged from a London psychiatric hospital. Using multiple assessment techniques, he found that only 31 percent of the discharged patients had made a lasting recovery; 52 percent had recurrent episodes of depression; and another 17 percent remained continuously ill. Of particular note was the finding that approximately 75 percent of the sample had received no further treatment following discharge. Although diagnostic criteria again do not correspond with current nosology and the sample was somewhat small, the lengthy follow-up period and careful attempt to examine the course of illness offset these weaknesses. These findings reveal that, though many elderly patients hospitalized for depressive illness are able to remain in the community following discharge, a significant proportion of them still suffer from recurrent depressive episodes. This suggests that the therapeutic effectiveness of inpatient hospitalization for depressive illness in late life was quite limited prior to the development of antidepressant medications. The best estimate, given the absence of an untreated control group, is full recovery in only one-third of the treated geriatric patients.

By the late 1960s, the use of tricyclic antidepressants was well integrated into both inpatient and outpatient psychiatric practice. Psychiatrists increasingly used electroconvulsive therapy in old persons as part of comprehensive inpatient treatment, and posthospitalization services improved. A number of follow-up studies were conducted to test the hypothesis that these changes in psychiatric inpatient treatment had significantly improved the long-term prognosis of depressive illness in late life.

Replicating his earlier study, Post (1972) followed a sample of 92 elderly consecutive admissions (1965–1966) with diagnoses of major depressive illness for 3 (rather than 6) years after discharge from a London psychiatric hospital. Complete recovery was observed in only 26 percent of the discharged geriatric patients. Recurrent depressive episodes were noted in 62 percent, and 12 percent remained continuously ill after discharge. Statistical analyses revealed no significant differences in recovery rates between this sample and the earlier 1950 sample. Pretreatment differences between the samples may explain these surprising findings. Only 15 percent of the 1950 sample had received treatment for their depressions prior to admission. In contrast, 61 percent of the 1966 sample were treated either by their family physician or in outpatient facilities prior to hospitalization. Interestingly, the later sample was also much more likely to receive posthospital psychiatric care. Ninety-three percent of those discharged in 1966 received additional treatment (largely with tricyclic medication) compared to only 26 percent in the 1950 sample. The introduction of new and more comprehensive treatments for elderly depressed patients did not improve the therapeutic effectiveness of geriatric inpatient programs. This may be due, however, to greater success in the community. Only seriously disturbed patients or patients who already were embarked on a chronic course of illness were hospitalized.

More recent studies of long-term prognosis reported sustained recovery rates ranging from 35 to 48 percent and chronic depression estimated at 22 to 26 percent (Cole, 1983; Gordon, 1981; Murphy, 1983). These figures are higher than those reported by Post (1966; 1972), but recent follow-up periods were much shorter. It is reasonable to expect that over a longer course both sustained recovery and chronic rates would decline. The more recent studies employed stringent diagnostic criteria but had serious design flaws. All studies failed to specify either the nature of treatments applied, who was treating the patients, or what percentage of patients had received treatment for their illness prior to admission. Cole (1983), using Feighner criteria (Feighner, Robins, Guze, Woodruff, & Winokur, 1972), studied only 38 consecutive admissions and failed to employ objective outcome criteria. Recovery rates had to be estimated from Gordon's (1981) study of consecutive admissions to an inpatient facility. Murphy's (1983) study was conducted on a large sample using Feighner research criteria for depressive illness for both diagnosis and follow-up. Because Murphy combined patients receiving inpatient and/or outpatient treatment in statistical analyses, it is impossible to arrive at an estimate for the therapeutic effectiveness of inpatient treatment for geriatric depressive disorder.

All of the inpatient treatment studies reviewed were conducted in Europe or Canada. The empirical studies conducted in the United States either used mortality as an outcome criterion (Black, Warrack, & Winokur, 1985a, 1985b; Martin, Cloninger, Guze, & Clayton, 1985), did not consider the course of illness during the follow-up period (Duckworth, Kedward, & Bailey, 1979), or presented outcome data that did not permit a valid assessment of long-term psychiatric status (Lowenthal et al. 1967). No study specified the nature of the treatment received in the inpatient setting. No systematic studies of cross-national differences in treatments for psychogeriatric disorders have been conducted.

Psychogeriatric patients in the United States tend to be diagnosed with senile dementia at higher rates than in the United Kingdom (Gurland, 1980). Elderly inpatients treated for a functional disorder are more rapidly discharged from hospitals in the United States and Canada than in the United Kingdom, but with no appreciable effect on mortality or inpatient status at 90-day follow-up (Duckworth et al., 1979). Assuming that there are no significant cross-national differences in inpatient treatment, the highest rates reported in the literature can be considered the best estimate of the therapeutic effectiveness of inpatient hospitalization for geriatric depression. Complete recovery can be expected in less than half of elderly patients who have depressive disorders and are treated in inpatient settings. It is also important to remember that elderly depressed patients in inpatient settings may have been treated unsuccessfully elsewhere and thus pose a difficult treatment problem.

Antidepressant Medication

Antidepressant medication is the primary form of treatment for patients of all ages suffering from a major depressive illness (Bieleski & Friedel, 1976; Forde & Sbordone, 1980). A review of 146 controlled double-blind studies using random assignment to treatment groups established the efficacy of both tricyclic antidepressants and monoamine oxidase inhibitors in the treatment of depression in adult men and women (Morris & Beck, 1974). However, the efficacy of these drugs for the treatment of geriatric depression has not been established unequivocally.

As of 1982, only 25 published studies on drug treatments for geriatric depression could be located, and all but a few were either uncontrolled, involved open trials, or used a treatment period of shorter duration than that required to establish drug efficacy (see reviews by Strauss & Solomon, 1983; Weissman & Myers, 1979). Drug trials published since 1982 on the efficacy of various psychotropic agents used in the treatment of geriatric depression were characterized by the same weaknesses in research design (Feighner & Cohn, 1985; Lakshmanan, Mion, & Frengley, 1986). Particularly noteworthy is the failure of most investigators to use established research criteria for selecting patients with depressive disorder. The following critical review is largely based on two recently published reviews (Raskin, 1978; Strauss & Solomon, 1983).

Tricyclic Antidepressants. Eight tricyclic antidepressants have proven efficacy in the treatment of depression in adults (Morris & Beck, 1974). Of these, only doxepin and imipramine have been subject to systematic investigations on geriatric populations. Six published studies on these medications were located (Friedel & Raskind, 1975, Gerner, Estabrook, Stever, & Jarvik, 1980; Grauer & Kral, 1960; Lakshmanan et al., 1986; Schmied, 1962; Zung, Gianturro, Pfeiffer, Wang, & Potkins, 1974). Only three employed a double-blind, placebo-controlled design (Gerner et al., 1980; Lakshmanan et al., 1986; Zung et al., 1974). Zung et al. (1974) compared the efficacy of imipramine and Gerovital H-3 with placebo in depressed men and women over age 60. Strict inclusion criteria for depressive disorder were not employed. Subjects treated with both imipramine and Gerovital H-3 showed significant improvement on a number of rating scales when compared to placebo controls. The dose was low and the treatment period was too short to establish the effectiveness of imipramine, especially because strict response criteria were not applied.

Similar problems were found in the study reported by Lakshmanan et al. (1986). The efficacy of low doses of doxepin was examined in a three-week double-blind, placebo-controlled trial in 24 geriatric rehabilitation patients. Both doxepin- and placebo-treated subjects showed significant improvements. The efficacy of both imipramine and the tetracyclic antidepressant trazodone were established in a double-blind, placebo-controlled trial conducted on patients aged 60 to 90 who met research diagnostic criteria for unipolar depressive disorder (Gerner et al., 1980). This study met almost all evaluation criteria; only serum drug levels and compliance rates were omitted. The authors concluded that, despite equal efficacy, trazodone was the preferred drug because of fewer side effects.

Monoamine Oxidase Inhibitors. No studies evaluating the monoamine oxidase inhibitors that are currently available in the United States were found. Three studies were located that evaluated the efficacy of improniazid and nialamide in geriatric populations, but these two drugs have been withdrawn from the U.S. market. Two studies were open and uncontrolled (Ayd, 1962; Settel, 1958). Results of the third double-blind, placebo-controlled study proved inconclusive (Shapiro, Dussik, Galentino, & Asekoff, 1960).

Other Antidepressants. Other antidepressant medications with chemical compositions and mechanisms of action that are dissimilar to the tricyclic antidepressants and monoamine oxidase inhibitors are being evaluated for treatment of depression in the elderly. As was discussed earlier, the tetracyclic antidepressant trazodone was proven effective in a well-designed clinical trial (Gerner et al., 1980). The effectiveness of nomifensine (Moizeszowicz & Subira, 1977), viloxazine (Mukherjee & Holland, 1979), mianserin (Fleischhauer, 1980), and cyprodemanol (Genevieve, cited in Strauss & Solomon, 1983) were investigated, but in open and/or uncontrolled studies with other serious design flaws that compromise the validity of the findings. Fluoxetine was found to be as effective as the tricyclic doxepin in significantly reducing symptoms of depression with fewer side effects (Feighner & Cohn, 1985). The efficacy of doxepam compared to a placebo has not been established. Thus, future trials against a suitable placebo control are still required.

Lithium. The use of lithium salts for the treatment of unipolar depression is controversial. Clinical reports suggest that lithium has the same therapeutic effect for both elderly and younger patients (Foster, Gershell, & Goldfarb, 1977). Bushley, Rathey, and Bowers (1983) reported good outcome with lithium treatment in a group of very elderly nursing home residents diagnosed with either bipolar or unipolar depressive illness. In contrast, Hewick, Newbury, Hopwood, Naylor, and Moody (1977) found that elderly depressed patients were less likely than younger patients to have therapeutic blood levels of lithium with treatment by lithium salts. This was a retrospective study of patients, aged 21 to 84, who were prescribed lithium prior to entry in the study. Double-blind, placebo-controlled studies of the therapeutic effectiveness of lithium salts for the treatment of unipolar depression in the elderly could not be located.

Antipsychotic Drugs. Four studies were located that assessed the effectiveness of antipsychotic medications used alone or in combination with other psychotropic drugs for treating depression. None of the authors reported diagnostic criteria. Thus, it was unclear whether the elderly patients studied presented with psychotic depression or were treated with antipsychotic medications in the absence of psychotic symptoms. Three of the four studies were either uncontrolled (Brook & McDonald, 1961), employed too small a control group (Kristof, Lehmann, & Ban, 1967), or were of questionable duration to establish drug efficacy (Brodie, McGhie, O'Hara, Valle-Jones, & Schiff, 1975). The combination of perphenazine and amitriptyline was found to significantly reduce symptoms of depression compared to chlordiazepoxide in a blind cross-over study (Beber, 1971). Chlordiazepoxide is a commonly prescribed anxiolytic. It would seem that more appropriate comparisons would test the efficacy of combination treatment against amitriptyline (tricyclic) alone and placebo control groups.

Gerovital H-3. Gerovital H-3 is included in this review because of its reputation as an antiaging drug that can also elevate mood in older depressed men and women (Ostfeld, Smith, & Stotsky, 1977). Of four clinical trials reviewed, two used open, uncontrolled research designs (Cohen & Dittman, 1974; Sakalis, Oh, Gershon, & Shopsin, 1974). Kurland and Hayman (1976), using strict exclusion criteria to select mildly depressed subjects for a double-blind, placebo-controlled study, found that significantly greater improvement occurred with Gerovital H-3 compared to placebo. The investigation conducted by Zung et al. (1974) found Gerovital H-3 superior to placebo. Diagnostic criteria were not presented, so it is unclear whether patients with major depressive disorders of those reporting symptoms of depression were successfully treated.

Summary. Only seven of the drug studies reviewed met minimal research criteria of random assignment to groups, inclusion of an adequate control group, and double-blind administration of treatments. The findings of these studies indicate that imipramine and trazodone appear effective for the treatment of depressive disorders in the elderly and that lithium has some potential when used cautiously. Fluoxetine warrants further study. Amitriptyline combined with perphenazine may also be effective but should be limited to elderly patients with psychotic depressions because the nature of the depressive disorder was not clarified in the report establishing its efficacy. Gerovital H-3 may also have some potential for the treatment of mild symptoms of depression.

It is important to note that the elderly treated with antidepressants are at risk for potentially serious side effects. Adverse drug reactions have been noted for all antidepressants reviewed. The most dangerous side effect is cardiac toxicity (Salzman, 1985). Antidepressants can also produce anticholinergic side effects ranging from dry mouth and blurred vision to memory deficits and confusional state.

Psychotherapy

Psychotherapy alone and in combination with psychotropic medications has been shown to be effective for the treatment of young and middle-aged adults suffering from acute depressive disorders. The efficacy of these treatments in geriatric populations has been studied only recently. Antidepressant medications are contraindicated for elderly patients with medical problems (for example, cardiac arrhythmias) and carry significant risk for adverse reactions. It is important, therefore, to establish the efficacy of psychotherapy alone, as well as in combination with more typical drug therapy.

Psychotherapy Alone. Both individual and group psychotherapy have been studied in geriatric populations. Only four empirical investigations of psychotherapy in elderly depressives were located, but all are characterized by good research design and include a range of psychotherapeutic approaches. All studies used adequate diagnostic criteria for major unipolar depression and exclusion criteria for patients with concurrent psychiatric disorders, serious phyical illness, and more than mild symptoms of dementia. Appropriate comparison groups were used, but only Fry (1984) included an untreated control group. Reliable and valid instruments were used to measure change, and follow-up periods were included in three of the four studies. Samples were small (less than 50 subjects) and drop-out rates ranged from 20 to 40 percent.

Significant reductions in depressive symptoms were found in two studies of brief individual psychotherapy (Fry, 1984; Gallagher & Thompson, 1982). Therapeutic efficacy was equivalent for cognitive, behavioral, and psychodynamic therapies. Improvement during a one-year follow-up was maintained more effectively by patients treated with cognitive or behavioral therapy than by those who received more insight-oriented psychotherapy (Gallagher & Thompson, 1982). Outcome was better for geriatric patients with nonendogenous depression (Gallagher & Thompson, 1983). Even so, 50 percent of the patients with endogenous depression had not relapsed during the posttreatment year.

Supportive, psychodynamic, and cognitive-behavioral group psychotherapies were also shown to be effective for the treatment of geriatric depression (Gallagher, 1981; Steuer et al., 1984). Outcomes slightly favored cognitive-behavioral compared to psychodynamic approaches (Steuer et al., 1984). Only Steuer et al. presented rates of improvement. Complete remission was observed in 40 percent of patients treated; some depressive symptoms were evident in 40 percent, and depressive illness was diagnosed in another 20 percent.

Therapeutic effectiveness was observed across a wide range of psychotherapeutic approaches. Only two studies included untreated or placebo-controlled groups in the research design. Thus, for three of the four studies, it is uncertain whether the observed changes were due to the treatments applied or to uncontrolled factors. Treatments ranged from individual sessions conducted 3 times a week for 4 weeks (Fry, 1984) to 10 weeks of twice-weekly group therapy followed by 26 weeks of weekly group meetings (Steuer et al., 1984). Only short-term psychotherapies were studied. No systematic investigations of long-term psychotherapy for elderly depressed patients could be located.

Psychotherapy and Pharmacotherapy Combined. The typical course of treatment for elderly men and women with depressive disorders is a combination of psychotherapy and antidepressant medication. Physicians in general medical practice are the principal source of psychiatric care for the elderly (Cohen, 1976; Richter, Barsky, & Happ, 1983; Shephard, 1976) with referral to outpatient psychiatric clinics or psychiatrists likely only for psychotic presentation of symptoms or chronic disorders (Mann, Jenkins, & Belsey, 1981; Richter et al., 1983). Four studies of the treatment effectiveness of psychotherapy combined with psychotropic medications provided are reviewed.

One hundred sixty-eight elderly depressed patients seeking treatment at a group medical practice were studied over a 22-month period (Richter et al., 1983). Diagnosis was made by the primary care physician; no corroboration of the diagnosis was reported. Most depressed patients also had chronic medical conditions. All patients received supportive counseling by the physician and 31 percent (n = 52) also were treated with one of four tricyclic antidepressants (amitriptyline, desipramine, doxepin, or imipramine). The duration of therapy ranged from 1 to 30 months with a median of 5 months. Therapeutic response was judged by patient and physician assessment of improved mood and relief of associated somatic symptoms as noted in the patient record. Partial or full recovery was reported for 72 percent of the patients treated with combined drug therapy and supportive counseling; 28 percent showed no sustained improvement. Anticholinergic or sedative side effects were noted in 23 percent of the treated patients.

A 12-month follow-up study (Mann et al., 1981) was conducted among patients with neurotic illness seeking treatment in two group general medical practices located outside London. A representative sample of 100 patients was selected from a larger study of patients with psychiatric illness noted by the physician. Fourteen patients over the age of 65 were selected, 6 of whom had diagnosed depressive neurosis. Diagnoses were based on the International Classification of Diseases, Version VIII, and were verified by a psychiatrist. Standard treatments of supportive counseling by the physician, supplemented in some cases with psychotropic medication, were given. The course of illness over the 12-month study period was rated. One-third of the cases showed complete recovery within the first 6 months of treatment; one-third showed an intermittent course, and one-third were continuously ill. Patients who were older, diagnosed as depressed, and showed more severe symptoms at outset were more likely to be treated with psychotropic medications; they also were more likely to show a chronic course of illness over the year. Only a few elderly depressed patients were studied. However, a major strength of this study is that subjects were selected to be representative of patients in group practice who manifest a depressive neurosis. This study, like the Richter et al. (1983) investigation, is limited by the use of unstandardized diagnostic procedure and lack of objective outcome criteria.

Cole (1985) satisfied most research design criteria in a follow-up of elderly depressed patients treated in outpatient geropsychiatry programs. Fifty-five patients were selected from consecutive referrals; 62 percent met Feighner criteria for primary depressive illness, and 38 percent presented moderate to severe depressive symptoms but did not satisfy criteria for primary depression. A history of prior depressive illness was noted in 35 percent of the patients. All patients were treated with combinations of tricyclic antidepressants and psychotherapy. Compliance was monitored with 64 percent of the patients compliant for the entire 20-month treatment period (this included initial treatment and maintenance therapy). Fifteen percent dropped out of treatment. The follow-up period ranged from 2 to 5 years with a mean of 4 years. Outcome over the course of the follow-up period was rated. Only 18 percent of the sample remained in remission during follow-up; 52 percent had some relapses, and another 30 percent were continuously ill. These findings were supported by a 2-year follow-up of patients treated in a Canadian geriatric psychiatry outreach program (Houston, 1983). The percentage of successful outcomes was similar to that observed in general medical practice. Unsophisticated research methods, however, seriously compromise the findings.

Prevention Programs

Most studies have examined the effectiveness of interventions for major depressive disorders. The elderly also tend to experience a disproportionately high number of depressive symptoms not currently part of a major depressive disorder. These symptoms may be a precursor to a later depressive illness. Treatment programs designed to reach elders whose symptoms may not be so severe as to require professional treatment have recently been developed. An educational program to teach elders how to cope with depression was effective under both nonprofessional and professional leadership (Thompson, Gallagher, Nies, & Epstein, 1983). Meditation–relaxation classes offered at senior centers helped alleviate targeted symptoms of depression as well as symptoms of anxiety (DeBerry, 1982). Only DeBerry's (1982) clinical trial included an appropriate control group. Both programs appeared to be helpful. A better test of prevention may be a long-term follow-up to ensure that depressive illness indeed did not develop.

Summary

Findings from all studies reviewed suggest that elderly patients treated in inpatient facilities for major depressive disorders are often hospitalized after other forms of treatment have failed. Successful outcomes were observed in approximately one-third of patients discharged. Most elderly patients seek treatment for depression from primary care physicians. Typically, depression is successfully treated with a combination of supportive therapy and psychotropic medication. A suitable empirical literature emerged only for the study of individual and group psychotherapy for elderly depressed patients. These studies yielded the best estimates for therapeutic outcome. Complete remission was observed for one-third to one-half of the elderly depressed patients who completed treatment. Estimates were comparable across all forms of treatment. Overall, it appears that successful treatments for geriatric depression are available and that some of the patients with the worst prognoses can be successfully treated.

The literature abounds with suggestions for modifications of treatments for geriatric depression (Grotjahn, 1978; Ingebretsen, 1977; Kovacs, 1980;

Salzman, 1985). No studies systematically examined the relative efficacy of modified programs. Brief cognitive and behavior therapies were proven more effective than brief psychodynamic therapies. More research is needed comparing various brief therapies to long-term therapies before brief cognitive behavioral approaches are recommended unilaterally for the treatment of geriatric depression.

Finally, pilot research suggests that educational classes to help community-resident elderly monitor symptoms of depression may eventually prove effective for preventing major depressive illness. Long-term trials, however, are needed to establish true "prevention." Of note is the absence of studies that examine treatments for both physical and psychological problems. No programs attempting to educate the elderly about the links between physical illness and emotional distress were located.

Senile Dementia

Senile dementias are primarily disorders of old age and are the only psychiatric disorders for which prevalence rates consistently increase over the life span (see chapter 1). There are no known cures of Alzheimer's type and other dementias. The cognitive and behvioral problems accompanying senile dementia can, however, be treated (Cassel & Jameton, 1981; Jarvik & Kumar, 1984).

Diagnosis

Senile dementia is not a unitary disorder with a single cause or set of causes. Thus, diagnosis is often quite difficult. Several studies have shown that many patients thought to have a primary dementing illness were found, upon careful reassessment in hospital, to have potentially treatable or "reversible" dementias (Cummings, Benson, & LoVerma, 1980; Fox, Toper, & Huckman, 1975; Freemon, 1976; Freemon & Rudd, 1982; Hutton, 1981; Larson, Reifler, Featherstone, & English, 1984; Marsden & Harrison, 1972; Smith, Kiloh, Ratnaverle, & Grant, 1976). Indeed, these investigators typically reported that 10 to 30 percent of patients evaluated for suspected dementia had reversible dementias. Follow-up studies have found that from one-fourth to one-half of patients with diagnoses of dementia at discharge from psychiatric hospitals show no serious cognitive deficits at follow-up (Bergmann, 1977; Kendell, 1974; Nott & Fleminger, 1975; Ron, Toone, Garralda, & Lishman, 1979). These findings have led to increased awareness of the importance of precise differential diagnosis (Eisdorfer & Cohen, 1980; Katzman, 1982; McKhann et al., 1984). There appears to be substantial diagnostic error in the evaluation of senile dementia. Inconsistent methods across studies and several design flaws preclude estimates of the actual error rates. Most studies did not include a follow-up period that would demonstrate if symptom remission occurred in patients with diagnoses of reversible dementia (Freemon, 1976; Freemon & Rudd, 1982; Hutton, 1981; Marsden & Harrison, 1972). Samples often included more middle-aged than elderly patients (Cummings et al., 1980; Marsden & Harrison, 1972; Nott & Fleminger, 1975; Ron et al., 1979; Smith et al., 1976). The careful prospective study of Larson et al. (1984) is presented in detail.

Patients who were referred for internal medicine evaluation and met DSM-III criteria for senile dementia were selected for study. Exhaustive medical and laboratory evaluations were conducted for each of the 107 patients selected. Alzheimer's-type dementia was diagnosed in 69 percent of the patients evaluated; multi-infarct dementia in 4 percent; alcohol-related dementia in 4 percent; and other irreversible dementia in 3 percent. Fifteen patients evaluated were found not to be demented. Objective features of dementia were absent, despite subjective complaints of memory impairment. Depression was diagnosed in 7 of these patients and cerebrovascular accident in another 3; the remainder received diagnoses of multiple sclerosis, acne rosacea, peripheral neuropathy, drug-induced lupus erythematosus, or benign senescent forgetfulness. Fifteen patients were diagnosed with potentially reversible dementia.

The most common causes of reversible dementias were medication side effects and hypothyroidism. The patients with potentially reversible dementia presented with significantly shorter duration of symptoms, an inconsistent pattern of findings on mental status examinations, and polypharmacy. Drugs implicated were sedative-hypnotic agents and antihypertensive medications. Previously unrecognized but treatable diseases were diagnosed in 48 patients; depression was diagnosed in well over 50 percent of these patients. Follow-up assessments were made on 72 percent of the patients at least 6 months after the initial evaluation. Significant improvements in cognitive functioning, as measured by Mini-Mental State and Dementia Rating Scale scores, were found in 16 patients. Of the patients showing improvement, 11 had been diagnosed as having reversible dementia, and 5 had been diagnosed as irreversible. Thirteen patients with reversible dementia were followed for an additional 18 months. Eight patients had progressive deterioration consistent with Alzheimer's-type dementia. The condition proved completely reversible for only 3 patients; 2 patients continued to show evidence of dementia but with no progression of symptoms over the follow-up period.

The authors concluded that the reversible–irreversible, treatable–untreatable dichotomy has limited practical value in the treatment of senile dementia. They recommend a model that views the elderly patient with cognitive impairment as at high risk for various coexistent treatable conditions. These findings highlight the importance of comprehensive evaluation of dementia and the potential for significant improvement in cognitive functioning with appropriate treatment. Though it appears that there was an underlying progressive illness in most patients, level of functioning was significantly improved with treatment of previously undiagnosed medical disease. Also of note was the role of iatrogenesis in potentially treatable dementias; the most common causes of reversible dementia were medication side effects. Psychotropic medications were implicated in the majority of cases.

Drug Treatments for Cognitive Impairment

A number of psychoactive agents have been investigated in the treatment of senile dementia. The most frequently studied are cerebral vasodilators, central nervous system stimulants, procaine hydrochloride, and cholinomimetic agents. Only findings from randomized, double-blind controlled studies are presented. Discussion of these investigations is based in large part on current published reviews (Bagne, Pomara, Crook, & Gershon, 1986; Funkenstein, Hicks, Dysken, & Davis, 1981; Reisberg, Ferris, & Gershon, 1980).

Vasodilators. Vasodilators increase blood flow to the brain by action on the blood vessels. Their use is based on findings that reduced cerebral blood flow is characteristic of patients with most forms of dementia (O'Brien, 1977). Seven controlled studies examined the effect of papaverine on cognitive impairment and mood disturbance (Bazo, 1973; Branconnier & Cole, 1977; Branconnier, Cole, & Gardos, 1978; Lu, Stotsky, & Cole, 1971; McQuillan, Lopec, & Vibal, 1974; Ritter, Nail, Tatum, & Blazi, 1971; Rosen, 1975; Stern, 1970). Four studies reported significant improvement in mood and/or performance on memory tests (Branconnier & Cole, 1977; Branconnier et al., 1978; McQuillan et al., 1974; Ritter et al., 1971; Stern, 1970). Shortcomings were noted, however, in all studies. Branconnier and Cole (1977; Branconnier et al., 1978) observed improvement with papaverine on some indices and increased impairment on others. One rater was not blind in the Stern (1970) study, thereby compromising assessment of change. Members of the placebo control group also showed significant improvement, although to a lesser degree than paparevine-treated subjects (Ritter et al., 1971). The sample size was too small to allow definitive conclusions from the lengthy trial by McQuillan et al. (1974).

Hydergine is the most frequently studied of the vasodilators. Funkenstein et al. (1981) reviewed 18 efficacy studies of Hydergine that met research criteria for a carefully controlled study. Fourteen of the studies found significant improvements in memory, mood, and social functioning for Hydergine-treated patients compared to placebo controls. In 3 of the studies, gains in mood and sociability were not accompanied by significant improvements in test performance. All studies used elderly subjects with diagnosed organic brain syndrome, but severity of disorder was rated as "mild" in some patients. Many studies used a behavioral rating scale as the sole measure of functioning without including objective measures of cognitive performance. The effect sizes across studies also tended to be small. Lengthy trials suggested that some of the effects may be due to learning or to possible antidepressant properties of the drug. More recent reviews continue to conclude that major questions about the indications for use, optimal dose, and effectiveness of Hydergine remain unanswered (Hollister & Yesavage, 1984; Loew & Weil, 1982).

Central Nervous System Stimulants. Central nervous system compounds were studied for their potential effects on attention and psychomotor performance. Pentylenetetrazol and methylphenidate are the central nervous system stimulants most widely investigated in geriatric populations.

Lehman and Ban (1975) reviewed 16 controlled studies of pentylenetetrazol in elderly men and women with diagnosed chronic brain syndrome. Drug efficacy was found in only 5 studies with changes largely found on behavioral rating scales. Reporting the findings of their own carefully controlled evaluation, these authors found no differences between pentylenetetrazol-treated subjects and controls on a wide range of psychiatric, psychometric, and electrophysiological measures.

Negative results from controlled studies refuted positive clinical reports of the efficacy of methylphenidate. Two placebo-controlled, double-blind studies used objective tests to measure cognitive function and found no positive effects on performance associated with administration of methylphenidate (Gilbert, Donnelly, Zimmer, & Kubis, 1973; Reisberg et al., 1980).

Procaine Hydrochloride. Jarvik and Milne (1975) comprehensively reviewed the literature on procaine hydrochloride (Gerovital H-3). Gerovital H-3 was developed in Rumania and has been acclaimed for its rejuvenating properties. Studies of Gerovital H-3 in the treatment of patients with memory impairment have largely failed to include sufficiently adequate controls to allow a true test of efficacy. Some studies suggest that the compound improves mood. There is, however, no evidence regarding its therapeutic effectiveness for memory impairment.

Cholinomimetic Drugs. The cholinergic system has been implicated in memory processes and may play a central role in Alzheimer's disease-related memory impairment (Drachman & Leavitt, 1974). Cholinomimetic agents have been given to Alzheimer's patients with mixed results. Physostigmine was shown to reduce inappropriate behavior (Smith & Swash, 1978) and improve symbol copying (Muramoto, Sugishita, Sugita, & Toyakura, 1979) in clinical trials with single patients. No significant differences on cognitive testing between placebo and drug groups were found in two double-blind, placebo-controlled studies of lecithin (Fisman et al., 1981; Smith, Swash, & Exton-Smith, 1979). Inconsistent results were also observed across evaluations of drug trials combining physostigmine and lecithin (Thal, Fula, Masur, & Sharpless, 1983; Wettstein, 1983). Moderate improvements were found for less impaired subjects in an evaluation of the combination of lecithin and tetrahydroaminoacridine (Kaye et al., 1982).

The most promising study to date was reported by Summers, Majovski, Marsh, Tachiki, and Kling (1986). An optimal dose of tetrahydroaminoacridine (THA), a centrally active anticholinesterase, was titrated in an open trial for 17 patients with a clinical diagnosis of undifferentiated dementia. A double-blind, placebo-controlled crossover study using individualized optimal doses was then conducted over a 3-week period on 15 subjects. Significant improvements over the treatment period were found on global assessments of behavior and cognitive tests; no improvements were observed on any learning task among the most severely demented subjects. Treatment versus placebo differences were statistically significant for all except the most severely demented subjects. Twelve subjects received long-term treatment with THA for an average duration of 12.6 months (range: 3 to 26 months). Dramatic improvements were reported for 3 subjects who resumed premorbid leisure and employment activities. Other subjects showed significant improvements in self-care. Transient side effects were experienced by a little over one-half of the subjects; all side effects were successfully treated by a dose reduction and/or administration of oral glycopyrrolate.

No drug has consistently demonstrated that it can slow or reverse the cognitive impairments of senile dementia. The few positive findings were compromised by shortcomings in study design and sample size. The diagnostic criteria for dementia often went unreported. It is likely that patients with quite different diseases were studied in each trial. Success criteria were not defined in advance. Many studies relied on one or two global rating scales of cognitive and behavioral deficits that have unproven reliability and validity. Guidelines for evaluating drugs in Alzheimer's disease have been published (Bagne et al., 1986; Isaacs, 1979). Until adequate assessments of drug efficacy are reported, positive findings can be viewed only as indicators of potentially promising drugs for treating dementia-related cognitive impairments. Cholinomimetic compounds especially warrant further clinical investigations.

Drug Treatments for Behavioral Impairment

Research on drug treatments for dementia has focused on cognitive dysfunction. The behavioral sequelae of Alzheimer's disease and other senile dementias have been relatively neglected. Helms (1985) reviewed 21 studies of the efficacy of antipsychotic medications in the treatment of the behavioral complications of dementia. Of these, only 8 were randomized, double-blind, placebo-controlled trials. The earliest controlled trial (Seager, 1955) showed marked improvement associated with chlorpromazine compared to placebo in female inpatients with chronic brain syndrome. Improvement was rated using a clinical global improvement scale. Psychiatric nosology has changed radically since this early trial. Instruments that allow more detailed evaluation of behavioral problems associated with psychiatric disorders have been developed and validated.

Only three studies using current diagnoses and multiple evaluations of behavior were found. Rada and Kellner (1976) found less manifest psychosis in patients treated with thiothixene. Patients with psychotic as well as non-psychotic organic brain syndrome were studied. Results were not presented separately for each diagnostic subtype. Two studies demonstrated moderate benefit with loxapine (Barnes, Raskind, Scott, & Murphy, 1981; Petrie et al., 1982), and Petrie et al. (1982) found haloperidol to be as effective as loxapine. Thioridazine showed no benefit when compared with placebo (Barnes, Veith, Okimoto, Raskind, & Bumbrecht, 1982). Adverse drug reactions were reported in all trials; 10 percent of the subjects were withdrawn because of side effects.

Some antipsychotic compounds proved efficacious in the treatment of the behavioral complications of dementia. Careful monitoring is required because of potentially adverse effects.

Behavioral Treatments

Behavioral therapies are becoming more widely used in the treatment of the behavioral problems associated with senile dementia. Specific problem behaviors are identified and operant conditioning techniques are employed to bring about behavior change. Empirical investigations of therapeutic efficacy consistently used single case designs. Only studies that included a suitable baseline are reviewed.

Responsive verbal behavior was successfully reinstated in a 58-year-old psychotic inpatient with chronic brain syndrome who had been mute for 5 years (Sabatasso & Jacobsen, 1970). Reinforcement, behavior shaping, and modeling were used. Verbal behavior generalized to situations on the ward and remained consistent at 12-month follow-up. Libb and Clements (1969) increased physical activity by means of material reinforcement in a token economy system in 3 of 4 treated inpatients with chronic brain syndrome. Brody, Kleban, Lawton, and Silverman (1971) developed individually tailored programs for elderly women with chronic brain syndrome who lived in a residential care facility. Excess disabilities—functional impairments over and above those induced by organic impairment—were targeted for change. Patients treated showed significant improvement compared to a control sample after a year of treatment. Follow-up at 9 months after treatment revealed no significant differences between groups.

Pinkston and Linsk (1984) had remarkable success in teaching operant conditioning techniques to 21 family caregivers who then applied the techniques to problem behaviors exhibited by their mentally and physically impaired relatives. Eleven patients had some form of organic cognitive impairment. Diagnostic procedures were not specified. A staff member recorded a 1.5-hour observation of specific client behaviors and the family's interaction with the client in the client's home. Problem behaviors were selected and desired outcomes specified. Family members were then taught to record behaviors with a reliability check by the observer conducted within the week. Caregivers were instructed in behavioral procedures. Instruction included orientation to operant and social learning theory with specific examples and applications procedures through modeling, role play, corrective feedback, and discussion of data.

All monitoring and intervention responsibilities were transferred to the caregiver. Termination of the education–treatment program occurred after 2 months of successful goal attainment. Thirty-four problem behaviors were targeted. Treatment methods focused on cueing, contracting, and reinforcement. Significant improvements were observed in 73 percent of all behaviors. Interventions designed to promote positive behaviors (for example, reading, sociability) were found to be more successful than those designed to eliminate negative behaviors (for example, repetitive questioning, verbal aggression). Follow-up at 6 months posttreatment revealed that improvement was maintained for 78 percent of the targeted behaviors. This study clearly demonstrates the efficacy of behavioral intervention techniques applied by caregivers. The severity of cognitive and behavioral impairments of clients were not rated, nor were results presented separately by diagnosis. The effects were substantial and warrant further research.

Day Treatment Centers

Adult day-care centers provide a therapeutic milieu for elderly clients suffering from a variety of mental and physical impairments. Centers offering a structured environment outside the home free family caregivers for employment, errands, rest, and recreation. No controlled studies of the therapeutic effects of adult day-care services were located. Mace (1984) surveyed 346 day-care centers across the nation that provided services to the demented elderly. All centers established a social milieu in which the staff monitored the clients' general health, provided recreational activities, and worked to maintain daily living skills. Disturbed behavior tended to decrease: 71 percent of the centers reported that their demented clients became less agitated and 67 percent reported that they paced and wandered less. Eighty-four percent noted that their demented clients formed friendships with other clients. The data are based on subjective reports and do not reflect measured change.

Family Support Groups

Spouses are the major care providers for the impaired elderly, followed by children, in-laws, and friends (Moon, 1983). Those caring for demented family members often report feelings of stress and burden and generally have low morale (Fengler & Goodrich, 1979; Safford, 1980; Zarit, Reeuer, & Bach-Peterson, 1980). There are a number of descriptions in the literature of various support group models (Barnes et al., 1981; Fuller, Ward, Evans, Massam, & Gardner, 1979; LaVorgna, 1979; Lazarus, Stafford, Cooper, Cohler, & Dysken, 1981; Steuer & Clark, 1982; Zarit & Zarit, 1983). These will be discussed in detail in chapter 6. Only one controlled outcome study was located.

Kahan, Kemp, Staples, and Brummel-Smith (1985) found significant reductions in family burden and increases in knowledge of Alzheimer's disease among participants in an 8-week support group for caregivers. Control subjects reported significant increases in family burden over the same time period. This group used an educational–support model. More research is needed on other treatment educational approaches.

Summary

Despite the poor prognosis for Alzheimer's disease and other dementias, successful treatments are available for the behavioral complications of senile dementia. Antipsychotic medications have proven effective but carry a high risk for adverse reactions. Continued use of antipsychotic medication may lead to the emergence of tardive dyskinesia. Behavioral treatments appear to be most effective and can be used successfully by family caregivers in the home. Support groups for family caregivers are becoming increasingly available but have no proven therapeutic effectiveness. Major research efforts have focused on drug treatments for the cognitive dysfunctions associated with senile dementia. No one drug has proven effective, but cholinomimetic compounds hold some promise for the future.

The empirical literature on treatments for senile dementia is seriously flawed by the lack of diagnostic specificity in most studies. Despite an ever-growing body of research, exactly who has been studied remains unclear. It is impossible to say with any certainty who can be successfully treated with which interventions. Even in carefully controlled drug trials, the characteristics of the patients experiencing adverse reactions and the specific nature or severity of the problem are rarely specified. Replications of positive findings on elderly men and women who have been carefully diagnosed are essential before drawing definitive conclusions about treatment effectiveness.

Dementia is a disorder of late life. Even so, the most effective treatment proved to be one that has been used successfully for behavioral problems in clients of all ages. The educational–treatment program designed to teach behavioral techniques to family caregivers was modeled after parent effectiveness training programs. No modifications were needed in order to achieve equal success with the elderly.

Anxiety Disorders

Recent epidemiological studies have shown that phobias and generalized anxiety are among the most prevalent psychiatric disorders of late life (see chapter 1). Numerous therapeutic options are available. Only the efficacy studies that sampled from geriatric populations are reviewed.

Phobias

Phobias were found to be the most prevalent psychiatric disorder among elderly women and second only to severe cognitive impairment among elderly men in the NIMH Epidemiological Catchment Area studies (Myers et al., 1984). Onset of simple phobias and social phobias typically occurs in early childhood or adolescence; onset in old age is rare (Sheehan, Sheehan, & Minichiello, 1981; Thyer, Parrish, Curtis, Nesse, & Cameron, 1985). Agoraphobia typically begins in early adulthood, but late onset is not as rare for agoraphobia as other phobias (Thyer et al., 1985). These findings suggest a chronic course for the elderly men and women suffering from phobic disorders in late life.

Numerous approaches were found to be effective for the treatment of phobias (Schuckit, 1981), with particular success noted for behavioral therapies as part of a program using multiple treatment methods (McPherson, Brougham, & McLaren, 1980; Popler, 1977; Rapp, Thornas, & Reyes, 1983; Weekes, 1973; Zitrin, Klein, & Woerner, 1980). No systematic clinical trials on geriatric populations were found. Only two case reports of successful behavioral treatments of elderly patients with phobic disorders were located (Garfinkel, 1979; Wanderer, 1972); both patients suffered from phobias (agoraphobia, aerophobia) and related depressions for most of their adult lives. Garfinkel (1979) reported two modifications of the standard desensitization techniques that she applied in her treatment of an elderly woman with chronic agoraphobia. The relaxation training period was simplified and prolonged and the patient's cooperation was systematically reinforced by permitting her free time to discuss current problems. The need for modification was attributed to the patient's social isolation and lack of introspectiveness—characteristics of the elderly that are generally considered obstacles to therapy.

Phobias, particularly agoraphobia, often coexist with depressive disorders (Bowen & Kohout, 1979; Dealy, Ishila, Avery, Wilson, & Dunner, 1981; Munjack & Moss, 1981). Beber (1971) compared the therapeutic efficacy of an amitriptyline–perphenazine combination to the anxiolytic chlordiazepoxide in elderly depressed inpatients who also had symptoms of anxiety. Chlordiazepoxide was more effective in relieving symptoms of anxiety, and the amitriptyline–perphenazine compound proved effective for alleviating depressive symptoms. A large double-blind, placebo-controlled study of diazepam for the treatment of anxiety and depression was conducted by Cromwell (1973). Improvement on 9 of 18 targeted symptoms of anxiety was found for diazepam-treated subjects. Diagnostic criteria were not specified and the study protocol did not prohibit the use of other medications. It is unclear whether the positive changes reported were due to diazepam or the successful treatment of other disorders.

It appears that behavioral treatments and the use of anxiolytic medications hold promise for the treatment of phobias in late life. Further systematic studies that take into account multiple diagnoses are needed, however, before definitive conclusions about the relative efficacy of various treatments can be drawn.

Generalized Anxiety

Generalized anxiety was found to be the most prevalent of four psychiatric disorders (major depression, agoraphobia-panic, other phobia, generalized anxiety) studied in elderly respondents participating in a national survey of prescription psychotropic drug use (Uhlenhuth, Balter, Mellinger, Cisin, & Clinthorne, 1983). Further analyses (Mellinger, Balter, & Uhlenhuth, 1984) revealed that those who used anxiolytics regularly tended to be older women with chronic physical health problems. Anxiolytics were largely prescribed by physicians in general medical practice and follow-up occurred approximately every four months. These findings were consistent with findings from other studies of general medical practice (Freeman, 1979; Skegg, Doll, & Perry, 1977).

There is little controlled research on the efficacy of anxiolytic drugs for the treatment of generalized anxiety in the aged. The majority of studies on geriatric populations examined the efficacy of benzodiazepines as a hypnotic rather than an anxiolytic agent (for example, Bannen & Resnick, 1973; Fillingham, 1982; Reeves, 1977). Because anxiety is often associated with insomnia, studies of the efficacy of benzodiazepines for the treatment of geriatric insomnia are reviewed.

Sleep disturbances are common in the elderly. Indeed, complaints of insomnia are much more prevalent among old compared to young men and women in the general population (Ballinger, 1976; Karacan et al., 1976; Tune, 1969). Physical illness (Kales & Tan, 1969) and organic sleep pathology (for example, sleep apnea, nocturnal myoclonus) undoubtedly play a role in the insomnia seen in some elderly men and women (Kupfer & Crook, 1984). The role of psychopathology in geriatric insomnia remains disputed. In younger adults, associations between various forms of psychopathology and insomnia are strong (Kales, 1983; Kales & Kales, 1984). Some investigators have claimed no such association in the elderly (Roehrs, Lineback, Zorick, & Roth, 1982). In a recent study, both anxiety and physiological factors appeared to be involved in the symptom of insomnia in the elderly (Bliwise, Bliwise, & Dement, 1985).

Insomnia at all ages is most typically treated with sedative-hypnotic medications. Benzodiazepines are the most commonly prescribed hypnotics. The findings of controlled studies consistently favored various benzodiazepine compounds for effective treatment of insomnia in the elderly (Dehlin & Bjornson, 1983; Martinez & Serna, 1982; Reeves, 1977). These compounds should be prescribed judiciously, for the elderly are at risk for adverse effects with prolonged use of benzodiazepine hypnotics (Evans & Jarvis, 1972; Martilla, Hammel, & Alexander, 1977; Reeves, 1977). Drowsiness, blurring of vision, unsteady gait, confusion, disorientation, and falls were side effects frequently observed in clinical trials. A number of investigators also observed withdrawal symptoms following cessation of long-term administration of benzodiazepine compounds (Lader & Petursson, 1983; Martilla et al., 1977; Rickels, Case, Downing, & Winokur, 1983).

A behavioral treatment program for geriatric insomnia was studied by Puder, Lacks, Bertelson, and Storandt (1983). Single-case designs were used to compare sleep patterns with behavioral treatment to sleep under a counterdemand condition. Reported latency to sleep onset was reduced and self-reported quality of sleep significantly improved under behavioral treatment compared to the control period. In a study previously discussed, DeBerry (1982) demonstrated the efficacy of meditation–relaxation techniques for alleviating symptoms of anxiety and depression in a group of elderly women.

Summary

In spite of the prevalence of phobias and generalized anxiety in the elderly, the efficacy of most currently used treatments has not been established in this population. Research has focused on pharmacologic agents, particularly benzodiazepines. Benzodiazepines were found to be effective for the treatment of insomnia in older adults. The efficacy of benzodiazepine compounds for relieving other symptoms of generalized anxiety has not, however, been systematically investigated in geriatric populations.

Behavioral treatments hold some promise for effective treatment of anxiety disorders. Desensitization techniques for the treatment of phobias warrant further research, particularly as clinical case reports suggest their efficacy for patients with chronic phobias.

Current nosology for anxiety disorders was not used in any study reviewed, nor were exclusion criteria reported for the majority of investigations. The duration of illness was noted only in the two clinical case reports. Given the varied symptoms of anxiety and the range of manifestations of disorder, the specific nature of the problem being treated was not clearly defined in most studies.

Alcohol Abuse

Community studies have revealed that alcohol abuse is a significant mental health problem, especially for elderly men (see chapter 1). The problems and effective treatments for alcohol abuse in late life have been extensively reviewed elsewhere (Hartford & Samorajski, 1984; Martin & Streissguth, 1982). This review focuses only on the issue of age-specific treatments for alcohol abuse in the elderly.

In recent years there has been a growing emphasis on alcoholism treatment programs designed specifically for the elderly (Foster, 1980; Hinrichsen, Dunham, & Janik, 1981). Some of the problems cited that presumably demonstrate a need for age-specific services included health problems that preclude drug therapy; decreased physical tolerance for alcohol; transportation problems; negative reactions to younger alcoholics who may also abuse illegal substances; and intellectual impairment. Studies of age-related differences in outcome consistently found no differences in treatment outcome between older and younger alcoholics (Janik & Dunham, 1983; Myerson & Mayer, 1966; Wiens, Menustik, Miller, & Schmitz, 1982–1983). Some investigators reported a better prognosis for elderly compared to younger clients (Blaney, Radford, & MacKenzie, 1975; Mishara & Kastenbaum, 1980; Wilkinson, 1971). The most comprehensive study was done by Janik and Dunham (1983) using data drawn from a national data base of 550 alcoholism treatment programs. Treatment programs served all age groups and provided comprehensive inpatient and outpatient services. Data were obtained on all patients aged 60 and above who had been randomly selected for 6-month, posttreatment interviews. Data on 8 percent of the follow-up patients under age 60 were obtained for purposes of comparison. Variables studied included social background characteristics; pretreatment alcohol use patterns; prior helpseeking for alcohol problems; treatment received; posttreatment alcohol use; and counselor assessment of change. Appropriate univariate and multivariate statistical analyses were performed. The only significant age differences in outcome indicated that treatment was less effective for middle-aged compared to younger and older alcoholics. The large sample size and breadth of variables studied were major strengths of this investigation. This elderly sample had, however, already entered into the treatment system. If elderly alcoholics experience age-related barriers to entering treatment (Shane, Weeden, & Lurie, 1985), the sample studied may be biased toward more motivated clients.

Studies did not address age-related problems to entering treatment or the need for age-specific alcohol outreach programs. Once elderly alcoholics enter treatment, it appears that they can be effectively helped in age-integrated treatment programs. Whether they would be better served in specialized programs for the elderly remains unknown.

Schizophrenia and Paranoid Disorders

The actual extent of schizophrenia, paranoia, and paraphrenia as mental health problems of the elderly is uncertain (see chapter 1). Investigations of treatments for late-life schizophrenia and paranoid disorders are reviewed below.

The short- and long-term prognosis for elderly schizophrenics and elderly patients suffering from paranoid disorders improved dramatically following the development of antipsychotic drugs. Comparing outcome before and after the introduction of phenothiazines, Post (1966; 1977) reported that 100 percent of his elderly psychotic patients admitted before systematic use of these drugs remained psychotic; 75 percent of a subsequently admitted cohort made complete recoveries following drug treatments. Blessed and Wilson (1982) found that approximately 20 percent of patients with paraphrenia were discharged from psychiatric hospitals by two years after admission in 1948–1949 compared to over 75 percent discharged by 2 years in 1976. Both of these investigations were conducted in England. Comparable changes were reported for the United States and Canada by Duckworth et al. (1979).

Well-controlled studies repeatedly demonstrated the efficacy of antipsychotic medications for the treatment of schizophrenia (see review by Davis, 1976) and a high rate of relapse when drug therapy was discontinued (see review by Ban, 1969). Several double-blind, placebo-controlled studies of drug treatments for elderly chronic schizophrenics and paraphrenics were located (Lehman, Ban, & Saxena, 1972; Raskind, Alvarez, & Herlin, 1979; Sugarman, Williams, & Adlerstein, 1964; Tobin, Brosseau, & Lorenz, 1970). All found significant improvement with antipsychotic drugs compared to placebo. Few studies, however, used a completely geriatric sample; most included patients 50–55 years of age and older.

Antipsychotic medications carry significant risks for side effects (Branchey, Lee, Amin, & Simpson, 1978), with the elderly particularly at risk for tardive dyskinesia (Johnson, Hunt, & Rey, 1982; Smith & Baldessarini, 1980). Toenniessen, Casey, and McFarland (1985) studied psychiatric inpatients over the age of 55 with observable abnormal involuntary movements. Over 50 percent of the patients studied exhibited these symptoms of tardive dyskinesia. Presence of the disorder was associated with duration of treatment with antipsychotic medication and tended to occur within the first 2 years of treatment. This study was limited by a small sample size and cross-sectional design. These weaknesses were offset by detailed, reliable ratings of involuntary movements, the availability of good drug histories, and appropriate multivariate statistical analyses.

Several efficacy studies of nonpharmacological treatments for elderly chronic geriatric inpatients were located. In a well-controlled study, Wolk and Goldfarb (1967) examined the effects of group psychotherapy on elderly chronic schizophrenic patients and recently admitted patients with organic brain syndrome. Patients were randomly assigned to treatment or no treatment conditions. Significant improvements in the areas of depression, interpersonal relations, and memory impairment were found after 1 year of treatment for group therapy patients when compared to control patients. Memory improved only in chronic schizophrenics. The introduction of token economy systems onto chronic geriatric wards proved successful for increasing social interaction among patients and with staff (Hoyer, Kafer, Simpson, & Hoyer, 1974; Mueller & Atlas, 1972), increasing participation in ward activities (Althowe & Krasner, 1970), and reducing self-injurious behavior. Remotivation therapy and conventional group therapy also proved effective for 39 geriatric inpatients (Birkett & Boltuch, 1973).

The issue of the therapeutic effectiveness of age-segregated compared to age-integrated programs for the institutionalized elderly was studied at two institutions (Kahana & Kahana, 1970). Newly admitted elderly patients were randomly assigned to standard geriatric wards or general adult mental hospital wards. Both organic and psychotic patients were studied. Treatment outcome supported age-integrated programs. No systematic studies of milieu therapies with elderly chronic schizophrenics were located.

All the studies reviewed used small samples and only Wolk and Goldfarb (1967) and Kahana and Kahana (1970) included a control group for comparison. Descriptions of the samples and ward settings were minimal, and the treatment administrator was often unspecified. No follow-up of patients was made. Thus, we do not know whether the positive gains presumably due to treatment were retained.

The nursing home has replaced the mental hospital as the primary site for treatment of older chronically mentally ill patients. An exceptionally well-designed study compared treatment outcomes of elderly chronic schizophrenics and organic brain syndrome patients who were treated in either VA nursing homes or VA psychiatric hospital wards (Linn et al., 1985). All patients met DSM-III criteria for either schizoprhenia or primary degenerative dementia. Assignment to treatment condition was random. Evaluation of outcome was comprehensive, using reliable rating measures of self-care ability, psychological symptoms, and behavioral problems. Drug use did not significantly differ between sites. Chronic schizophrenics treated in nursing homes, compared to patients treated on psychiatric hospital units, became significantly less able to perform self-care tasks within the first six months of treatment. No differences in self-care ability between sites was observed for patients with organic brain syndrome, but greater anxiety, depression, and dissatisfaction with care were found at the 1-year follow-up for patients treated in a nursing home when compared to patients treated in the psychiatric unit. Comparisons favored the psychiatric unit as a treatment site. Although no greater psychiatric morbidity was observed with nursing home care, findings suggested that chronic patients became more dependent on staff for basic self-care. It appears that the care provided in psychiatric facilities is essential for the maintenance of basic abilities that would allow the elderly chronic schizophrenic to be discharged into the community.

Therapeutically effective treatments are available for elderly patients with chronic schizophrenia, but each has some attendant risks. Antipsychotic medications can be used to control symptoms but only for a limited course of treatment. The elderly are at much greater risk than younger schizophrenics of developing the involuntary movements associated with long-term use of antipsychotic medication. No research has been done on the best pharmacologic regimen for elderly schizophrenic patients. There may be a preferred course of treatment, alternating drugs, withdrawal of medication, and group or behavioral psychotherapy that would allow long-term treatment without serious risk of medical complications. Nonpharmacologic treatments appear effective for symptom management within institutions. Whether they produce enough positive changes to allow discharge into the community, however, is unknown. Age-integrated inpatient programs also seem to be more effective than specialized age-segregated programs. More research is needed in this area across institutions before definitive conclusions can be drawn. Nursing homes do not provide an optimal therapeutic environment for chronic schizophrenia. Medications can be appropriately administered, but placement with more physically ill peers appears to produce a deterioration of basic self-care skills that could eventually preclude a return to community residence. Only early studies specifically examined patients with paranoid disorders. Research is needed to evaluate the various treatment strategies for patients with paranoid disorders.

Prevention Programs

One of the central questions underlying this review is whether there are specific problems typically occurring in late life that should be addressed by the mental health profession in order to prevent the development of significant mental illness or further declines among men and women who already experience emotional distress. Programs targeted to bereavement, life satisfaction, and complications of medication are reviewed.

Bereavement

Elderly widows and widowers are at much greater risk of morbidity and mortality than their married peers (Maddison & Viola, 1968; Parkes, 1972). This may be due to a combination of the emotional stress of the period preceding the death, the psychological impact of the loss, and the physical stress incurred by the caretaker whose spouse suffered a lengthy illness (Kalish, 1977). Many programs have been established specifically for widows, many based on the widow-to-widow program, begun in Boston. Women who are widows are trained to serve as outreach workers for those more recently widowed (Silverman, 1969). The program attempts to ameliorate the loneliness and isolation of widows while simultaneously providing an empathic peer who can provide support through the first phases of grief. An initial evaluation suggested that widows who participated in the program benefited from their participation (Silverman, 1969).

Lieberman and Videka-Sherman (1986) found significant reductions in psychological symptoms among widows who participated in self-help groups compared to widows who were invited but chose not to join the groups. The primary mechanism of change appeared to be the replacement of social contacts lost through widowhood. Although widows who decided not to join the groups were not an equivalent comparison group, the large sample size, use of reliable outcome measures, and lengthy follow-up period were major strengths of this study (see chapter 6 for further discussion of self-help groups).

Life Satisfaction

The elderly experience more losses in late life than younger adults (Berezin, 1980; Palmore, 1973). These losses can have a negative impact on life satisfaction (Larson, 1978). Loss of one's home in late life is a significant stressor. For many elderly people, the decision to relocate to a new home, a retirement community, or a skilled nursing facility is an involuntary one and can result in physical deterioration and death (Tobin & Lieberman, 1976). Szapocznik, Kurtines, Santisteban, and Perez-Vidal (1982) developed the Life Enhancement program for elderly men and women who were recent arrivals to a retirement home in an urban area. The program attempts to help those experiencing difficulties in adjusting to the retirement home to increase self-esteem by replacing lost activities and social commitments with new, rewarding activities. The program begins with a guided life review in which past skills and rewarding activities are identified. The counselor then suggests activities either in the home or in the neighborhood that are similar to old activities and could possibly provide the same emotional rewards. Counselors often make phone calls and arrange introductory meetings for their clients. Encourgement is provided and alternate arrangements made until the new activities are incorporated into the client's routine. The program also can be used in noninstitutional settings with private clients. No systematic evaluation of the program was made. Case vignettes demonstrating successful outcome, however, were presented.

Senior Actualization and Growth Explorations (SAGE) was developed in Berkeley for men and women over the age of 65 who were experiencing some of the stresses and strains of late life. It is a 9-month group program with the stated goal of "holistic health." Group activities include physical exercises and dance designed to encourage continued physical activity; meditation and yoga; discussions of negative attitudes about the elderly; and sharing of positive and negative aspects of late life. In a systematic evaluation of outcome, Lieberman and Bliwise (1979) found significantly improved self-esteem and reductions in psychological symptoms in the elderly who participated in the groups compared to men and women in a wait-list control group. Participants in the program were highly educated and successful men and women. Findings supporting positive outcome may not generalize to other geriatric populations.

Thompson et al. (1983) developed and evaluated an educational program of "life satisfaction classes" that teach elders how to cope with depression. Using behavioral charting techniques, elderly men and women were helped to recognize the strong association between depressed mood and involvement in unpleasant activities or nonactivity. By the end of the training sessions, most participants reported significantly better mood and increased involvement in pleasant activities. The program was equally effective under professional and nonprofessional leadership.

Medication Use

Most older men and women use more than one prescription drug, of which 25 percent are some form of psychotropic medication (Ostrom, Hammarlund, Christensen, Plein, & Kethley, 1985). Psychotropic medications are frequently implicated in the development of psychiatric symptoms, particularly depression (Salzman & Shader, 1978) and confusional states (Davison, 1978). All psychotropic medications carry potential risks for the elderly for serious side effects, especially with prolonged use. Drug interactions also produce serious physical and neurological problems (Davis, 1976; Sriwatanakul, 1983). In response to some of the problems associated with medication use in the elderly, Hammarlund, Ostrom, and Kethley (1985) developed an educational program for community-resident elderly. Registered pharmacists gave instruction in drug use and drug counseling to 183 elderly apartment residents. Approximately 1 year after completion of the program, a final assessment of the 39 residents who were initially found to have the greatest number of problems with drug use revealed a significant 11 percent decrease in the number of prescription medications taken and a significant 39 percent decrease in the number of medication behavior problems.

There is some evidence that age-specific prevention programs can help elderly men and women cope with some of the problems of late life. The evaluations of programs are not complete. Greater care needs to be given to the design of evaluation studies. Long-term follow-up is needed to demonstrate that the programs indeed prevent the development of emotional problems or further deterioration in the client already experiencing emotional distress.

General Considerations

In general, the literature on psychotherapeutic efficacy is flawed by poor research design. The research on psychopharmacology consistently employed the best methods. Even so, the majority of studies still had major shortcomings. Adequate studies are defined as those using specified inclusion and exclusion criteria to select samples; double-blind procedures where possible; random or specified assignment to treatment groups; specification of who is administering interventions as well as the nature of the intervention; use of reliable assessment measures; and application of statistical techniques in data analysis. Relatively few studies meet these criteria. Although the research has been synthesized in order to answer the three questions posed in the review, conclusions are preliminary at best.

Which interventions have proven to be most effective for treating the major psychiatric disorders of late life?

Therapeutically effective treatments exist for all the major psychiatric disorders typically found in older men and women. Psychotropic medications are particularly effective for depression, anxiety disorders, insomnia, and psychotic symptoms that either accompany Alzheimer's disease or are part of late-life schizophrenia or paranoid disorders. There are, however, major risks attendant to prescribing drug therapy for elderly psychiatric patients. Many have physical problems and are taking other prescription medications that can interact with psychotropic drugs. Dizziness, drowsiness, cardiac problems, memory impairment, and confusional states are typical side effects found in elderly patients treated with psychotropic medications. Elderly patients are also at high risk for tardive dyskinesia with prolonged use of antipsychotic medications.

Behavioral treatments consistently emerged from efficacy studies as effective approaches for treating late-life psychiatric disorders. Adequate single-case designs were typically used. Even so, this was not a particularly strong body of research. Diagnostic criteria were rarely specified. Simple baseline-training designs were employed instead of more sophisticated designs that include reversal or counterdemand conditions and repeated assessment of learned responses. Long-term follow-ups were rare, so the long-term prognosis with behavioral treatment is largely unknown.

Only one systematic study of psychiatric treatment in nursing homes was found—in spite of the large percentage of mentally ill elderly placed in nursing home care. This excellent study suggested that nursing homes are not the placement of choice even for patients with organic brain syndrome.

Success rates for the treatment of depression were consistent across most available treatments. Complete remission of symptoms was found for less than half the patients treated, and approximately 20 percent of the elderly patients remained continuously ill throughout treatment and follow-up periods. The characteristics of patients who succeeded and those who failed in treatment were never clearly specified. There is some indication, however, that patients who enter treatment with severe symptoms or an already chronic course of illness have the worst prognosis. The most methodologically sound efficacy studies were of individual and group psychotherapy for elderly patients treated for depression. Both individual and group psychotherapy were found to be effective. Cognitive and behavioral psychotherapies also appear to hold more promise than psychodynamic psychotherapies. However, only studies of brief psychotherapies were located. Brief psychodynamic psychotherapies are thought to be most effective with patients for whom a focal conflict can be quickly identified. Similar constraints for cognitive or behavioral therapies were not discussed. Because assignment to treatment conditions was random, there may have been more "unsuitable" cases in the brief psychodynamic psychotherapy conditions. Most elderly people treated for depression receive antidepressant medications from physicians in general medical practice. Treatment failures occurred in 20 to 30 percent of the cases; referral for more specialized care was rare. Given the strong links between depression and physical illness, it is surprising that no programs attempting to educate the elderly about the links between physical and emotional illness could be found.

No effective treatment for the cognitive dysfunctions of senile dementia has been found. Cholinomimetic compounds, however, hold some promise for further investigation. Effective treatments are available for the behavioral sequelae of dementia. Antipsychotic medications reduce behavioral problems attendant to cognitive deterioration. Behavioral treatments are also effective for successful management of behavioral problems. One excellent study demonstrated that caregivers can easily learn and apply behavioral techniques in their home management of the patient. Programs exist for caregivers who are at risk themselves for emotional problems. The efficacy of these programs, however, has not been established.

Various anxiolytic agents are widely used in the treatment of anxiety disorders in late life. Benzodiazepine compounds are among the most commonly prescribed drugs for geriatric medical and psychiatric patients. They have proven efficacy for the treatment of geriatric insomnia but carry high risks for side effects. Behavioral treatments for anxiety appear promising. Of particular note are systematic desensitization techniques for the treatment of chronic phobias. Anxiety can have numerous manifestations in late life. It is surprising that so few descriptive studies of anxiety disorders and treatments for these disorders were found.

The need for age-specific alcohol treatment programs is an unresolved issue. The most comprehensive study, however, suggests that there is no great need for age-segregated alcohol services. The elderly appear to be able to benefit from current age-integrated programs at a rate greater than or equal to younger alcoholics.

Effective pharmacologic and nonpharmacologic treatments are available for treating late-life psychotic disorders. The risk for tardive dyskinesia resulting from long-term use of antipsychotic medications is quite high in the elderly. Group psychotherapy and behavioral treatments applied in nursing home settings were effective for some chronic inpatients. No long-term follow-ups of patients were done to determine whether successful treatment in the inpatient setting improved chances for a successful community placement. In today's mental health system, chronic schizophrenics have been reinstitutionalized in nursing homes. Only one systematic study of VA nursing home care was found. It demonstrated that nursing homes do not provide optimal mental health care either to chronic schizophrenics or to patients with organic conditions.

Is there evidence that interventions need to be revised for maximum effectiveness with elderly patients?

There is a growing clinical literature on the modifications necessary for successful psychotherapeutic treatment of the elderly. Specific changes in therapeutic procedures have only been systematically investigated, however, in the empirical literature on geriatric psychopharmacology. Although the literature is not large, there is evidence that therapeutic benefit with less risk for medical complications occurs at lower doses in the elderly for most psychotropic drugs. Medical conditions (for example, cardiac conditions) for which psychotropic medication use is contraindicated have been identified. Missing from the literature are systematic studies of optimal treatment. For example, elderly schizophrenics may be maintained on antipsychotic drugs for longer periods of time if washout periods are regularly scheduled into the drug therapy. Even lower doses of psychotropic drugs than are currently recommended may be therapeutic if drug therapy is combined with psychotherapy. Only well-controlled comparative research focused on identifying optimal treatment plans will allow assessment of these possibilities.

Clinicians have recommended that therapy with the institutionalized elderly be quite brief, perhaps no longer than 15 minutes, that interventions bolster patient self-esteem, and that the therapist encourage the patient's dependence. Numerous case reports suggest the efficacy of this approach, but the recommended techniques have never been systematically evaluated.

Other modifications suggested in the literature are a more active role on the part of the therapist; a supportive focus for the therapy rather than insight orientation; active problem-solving in the therapy; limiting therapy to short-term work; and the use of systematic reminiscence in the therapy. The only controlled comparisons of age-specific modifications were the studies of age-integrated psychiatric wards compared to age-segregated wards. Findings favored age-integrated treatment. Additional support for age-integrated treatment programs was provided by the national data base of alcohol treatment programs. Older alcoholics did as well as younger alcoholics and somewhat better than middle-aged alcoholics in age-integrated treatment programs. More studies are needed on a wider variety of treatment programs before it can be concluded that age-integrated programs are more therapeutically effective for older patients.

No controlled studies compared suggested modifications for the elderly with more standard techniques. However, de facto evidence in the psychotherapy studies reviewed deserves mention. Treatment sessions were extended to 90 minutes in the psychotherapy studies of Gallagher and associates (Gallaher & Thompson, 1982; 1983). Sessions were extended because clinical impressions suggested that the elderly needed more time to get started in the therapy. There may be a greater need for closure, or older patients may have more trouble organizing thoughts and feelings. Controlled comparative research including examinations of the process of psychotherapy would be needed to evaluate such modifications. Systematic desensitization techniques were modified in the treatment of an elderly woman with chronic agoraphobia and accompanying depression. A simplified and extended relaxation training period was used. Time was added for discussion as a reinforcement for cooperation. Multiple treatment modes were used to meet multiple needs. Combined treatments may be needed in late life because disorders have had a prolonged course or because the elderly are likely to experience multiple losses that can lead to multiple problems.

Clearly, there is a large gap in the literature on age-specific treatments. Comparative research is needed, but is not possible until treatments are specified and good techniques for measuring what happens in psychotherapy are developed.

> *Are there specific problems typical of late life that should be addressed by the mental health profession in order to prevent either the development of significant mental health problems or further declines among men and women already experiencing emotional distress?*

The research reviewed showed that a variety of experimental programs helped the elderly alleviate distress associated with typical losses of late life. None of the elderly men and women studied had diagnosable psychiatric disorders, but all were experiencing distress. Bereavement, life satisfaction, and medication behavior problems were areas targeted by these programs. Treatment was education-oriented. Evaluations suggested that the programs were of some benefit to the elderly. Follow-up research is needed in all areas, however, to determine whether programs prevented the development of significant emotional disorders at a later date. The community-based medication education program was the only treatment program found that specifically addressed the relationship between physical and mental illness in late life. This area certainly holds promise for further research.

Specific Research Recommendations

Research is needed in a number of areas, but at least four research programs are suggested by gaps in the literature on treatment effectiveness for the mental disorders of late life.

Chronic Disorders

Many of the elderly who seek treatment for psychiatric problems in late life are suffering from chronic disorders. Little is known about the long-term course of mental health problems or about outcomes for chronic patients versus patients with late-onset disorders. There is some indication in the literature that elderly patients with chronic disorders have a poorer prognosis than those with late-onset illness and may be repeated "treatment failures." Follow-up studies provide a needed start, but the short follow-up periods used in most investigations may not give an accurate picture of the true course of the illness for the chronic patient. Good descriptive studies presenting the economic, social, and physical circumstances as well as the nature and course of the psychiatric illness are needed. Also of interest are the patients who have been treated successfully for psychiatric disorders earlier in life and again experience difficulties in late life. The many losses of late life may have a greater impact on those already vulnerable from earlier illness.

The need for specific treatment programs for chronic patients should also be systematically addressed. The chronic patient who has already had a number of prior treatment experiences may require specialized multimodal treatment programs. The case reports on treatments for elderly patients suffering from life-long agoraphobia—a particularly treatment-resistant disorder at all ages— suggest that simplifying programs and including systematic reinforcement for small gains are good places to start.

Age-Specific Treatments

Research on age-specific treatment strategies is quite limited. The few studies addressing the question of age-integrated versus age-segregated treatment programs suggest that age-integrated programs are more effective. Findings need to be replicated across a variety of treatment settings and strategies before definitive conclusions can be drawn. Outpatient group psychotherapy may be most effective when limited to older patients; an age mixture in therapy may be most efficacious for inpatient psychotherapy groups.

Time spent in therapy may need to vary from the standard 50 minutes. Inpatient therapy may need to be brief. Outpatient psychotherapy hours may need to be extended to allow the older patient more time to organize thoughts and feelings or to obtain a sense of closure at the end of the hour. Other issues related to time also need to be addressed. Comparative research is needed to determine whether specific modifications can most effectively address the life review in therapy. Short-term approaches have been recommended for the elderly, but no systematic research has addressed whether brief therapies are most effective for treating late-life disorders. Given the often chronic nature of late-life disorders, short-term strategies may not be the optimal approach.

The elderly may need more intensive, multimodal treatment programs. The success of the elderly treated in multifaceted alcohol abuse programs may serve as a model for treatment programs targeted for other disorders of late life. For example, discussion of the origins of social phobias in a self-help group may help elderly patients feel less embarrassed and alone. Relaxation training directed toward management of anxiety and behavioral techniques that use successive approximation of the social situation causing the most anxiety together can help the patient overcome debilitating anxiety associated with social phobias.

Continued participation in the self-help group could allow successfully treated patients to share their success with others, thereby reinforcing the positive outcome of treatment.

Finally, there is some indication that a more active stance on the part of the therapist is needed. In both behavioral and cognitive psychotherapy, the practitioner actively helps the patient to organize feelings and experiences. Preliminary research indicates that these approaches may be more successful, especially in treating late-life depression, than traditional psychodynamic psychotherapy. However, research that examines process in therapy and considers long-term outcome is needed.

Links between Physical and Mental Disorders

As noted in chapter 2, more knowledge of the role of physical illness in the etiology and course of mental illness is needed. Studies of treatment efficacy often excluded elderly men and women who are physically ill. Mental health professionals need to focus their efforts on developing treatment strategies that can effectively serve the physically ill elderly who also have mental health problems.

Of particular concern are the elderly in nursing homes, which are fast becoming the institutional setting for the treatment of chronic schizophrenia and senile dementias. It is unclear how many nursing home placements for these disorders are made because those placed also suffer from serious medical problems. It is known that most nursing homes do not provide adequate mental health services for their patients (see chapters 4 and 5). More research is needed, however, to determine how physical and emotional problems can best be treated in the nursing home setting.

Behavioral Therapy

Behavioral therapy appears to have promise for the treatment of a wide range of late-life psychiatric disorders. Of particular note is the successful use of behavioral techniques by family caregivers of demented patients. Many caregivers are elderly themselves. This area should be targeted for further research. Training programs for family caregivers allow mental health professionals to assist the family in a way that may prevent or substantially delay institutionalization. The therapeutic potential of behavioral intervention across a wide range of disorders makes it an important area for further research.

Selected Topics

Particular areas needing further research emerged from the review of treatment strategies for particular disorders. Though the use of psychotropic medications is widespread, there is not a large body of research on geriatric populations. Sample sizes tend to be quite small, and the research instruments used to measure outcome are often not the best available. Continued research on psychotropic medications, especially research focused on optimal dosage and most appropriate length of treatment, needs to be encouraged.

Research on Alzheimer's disease and other dementias is in its earliest phase. No effective treatment has been found for the mental impairment of senile dementia, but cholinomimetic compounds hold some promise. Research has not demonstrated that the educational and treatment programs targeted to family caregivers help alleviate their sense of burden. The role of respite programs and other day-care services in preventing or delaying institutionalization or helping to minimize the behavioral problems of dementia is unknown. The extent of stress experienced by paid caregivers and nursing home personnel caring for demented patients is also unknown; research in this area could eventually lead to the development of appropriate educational and support programs.

Research on chronic schizophrenia and paranoid disorders and their treatment in late life is quite sparse. Research is needed to identify effective treatment strategies and settings that will allow elderly chronic schizophrenics to live the remainder of their lives in the community.

Policy Recommendations

Much research remains to be done before definitive recommendations can be made about effective treatments for the most common psychiatric disorders of late life. The literature suggests areas needing program development, some that can be implemented immediately with current treatment methods and others that require long-term research and development.

Comprehensive Programs for Elderly with Senile Dementia

As the percentage of the population over the age of 65 increases, there will be a growing need for comprehensive services targeted to patients with senile dementia and their families. The mental health profession can respond to this growing need with comprehensive treatment programs. The CMHC can act as a coordinating agency to help families obtain an accurate diagnosis; educate all those involved about the disease; provide respite care for families; train family members in behavioral management techniques; and assist families with information and counseling when nursing home placement becomes necessary. The CMHC can also extend educational services and training in behavioral management techniques to nurses, nurse assistants, and others who provide direct care to the elderly patient with senile dementia.

Drug Trials in Geriatric Populations

Psychotropic medications are widely used by the elderly, but few medications have been adequately tested on geriatric populations. For example, only two of the antidepressants in current use (doxepin and imipramine) have been tested with randomized, double-blind, placebo-controlled clinical trials in elderly depressed patients. Because the elderly are at greater risk for adverse side effects for most drugs and require lower doses and possibly shorter drug trials than younger people, there is a need for adequate testing of new drugs before they are used widely on geriatric patients. A special ombudsperson or watchdog agency could monitor new drugs approved by the FDA, examine trends in drug prescription, or lobby pharmaceutical companies to ensure adequate tests before the release of drugs to the general market.

Geriatric Psychiatric Practitioners for General Practice

Geriatric psychiatric practitioners might work out of CMHCs and provide services to general practitioners and medical clinics in the catchment area. A geriatric psychiatric practitioner may be a master's nurse or psychologist who would provide assistance with diagnosis of mental health problems, assist with referrals to mental health agencies, and provide support and assistance to family caregivers. At present, most elderly people are reluctant to seek help from mental health professionals and are treated in general medical practice. Given the strong association between medical and psychiatric disorders in late life, a mental health practitioner who is integrated into medical practice may provide the best outreach possible.

Specialized Programs for the Chronically Mentally Ill

The problems of the chronically mentally ill are largely unrecognized, but there are some indications that the prognosis for treatment of chronic disorders in late life is poor. A long-term commitment would be needed to develop specialized services for the chronically mentally ill elderly. The goal would be to maintain or work toward adequate functioning in the community. Outreach to nursing homes and board-and-care facilities may be needed. Multiple treatment modalities ranging from remotivation therapy to behavior modification, adult day care, partial hospitalization, and psychotherapy would need to be developed. Programs should be targeted to specific needs of the chronically mentally ill. Coordination between clinicians and researchers would be needed to develop optimal treatment strategies.

Psychiatric Care in Nursing Homes

Comprehensive psychiatric programs are also needed in the nursing home. Programs should have community placement as a goal whenever possible, but poor physical health may preclude discharge to the community for many nursing home patients. Programs aimed at remotivation therapy, reality orientation, and behavior modification all hold promise for successful implementation in nursing homes. Family support groups in the nursing home may also help the patient and family to adjust to the placement and prevent the debilitating guilt that often keeps family members away. Development of special funding would be needed, however, to allow reimbursement for mental health services.

Prevention Programs

There is some evidence that age-specific prevention programs can help the elderly cope with some of the problems of late life. Programs targeted to specific late-life problems may help prevent the development of psychiatric disorder or further deterioration in patients already experiencing mental illness. Self-help groups for the bereaved and life-satisfaction classes are particularly promising. Prevention programs may also be the most appropriate for educating the elderly about the links between physical illness and emotional distress.

References

Althowe, J.M., & Krasner, L. (1970). Preliminary report on the application of contingent reinforcement procedures (token economy) on a "chronic" psychiatric ward. In R. Ulrich, T. Stachnik, & J. Mabry (Eds.), *Control of human behavior: Vol. 2. From cure to prevention* (pp. 214–229). Glenview, IL: Scott, Foresman.

Ayd, F.J. (1962). Nialamide therapy for the depressed geriatric patient. *Journal of the American Geriatrics Society, 10,* 432–435.

Bagne, C.A., Pomara, N., Crook, R., & Gershon, S. (1986). Alzheimer's disease: Strategies for treatment and research. In T. Crook, R.T. Bartus, S. Ferris, & S. Gershon (Eds.), *Treatment development strategies for Alzheimer's disease* (pp. 585–638). Madison, CT: Mark Powley.

Ballinger, C.B. (1976). Subjective sleep disturbance at the menopause. *Journal of Psychosomatic Research, 20,* 509–513.

Ban, T.A. (1969). *Psychopharmacology.* Baltimore, MD: Williams & Wilkins.

Ban, T.A. (1978). The treatment of depressed geriatric patients. *American Journal of Psychotherapy, 31,* 93–104.

Bannen, D.M., & Resnick, O. (1973). Lorazepam versus glutethimide as a sleep-inducing agent for the geriatric patient. *Journal of the American Geriatrics Society, 21,* 507–511.

Barnes, R.F., Raskind, M.A., Scott, M., & Murphy, C. (1981). Problems of families caring for Alzheimer patients: Use of a support group. *Journal of the American Geriatrics Society, 19,* 80–85.

Barnes, R.F. Veith, R., Okimoto, J., Raskind, M., & Bumbrecht, G. (1982). Efficacy of antipsychotic medications in behaviorally disturbed dementia patients. *American Journal of Psychiatry, 139,* 1170–1174.

Bazo, A.J. (1973). An ergot alkaloid preparation (Hydergine) versus papaverine in treating common complaints of the aged: Double-blind study. *Journal of the American Geriatrics Society, 21,* 63–71.

Berber, C.R. (1971). Treating anxiety and depression in the elderly: A double-blind crossover evaluation of two widely used tranquilizers. *Journal of the Florida Medical Association, 58,* 35–38.

Berezin, M.A. (1980). Intrapsychic isolation in the elderly. *Geriatric Psychiatry, 1,* 5–18.

Bergin, A., & Garfield, S. (Eds.). (1971). *Handbook of psychotherapy and behavior change.* New York: John Wiley & Sons.

Bergmann, K. (1977). Prognosis in chronic brain failure. *Age and Ageing, 6*(Suppl.), 61–66.

Bieleski, R.J., & Friedel, R.O. (1976). Prediction of tricyclic antidepressant response: A critical review. *Archives of General Psychiatry, 26,* 57–63.

Birkett, D.R., & Boltuch, B. (1973). Remotivation therapy. *Journal of the American Geriatrics Society, 21,* 368–371.

Black, D.W., Warrack, G., & Winokur, G. (1985a). The Iowa record-linkage study: Pt. 1. Suicides and accidental deaths among psychiatric patients. *Archives of General Psychiatry, 42,* 71–75.

Black, D.W., Warrack, G., & Winokur, G. (1985b). The Iowa record-linkage study: Pt. 3. Excess mortality among patients with functional disorders. *Archives of General Psychiatry, 42,* 82–88.

Blaney, R., Radford, I.S., & MacKenzie, G. (1975). A Belfast study of outcome in the treatment of alcoholism. *British Journal of Addiction, 70,* 41–50.

Blazer, D. (1983). The epidemiology of psychiatric disorder in the elderly population. In L. Grinspoon (Ed.), *Psychiatry update: The American psychiatric association annual review: Vol. 2* (pp. 247–261). Washington, DC: American Psychiatric Press.

Blessed, G., & Wilson, I.D. (1982). The contemporary natural history of mental disorder in old age. *British Journal of Psychiatry, 141,* 59–67.

Bliwise, N.G., Bliwise, D.L., & Dement, W.C. (1985). Age and psychopathology in insomnia. *Clinical Gerontologist, 4,* 3–9.

Bollerup, T.R. (1975). Prevalence of mental illness among 70-year-olds domiciled in nine Copenhagen suburbs. *Acta Psychiatrica Scandinavica, 51,* 327–339.

Bowen, R.C. & Kohout, J. (1979). The relationship between agoraphobia and primary affective disorders. *Canadian Journal of Psychiatry, 24,* 317–322.

Branchey, M.H., Lee, J.H., Amin, R., & Simpson, G.M. (1978). High- and low-potency neuroleptics in elderly psychiatric patients. *Journal of the American Medical Association, 239,* 1860–1862.

Branconnier, R.J., & Cole, J.O. (1977). Effects of chronic papaverine administration on mild senile organic brain syndrome. *Journal of the American Geriatrics Society, 25,* 458–462.

Branconnier, R.J., Cole, J.O., & Gardos, G. (1978). ACTH in the amelioration of neuropsychological symptomatology associated with senile organic brain syndrome. *Psychopharmacology Bulletin, 14,* 27–30.

Brodie, N.H., McGhie, R.L., O'Hara, H., Valle-Jones, G.C., & Schiff, A.A. (1975). Anxiety depression in elderly patients. *Practitioner, 215,* 660–664.

Brody, E.M., Kleban, M.H., Lawton, M.P., & Silverman, H.A. (1971). Excess disabilities of mentally impaired aged: Impact of individualized treatment. *Gerontologist, 11,* 124–132.

Brook, G.W., & McDonald, M. (1961). Effects of trifluoperazine in aged depressed female patients. *American Journal of Psychiatry, 118,* 932–933.

Bushley, M., Rathey, V., & Bowers, M.B. (1983). Lithium treatment in a very elderly nursing home population. *Comprehensive Psychiatry, 24,* 392–396.

Cassel, C.K., & Jameton, A.L. (1981). Dementia in the elderly: An analysis of medical responsibility. *Annals of Internal Medicine, 94,* 802–807.

Cohen, G.D. (1976). Mental health services and the elderly: Needs and options. *American Journal of Psychiatry, 133,* 65–68.

Cohen, S., & Dittman, K.S. (1974). Gerovital H-3 in the treatment of depressed aging patients. *Psychosomatics, 15,* 15–19.

Cole, M.G. (1983). Age, age of onset and course of primary depressive illness in the elderly. *Canadian Journal of Psychiatry, 28,* 102–104.

Cole, M.G. (1985). The course of elderly depressed out-patients. *Canadian Journal of Psychiatry, 30,* 217–220.

Cromwell, H.A. (1973). Management of anxiety/depression in geriatric patients. *Medical Times, 101,* 47–53.

Cummings, J., Benson, D.F., & LoVerma, S., Jr. (1980). Reversible dementia: Illustrative cases, definition and review. *Journal of the American Medical Association, 243,* 2434–2439.

Davis, J.M. (1976). Recent developments in the treatment of schizophrenia. *Psychiatric Annals, 6,* 71–103.

Davison, W. (1978). Neurological and mental disturbances due to drugs. *Age and Ageing, 7*(Suppl.), 119–126.

Dealy, R.S., Ishila, D.M., Avery, D.H., Wilson, L.G., & Dunner, D.L. (1981). Secondary depression in anxiety disorders. *Comprehensive Psychiatry, 22,* 612–618.

DeBerry, S. (1982). The effects of meditation—relaxation on anxiety and depression in a geriatric population. *Psychotherapy: Theory, Research and Practice, 19,* 512–521.

Dehlin, O., & Bjornson, G. (1983). Triazolam as a hypnotic for geriatric patients. *Acta Psychiatrica Scandinavica, 67,* 290–296.

Drachman, D.A., & Leavitt, J. (1974). Human memory and the cholinergic system: A relationship to aging. *Archives of Neurology, 30,* 113–121.

Duckworth, G.S., Kedward, H.B., & Bailey, W.F. (1979). Prognosis of mental illness in old age: A four-year follow-up study. *Canadian Journal of Psychiatry, 24,* 674–682.

Eisdorfer, C., & Cohen, D. (1980). Diagnostic criteria for primary neuronal degeneration of the Alzheimer's type. *The Journal of Family Practice, 11,* 553–557.

Eisdorfer, C., & Stotsky, B.A. (1977). Intervention, treatment, and rehabilitation of psychiatric disorders. In J.E. Birren & K.W. Schaie (Eds.), *Handbook of the psychology of aging* (pp. 724–750). New York: Van Nostrand.

Evans, J.G., & Jarvis, E.H. (1972). Nitrazepam and the elderly. *British Medical Journal, 4,* 487–491.

Feighner, J.P., & Cohn, J.B. (1985). Double-blind comparative trials of fluoxetine and doxepin in geriatric patients with major depressive disorder. *Journal of Clinical Psychiatry, 46,* 20–25.

Feighner, J.P., Robins, E., Guze, S.B., Woodruff, R.A., & Winokur, G. (1972). Diagnostic criteria for use in psychiatric research. *Archives of General Psychiatry, 26,* 57–63.

Fengler, A. & Goodrich, N. (1979). Wives of elderly disabled men: The hidden patients. *Gerontologist, 19,* 175–185.

Fillingham, J.M. (1982). Double-blind evaluation of temazepam, flurazepam, and placebo in geriatric insomniacs. *Clinical Therapeutics, 4,* 369–380.

Fisman, M., Merskey, H., Helmes, E., McCready, J., Colhoun, E.H., & Rylett, B.J. (1981). Double-blind study of lecithin in patients with Alzheimer's disease. *Canadian Journal of Psychiatry, 26,* 426–428.

Fleischhauer, J. (1980). Effects of mianserin in depression in elderly patients. *Current Medical Research and Opinion,* 6(Suppl.), 139–143.

Forde, C.V., & Sbordone, R.J. (1980). Attitudes of psychiatrists toward elderly patients. *American Journal of Psychiatry, 137,* 571–575.

Foster, J.R., Gershell, W.J., & Goldfarb, A.I. (1977). Lithium treatment in the elderly. *Journal of Gerontology, 32,* 299–302.

Foster, W.O. (1980). *Alcohol-related problems of the elderly: The federal response.* Paper presented at the annual convention of the National Council on Alcoholism, Seattle, WA.

Fox, J.H., Toper, J.L., & Huckman, M.S. (1975). Dementia in the elderly—a search for treatable illness. *Journal of Gerontology, 34,* 557–564.

Freeman, G.K. (1979). Drug-prescribing patterns in the elderly: A general practice study. In D.M. Peterson, B.P. Payne, & F.J. Whittington (Eds.), *Drugs and the elderly: Social and pharmacological issues* (pp. 223–229). Springfield, IL: C.C. Thomas.

Freemon, F.R. (1976). Evaluation of patients with progressive intellectual deterioration. *Archives of Neurology, 37,* 658–659.

Freemon, F.R., & Rudd, S.M. (1982). Clinical features that predict potentially reversible progressive intellectual deterioration. *Journal of the American Geriatrics Society, 30,* 449–451.

Friedel, R.O., & Raskind, M.A. (1975). Relationship of blood levels of Sinequan to clinical effects in the treatment of depression in aged patients. In J. Mendels (Ed.), *Sinequan (Doxepin HC1): A monograph of recent clinical studies* (pp. 51–54). Princeton, NJ: Excerpta Medica.

Fry, P.S. (1984). Cognitive training and cognitive-behavioral variables in the treatment of depression in the elderly. *Clinical Gerontologist, 3,* 25–45.

Fuller, J., Ward, E., Evans, A., Massam, K., & Gardner, A. (1979). Dementia: Supportive groups for relatives. *British Medical Journal, 1,* 1684–1685.

Funkenstein, H.H., Hicks, R., Dysken, M.W., & Davis, J.M. (1981). Drug treatment of cognitive impairment in Alzheimer's disease and the late life dementias. In N.E. Miller & G.D. Cohen (Eds.), *Clinical aspects of Alzheimer's disease and senile dementia* (pp. 139–160). New York: Raven.

Gaitz, C.M. (1985). The diagnosis and treatment of mental illness in late life. *Community Mental Health Journal, 21,* 119–130.

Gallagher, D.E. (1981). Behavioral group therapy with elderly depressives: An experimental study. In D. Upper & S. Ross (Eds.), *Behavioral group therapy* (pp. 110–118). Champaign, IL: Research Press.

Gallagher, D.E., & Thompson, L.W. (1982). Treatment of major depressive disorder in older adult outpatients with brief psychotherapies. *Psychotherapy: Theory, Research and Practice, 19,* 482–490.

Gallagher, D.E., & Thompson, L.W. (1983). Effectiveness of psychotherapy for both endogenous and nonendogenous depression in older adult patients. *Journal of Gerontology, 38,* 707–712.

Garfinkel, R. (1979). Brief behavior therapy with an elderly patient: A case study. *Journal of Geriatric Psychiatry, 12,* 101–109.

Gerner, R., Estabrook, W., Stever, J., & Jarvik, L. (1980). Treatment of geriatric depression with trazodone, imipramine, and placebo: A double-blind study. *Journal of Clinical Psychiatry, 41,* 216–220.

Gilbert, J.G., Donnelly, K.J., Zimmer, L.E., & Kubis, J.F. (1973). Effect of magnesium pemoline and methylphenidate on memory improvement and mood in normal aging subjects. *International Journal of Aging and Human Development, 4,* 35–51.

Goodstein, R.K. (1982). Individual psychotherapy and the elderly. *Psychotherapy: Theory, Research and Practice, 19,* 412–418.

Gordon, W.F. (1981). Elderly depressives: Treatment and follow-up. *Canadian Journal of Psychiatry, 26,* 110–113.

Grauer, H., & Kral, V.A. (1960). Use of imipramine (Tofranil) in psychiatric patients of a geriatric outpatient clinic. *Canadian Medical Association Journal, 83,* 1423–1426.

Grotjahn, M. (1978). Group communication and group therapy with the aged: A promising project. In L.F. Jarvik (Ed.), *Aging into the twenty-first century* (pp. 113–121). New York: Gardner Press.

Gurland, B.J. (1980). The assessment of the mental health status of older adults. In J.E. Birren & R.B. Sloane (Eds.), *Handbook of mental health and aging* (pp. 671–700). Englewood Cliffs, NJ: Prentice-Hall.

Hammarlund, E.R., Ostrom, J.R., & Kethley, A.J. (1985). The effects of drug counseling and other educational strategies on drug utilization of the elderly. *Medical Care, 23,* 165–170.

Hartford, J.T., & Samorajski, P. (1984). *Alcoholism in the elderly.* New York: Raven.

Helms, P.M. (1985). Efficacy of antipsychotics in the treatment of the behavioral complications of dementia: A review of the literature. *Journal of the American Geriatrics Society, 33,* 206–209.

Hewick, D.S., Newbury, P., Hopwood, S., Naylor, G., & Moody, J. (1977). Age as a factor affecting lithium therapy. *British Journal of Clinical Pharmacology, 4,* 201–205.

Hinrichsen, J.J., Dunham, R.G., & Janik, S.W. (1981). *Factors affecting utilization and effectiveness of alcoholism treatment services for elderly alcoholics* (Final report to the Administration on Aging). Washington, DC: Government Printing Office.

Hollister, L.E., & Yesavage, J. (1984). Ergoloid mesylates for senile dementias: Unanswered questions. *Annals of Internal Medicine, 100,* 894–898.

Houston, F. (1983). Two-year follow-up study of an outreach program in geriatric psychiatry. *Canadian Journal of Psychiatry, 28,* 367–369.

Hoyer, W.J., Kafer, R.A., Simpson, S.C., & Hoyer, F.W. (1974). Reinstatement of verbal behavior in elderly patients using operant procedures. *Gerontologist, 14,* 149–152.

Hutton, J.T. (1981). Results of clinical assessment for dementia: Implications for epidemiologic studies. In J.A. Mortimer & L.M. Schulman (Eds.), *The epidemiology of dementia* (pp. 62–69). New York: Oxford University Press.

Ingebretsen, R. (1977). Psychotherapy with the elderly. *Psychotherapy: Theory, Research and Practice, 14,* 319–332.

Isaacs, B. (1979). The evaluation of drugs in Alzheimer's disease. *Age and Ageing, 8,* 1–7.

Janik, S.W., & Dunham, R.G. (1983). A nationwide examination of the need for specific alcoholism treatment programs for the elderly. *Journal of Studies on Alcohol, 44,* 307–317.

Jarvik, L.F., & Kumar, V. (1984). Diagnosis: A complex problem. *Generations, 9,* 7–9.

Jarvik, L.F., & Milne, J.F. (1975). Gerovital H-3: A review of the literature. In S. Gershon & A. Raskin (Eds.), *Aging* (pp. 203–227). New York: Raven.

Johnson, G.F.S., Hunt, G.E., & Rey, J.M. (1982). Incidence and severity of tardive dyskinesia increases with age. *Archives of General Psychiatry, 39,* 486–491.

Kahan, J., Kemp, B., Staples, F.R., & Brummel-Smith, K. (1985). Decreasing the burden in families caring for a relative with a dementing illness: A controlled study. *Journal of the American Geriatrics Society, 33,* 664–670.

Kahana, E., & Kahana, B. (1970). Therapeutic potential of age-integration: Effects of age-integrated hospital environments of elderly psychiatric patients. *Archives of General Psychiatry, 23,* 20–29.

Kahana, R.J. (1979). Strategies of dynamic psychotherapy with a wide range of older individuals. *Journal of Geriatric Psychiatry, 12,* 71–100.

Kales, A. (1983). Biopsychobehavioral correlates of insomnia: Pt. 2. Pattern specificity and consistency with the MMPI. *Psychosomatic Medicine, 45,* 351–356.

Kales, A., & Kales, J.D. (1984). *Evaluation and treatment of insomnia.* New York: Oxford University Press.

Kales, A., & Tan, T.L. (1969). Sleep alterations associated with medical illnesses. In A. Kales (Ed.), *Sleep physiology and pathology: A symposium* (pp. 148–157). Philadelphia, PA: Lippincott.

Kalish, R.A. (1977). Death and dying in a social context. In R.H. Binstock & E. Shanas (Eds.), *Handbook of aging and the social sciences* (pp. 483–507). New York: Van Nostrand.

Karacan, I., Thornby, J.I., Anch, M., Holzer, C.E., Warheit, G.J., Schwab, J.J., & Williams, R.L. (1976). Prevalence of sleep disturbance in a primarily urban Florida county. *Social Science & Medicine, 10,* 239–244.

Katzman, R. (1982). The complex problem of diagnosis. *Generations, 7,* 8–10.

Kaye, W.H., Sitaram, N., Weingartner, H., Ebert, M.H., Smallberg, S., & Gillin, J.C. (1982). Modest facilitation of memory in dementia with combined lecithin and anticholinesterase treatment. *Biological Psychiatry, 17,* 275–280.

Kendell, R. (1974). The stability of psychiatric diagnosis. *British Journal of Psychiatry, 124,* 352–356.

Kovacs, M. (1980). Cognitive therapy in depression. *Journal of the American Academy of Psychoanalysis, 8,* 127–144.

Kristof, F.E. Lehmann, H.E., & Ban, T.A. (1967). Systematic studies with imipramine, a new antidepressive drug. *Canadian Psychiatric Association Journal, 12,* 517–520.

Kupfer, D.J., & Crook, T.C. (1984). *Physicians' guide to the recognition and treatment of sleep disorders in the elderly.* New Canaan, CT: Mark Powley.

Kurland, M.L., & Hayman, M. (1976). A procaine derivative for the treatment of depression in an outpatient population. *Psychosomatics, 17,* 96–102.

Lader, M.H., & Petursson, H. (1983). Long-term effects of benzodiazepines. *Neuropharmacology, 22,* 527–533.

Lakshmanan, M., Mion, L.C., & Frengley, J.D. (1986). Effective low dose tricyclic antidepressant treatment for depressed geriatric rehabilitation patients: A double-blind study. *Journal of the American Geriatrics Society, 34,* 421–426.

Larson, E.B., Reifler, B.V., Featherstone, H.J., & English, D.R. (1984). Dementia in elderly outpatients: A prospective study. *Annals of Internal Medicine, 100,* 417–423.

Larson, R. (1978). Thirty years of research on the subjective well-being of older Americans. *Journal of Gerontology, 33,* 109–129.

LaVorgna, D. (1979). Group treatment for wives of patients with Alzheimer's disease. *Social Work in Health Care, 5,* 219–223.

Lazarus, L.W., Stafford, B., Cooper, K., Cohler, B., & Dysken, M. (1981). A pilot study of an Alzheimer patients' relatives discussion group. *Gerontologist, 21,* 353–357.

Lehman, H.E., & Ban, T.A. (1975). Central nervous system stimulants and anabolic substances in geropsychiatric therapy. In S. Gershon & A. Raskin (Eds.), *Aging* (pp. 179–202). New York: Raven.

Lehman, H.E., Ban, T.A. & Saxena, B.M. (1972). Nicotinic acid, thioridazine, fluoxymesterone and their combinations in hospitalized geriatric patients: A systematic clinical study. *Canadian Psychiatric Association Journal, 17,* 315–319.

Libb, J.W., & Clements, C.B. (1969). Token reinforcement in an exercise program for hospitalized geriatric patients. *Perceptual and Motor Skills, 28,* 957–958.

Lieberman, M.A., & Bliwise, N. (Gourash). (1979). Evaluating the effects of change groups on the elderly: The impact of SAGE. *International Journal of Group Psychotherapy, 29,* 283–304.

Lieberman, M.A., & Videka-Sherman, L. (1986). The impact of self-help groups on the mental health of widows and widowers. *American Journal of Orthopsychiatry, 56,* 435–449.

Linn, M.W., Gurel, L., Williford, W.O., Overall, J., Gurland, B., Laughlin, P., & Barchiesi, A. (1985). Nursing home care as an alternative to psychiatric hospitalization: A Veterans Administration cooperative study. *Archives of General Psychiatry, 42,* 544–551.

Loew, D.M., & Weil, C. (1982). Hydergine in senile mental impairment. *Gerontology, 28,* 54–74.

Lowenthal, M.F., Berkman, P.L., Brissette, G.C., Buehler, J.A., Pierce, R.C., Robinson, B.C., & Trier, M.L. (1967). *Aging and mental disorder in San Francisco.* San Francisco, CA: Jossey-Bass.

Lu, L., Stotsky, B.A., & Cole, J.O. (1971). A controlled study of drugs in long-term geriatric psychiatric patients. *Archives of General Psychiatry, 25,* 284–288.

Mace, N. (1984). Day care for demented clients. *Hospital and Community Psychiatry, 35,* 979–994.

Maddison, D., & Viola, A. (1968). The health of widows in the year following bereavement. *Journal of Psychosomatic Research, 12,* 297–306.

Mann, A.H., Jenkins, R., & Belsey, E. (1981). The twelve-month outcome of patients with neurotic illness in general practice. *Psychological Medicine, 11,* 535–550.

Marsden, C.D., & Harrison, M.J.G. (1972). Outcome of investigations in patients with presenile dementia. *British Medical Journal, 2,* 249–252.

Martilla, J.K., Hammel, R.J., & Alexander, B. (1977). Potential untoward effects of long-term use of flurazepam in geriatric patients. *Journal of the American Pharmacology Association, 11,* 692–695.

Martin, J.C., & Streissguth, A.P. (1982). Alcoholism and the elderly: An overview. In C. Eisdorfer & W.E. Fann (Eds.), *Treatment of psychopathology in the aging* (pp. 243–280). New York: Springer.

Martin, R.L., Cloninger, R., Guze, S.B., & Clayton, P.J. (1985). Mortality in a follow-up of 500 psychiatric outpatients: Pt. 2. Cause-specific mortality. *Archives of General Psychiatry, 42,* 58–66.

Martinez, H.T., & Serna, C.T. (1982). Short-term treatment with quazepam of insomnia in geriatric patients. *Clinical Therapeutics, 5,* 174–178.

McKhann, G., Drachman, D., Folstein, M., Katzman, R., Price, D., & Stadlan, E.M. (1984). Clinical diagnosis of Alzheimer's disease. *Neurology, 34,* 939–944.

McPherson, F.M., Brougham, L., & McLaren, S. (1980). Maintenance of improvement in agoraphobic patients treated by behavioral methods. *Behavioral Research and Therapy, 18,* 150–152.

McQuillan, I.M., Lopec, C.A., & Vibal, J.R. (1974). Evaluation of EEG and clinical changes associated with Pavabid therapy in chronic brain syndrome. *Current Therapy Research, 16,* 49–58.

Mellinger, G.D., Balter, M.B., & Uhlenhuth, E.H. (1984). Prevalence and correlates of the long-term regular use of anxiolytics. *Journal of the American Medical Association, 251,* 375–379.

Mintz, J., Steuer, J., & Jarvik, L.F. (1981). Psychotherapy with depressed elderly patients: Research considerations. *Journal of Consulting and Clinical Psychology, 49,* 542–548.

Mishara, B.L. & Kastenbaum, R. (1980). *Alcohol and old age.* New York: Grune and Stratton.

Moizeszowicz, J., & Subira, S. (1977). Controlled trial of nomifensine and viloxazine in the treatment of depression in the elderly. *Journal of Clinical Pharmacology, 17,* 81–83.

Moon, M. (1983). The role of the family in the economic well-being of the elderly. *Gerontologist, 23,* 45–50.

Morris, J.B., & Beck, A.T. (1974). The efficacy of antidepressant drugs: A review of research (1958–1972). *Archives of General Psychiatry, 30,* 667–674.

Mueller, D.J., & Atlas, L. (1972). Resocialization of regressed elderly residents: A behavioral management approach. *Journal of Gerontology, 27,* 390–392.

Mukherjee, B., & Holland, R.P.C. (1979). Study of vivalan in geriatric patients suffering from depression. *Journal of Internal Medical Research, 7,* 588–591.

Munjack, D.J., & Moss, H.B. (1981). Affective disorder and alcoholism in families of agoraphobics. *Archives of General Psychiatry, 38,* 317–322.

Muramoto, O., Sugishita, M., Sugita, M., & Toyakura, Y. (1979). Effect of physostigmine on constructural and memory tasks in Alzheimer's disease. *Archives of Neurology, 36,* 501–503.

Murphy, E. (1983). The prognosis of depression in old age. *British Journal of Psychiatry, 142,* 111–119.

Muslim, H., & Epstein, L.J. (1980). Preliminary remarks on the rationale for psychotherapy of the aged. *Comprehensive Psychiatry, 21,* 1–12.

Myers, J.K., Weissman, M.M., Tischler, G.L., Holzer, C.E., Leaf, P.J., Orvaschel, H., Anthony, J.C., Boyd, J.H., Burke, J.D., Kramer, M., & Stoltzman, R. (1984). Six-month prevalence of psychiatric disorders in three communities. *Archives of General Psychiatry, 41,* 959–970.

Myerson, D.J., & Mayer, J. (1966). Origins, treatment and destiny of skid-row alcoholic men. *New England Journal of Medicine, 275,* 419–426.

Nott, P.N., & Fleminger, J.J. (1975). Presenile dementia: The difficulties of early diagnosis. *Acta Psychiatrica Scandinavica, 51,* 210–217.

O'Brien, M.D. (1977). Vascular disease and dementia in the elderly. In W.L. Smith & M. Kinsbourne (Eds.), *Aging and dementia* (pp. 79–90). New York: Spectrum.

Ostfeld, A., Smith, C.M., & Stotsky, B.O. (1977). The systemic use of procaine in the treatment of the elderly: A review. *Journal of the American Geriatrics Society, 25,* 1–19.

Ostrom, J.R., Hammarlund, E.R., Christensen, D.B., Plein, J.B., & Kethley, A.J. (1985). Medication usage in an elderly population. *Medical Care, 23,* 157–164.

Palmore, E.G. (1973). Social factors in mental illness of the aged. In E.W. Busse & E. Pfeiffer (Eds.), *Mental illness in later life* (pp. 41–52). Washington, DC: American Psychological Association.

Parkes, C.M. (1972). *Bereavement.* New York: International Universities Press.

Petrie, W.M., Ban, T.A., Berney, S., Fujimori, M., Guy, W., Ragheb, M., Wilson, W.H., & Schaffer, J.D. (1982). Loxapine in psychogeriatrics: A placebo and standard-controlled clinical investigation. *Journal of Clinical Psychopharmacology, 2,* 122–126.

Pinkston, E.M., & Linsk, N.L. (1984). Behavioral family intervention with the impaired elderly. *Gerontologist, 24,* 576–583.

Popler, K. (1977). Agoraphobia: Indications for the application of the multimodel behavioral conceptions. *Journal of Nervous and Mental Disease, 164,* 97–101.

Post, F. (1962). *The significance of affective symptoms in old age: A follow-up study of one hundred patients.* London: Oxford University Press.

Post, F. (1966). *Persistent persecutory states of the elderly.* Oxford: Pergamon Press.

Post, F. (1972). The management and nature of depressive illnesses in late life: A follow-through study. *British Journal of Psychiatry, 121,* 393–404.

Puder, R., Lacks, P., Bertelson, A.D., & Storandt, M. (1983). Short-term stimulus control treatment of insomnia in older adults. *Behavior Therapy, 14,* 424–429.

Rada, R.T., & Kellner, R. (1976). Thiothixene in the treatment of geriatric patients with chronic organic brain syndrome. *Journal of the American Geriatrics Society, 24,* 105–109.

Rapp, M.S., Thornas, M.R., & Reyes, E.C. (1983). Mega-doses of behavior therapy for treatment-resistant agoraphobics. *Canadian Journal of Psychiatry, 28,* 105–108.

Raskin, D.E. (1978). A selected review of anxiolytics, neuroleptics and antidepressants in psychogeriatrics. *Proceedings of the 19th CINP,* Vienna.

Raskind, M., Alvarez, C., & Herlin, S. (1979). Fluphenazine enanthate in the outpatient treatment of late paraphrenia. *Journal of the American Geriatrics Society, 27,* 459–463.

Rechtschaffen, A. (1959). Psychotherapy with geriatric patients: A review of the literature. *Journal of Gerontology, 14,* 73–84.

Redick, R.W., Kramer, M., & Taube, C.A. (1973). Epidemiology of mental illness and utilization of psychiatric facilities among older persons. In E.W. Busse & E. Pfeiffer (Eds.), *Mental illness in later life* (pp. 199–231). Washington, DC: American Psychiatric Association.

Redick, R.W., & Taube, C.A. (1980). Demography and mental health care of the aged. In J.E. Birren & R.B. Sloane (Eds.), *Handbook of mental health and aging* (pp. 57–71). Englewood Cliffs, NJ: Prentice-Hall.

Reeves, R.L. (1977). Comparison of triazolam, flurazepam, and placebo as hypnotics in geriatric patients with insomnia. *Journal of Clinical Pharmacology, 17,* 319–323.

Reisberg, B., Ferris, S.H., & Gershon, S. (1980). Pharmacotherapy of senile dementia. In J.O. Cole & J.E. Barrett (Eds.), *Psychopathology in the aged* (pp. 233–261). New York: Raven.

Richter, J.M., Barsky, A.J., & Happ, J.A. (1983). The treatment of depression in elderly patients. *The Journal of Family Practice, 17,* 43–47.

Rickels, K., Case, W.G., Downing, R.W., & Winokur, A. (1983). Long-term diazepam therapy and clinical outcome. *Journal of the American Medical Association, 250,* 767–771.

Ritter, R.H., Nail, H.R., Tatum, P., & Blazi, M. (1971). The effect of papaverine on patients with cerebral arteriosclerosis. *Clinical Medicine, 78,* 18–22.

Roehrs, T., Lineback, W., Zorick, F., & Roth, T. (1982). Relationship of psychopathology to insomnia in the elderly. *Journal of the American Geriatrics Society, 30,* 312–315.

Ron, M.A., Toone, B.K., Garralda, M.E., & Lishman, W.A. (1979). Diagnostic accuracy in presenile dementia. *British Journal of Psychiatry, 134,* 161–168.

Rosen, H.J. (1975). Mental decline in the elderly: Pharmacotherapy (ergot alkaloids versus papaverine). *Journal of the American Geriatrics Society, 23,* 169–171.

Roth, M. (1955). The natural history of mental disorder in old age. *Journal of Mental Science, 101,* 281–301.

Sabatasso, A.P., & Jacobsen, L.J. (1970). Use of behavioral therapy in the reinstatement of verbal behavior in a mute psychotic with chronic brain syndrome. *Journal of Abnormal Psychology, 76,* 322–324.

Sadavoy, J. (1981). Psychogeriatric care in the general hospital. *Canadian Journal of Psychiatry, 26,* 334–336.

Safford, F. (1980). A program for families of the mentally impaired elderly. *Gerontologist, 20,* 656–660.

Sakalis, G., Oh, D., Gershon, S., & Shopsin, B. (1974). A trial of Gerovital H-3 in depression during senility. *Current Therapeutic Research, 16,* 59–63.

Salzman, C. (1985). Geriatric psychopharmacology. *Annual Review of Medicine, 36,* 217–218.

Salzman, C., & Shader, R.I. (1978). Depression in the elderly: Pt. 2. Possible drug etiologies: Differential diagnostic criteria. *Journal of the American Geriatrics Society, 26,* 303–308.

Schmied, J. (1962). Values and significance of psychotropic drugs in geriatric practice. In H.T. Blumenthal (Ed.), *Medical and clinical reports of aging* (pp. 128–130). New York: Columbia University Press.

Schuckit, M.A. (1981). Current therapeutic options in the management of typical anxiety. *Journal of Clinical Psychiatry, 42,* 15–26.

Seager, C.P. (1955). Chlorpromazine in treatment of elderly psychotic women. *British Medical Journal, 1,* 882.

Settel, E. (1958). Marsilid for elderly persons. *Journal of Clinical and Experimental Psychopathology and Quarterly Review of Psychiatry and Neurology, 19*(Suppl.), 98–105.

Shane, P., Weeden, J.P., & Lurie, E.E. (1985). *Linkages between mental health and aging systems: Literature synthesis and findings from a census of state units on aging.* San Francisco, CA: Institute for Health & Aging, University of California.

Shapiro, A.K., Dussik, K.T., Galentino, G.C., & Asekoff, M. (1960). A browsing double-blind study of iproniazid in geriatric patients. *Diseases of the Nervous System, 21,* 286–287.

Sheehan, D.V., Sheehan, K.E., & Minichiello, W.E. (1981). Age of onset of phobic disorders: A reevaluation. *Comprehensive Psychiatry, 22,* 544–553.

Shephard, M. (1976). General practice, mental illness and the British national health service. *American Journal of Public Health, 64,* 230–232.

Silverman, P.R. (1969). The widow-to-widow program: An experiment in preventive intervention. *Mental Hygiene, 53,* 333–337.

Skegg, D.C.G., Doll, R., & Perry, J. (1977). Use of medicine in general practice. *British Medical Journal, 1,* 1561–1563.

Smith, C.M., & Swash, M. (1978). Possible biochemical basis of memory disorder in Alzheimer's disease. *Annals of Neurology, 3,* 471–473.

Smith, C.M., Swash, M., & Exton-Smith, A.N. (1979). Effects of cholinergic drugs on memory in Alzheimer's disease. In A. Glen & C.J. Whalley (Eds.), *Alzheimer's disease* (pp. 148–153). Edinburgh: Churchill Livingston.

Smith, J.M., & Baldessarini, R.J. (1980). Changes in prevalence, severity, and recovery in tardive dyskinesia with age. *Archives of General Psychiatry, 37,* 1368–1373.

Smith, S.J., Kiloh, L.G., Ratnaverle, G.S., & Grant, D.A. (1976). The investigation of dementia: The results in 100 consecutive admissions. *The Medical Journal of Australia, 2,* 403–405.

Sriwatanakul, M.G. (1983). Clinically significant drug interactions. *Rational Drug Therapy, 17,* 1–4.

Stern, F.H. (1970). Management of chronic brain syndrome secondary to cerebral arteriosclerosis with special reference to papaverine hydrochloride. *Journal of the American Geriatrics Society, 18,* 507–512.

Steuer, J., & Clark, E. (1982). Family support groups within a research project on dementia. *Clinical Gerontologist, 1,* 87–95.

Steuer, J.L., Mintz, J., Hammer, C.L., Hill, M.A., Jarvik, L.F., McCarley, T., Motoike, P., & Rosen, R. (1984). Cognitive-behavioral and psychodynamic group psychotherapy in treatment of geriatric depression. *Journal of Consulting and Clinical Psychology, 52,* 180–189.

Strauss, D., & Solomon, K. (1983). Psychopharmacologic intevention for depression in the elderly. *Clinical Gerontologist, 2,* 3–29.

Sugarman, A.A., Williams, H., Adlerstein, A.M. (1964). Haloperidol in the psychiatric disorders of old age. *American Journal of Psychiatry, 120,* 1190–1192.

Summers, W.K., Majovski, L.V., Marsh, G.M., Tachiki, K., & Kling, A. (1986). Oral tetrahydroaminoacridine in long-term treatment of senile dementia, Alzheimer's type. *New England Journal of Medicine, 315,* 1241–1245.

Szapocznik, J., Kurtines, W.M., Santisteban, D., & Perez-Vidal, A. (1982). Ethnic and cultural variations in the care of the aged. *Journal of Geriatric Psychiatry, 15, 257–281.*

Thal, L.J., Fula, P.A., Masur, D.M., & Sharpless, N.S. (1983). Oral physostigmine and lecithin improve memory in Alzheimer's disease. *Annals of Neurology, 13, 491–496.*

Thompson, L.W., Gallagher, D., Nies, G., & Epstein, D. (1983). Evaluation of the effectiveness of professionals and nonprofessionals as instructors of "Coping with Depression" classes for elders. *Gerontologist, 23, 390–396.*

Thyer, B.A., Parrish, R.T., Curtis, G.C., Nesse, R.M., & Cameron, O.G. (1985). Ages of onset of DSM-III anxiety disorders. *Comprehensive Psychiatry, 26, 113–122.*

Tobin, J.M., Brosseau, E.R., & Lorenz, A.A. (1970). Clinical evaluation of naloperidol in geriatrics patients. *Geriatrics, 25, 119–122.*

Tobin, S.S., & Lieberman, M.A. (1976). *Last home for the aged.* San Francisco, CA: Jossey-Bass.

Toenniessen, L.M., Casey, D.E., McFarland, B.H. (1985). Tardive dyskinesia in the aged: Duration of treatment relationships. *Archives of General Psychiatry, 42, 278–284.*

Tune, G.S. (1969). The influence of age and temperament on the adult human sleep–wakefulness pattern. *British Journal of Psychology, 60, 431–441.*

Uhlenhuth, E.H., Balter, M.B., Mellinger, G.D., Cisin, I.H., & Clinthorne, J. (1983). Symptom checklist syndromes in the general population: Correlations with psychotherapeutic drug use. *Archives of General Psychiatry, 40, 1167–1178.*

Wanderer, Z.W. (1972). Existential depression treated by desensitization of phobias: Strategy and transcript. *Journal of Behavior Therapy and Experimental Psychiatry, 3, 111–116.*

Weekes, C. (1973). A practical treatment of agoraphobia. *British Medical Journal, 2, 469–471.*

Weissman, M.M., & Myers, J.K. (1979). Depression in the elderly: Research directions in psychopathology, epidemiology, and treatment. *Journal of Geriatric Psychiatry, 12, 187–201.*

Wettstein, A. (1983). No effect from double-blind trial of physostigmine and lecithin in Alzheimer's disease. *Annals of Neurology, 13, 210–212.*

Wiens, A.N., Menustik, C.E., Miller, S.T., & Schmitz, R.E. (1982–1983). Medical-behavioral treatment of the older alcoholic patient. *American Journal of Drug and Alcohol Abuse, 9, 461–475.*

Wilkinson, P. (1971). Alcoholism in the aged. *Geriatrics, 34, 59–64.*

Williamson, P.N., & Ascione, F.R. (1983). Behavioral treatment of the elderly: Implications for theory and therapy. *Behavior Modification, 7, 583–610.*

Wolk, R.L., & Goldfarb, A.L. (1967). The response to group psychotherapy of aged recent admissions compared with long-term mental hospital patients. *American Journal of Psychiatry, 123, 1251–1257.*

Woods, R.T., & Britton, P.G. (1977). Psychological approaches to the treatment of the elderly. *Age and Ageing, 6, 104–112.*

Zarit, S., Reeuer, K., & Bach-Peterson, J. (1980). Relatives of impaired elderly: Correlates of feelings of burden. *Gerontologist, 6, 649–655.*

Zarit, S.H., & Zarit, J.M. (1983). Cognitive impairment. In P.M. Lewinsohn & L. Teri (Eds.), *Clinical geropsychology* (pp. 38–80). New York: Pergamon.

Zevon, M.A., Karuza, J., & Brickman, P. (1982). Responsibility and the elderly: Applications to psychotherapy. *Psychotherapy: Theory, Research and Practice, 19,* 405–411.

Zitrin, C.M., Klein, D.F., & Woerner, M.G. (1980). Treatment of agoraphobia with group exposure in vivo and imipramine. *Archives of General Psychiatry, 37,* 63–72.

Zung, W.W.K., Gianturro, D., Pfeiffer, E., Wang, H.S., & Potkins, S. (1974). Pharmacology of depression in the aged: Evaluation of Gerovital H-3 as an antidepressant drug. *Psychosomatics, 15,* 127–131.

4

Mental Health System Components and the Aged

James H. Swan
Mary E. McCall

Mental health care in the United States occurs within a multifaceted network of providers. Of central importance are the formal service providers of mental health care. Although this chapter refers to this network as a "system," the network's dominant characteristic is its fragmented nature—a nonsystem of mental health care. This is especially true of care for the elderly who suffer from mental disorders. Most care for such individuals is delivered by non–mental health providers: physicians; general hospitals; medical outpatient clinics; nursing homes; and residential care facilities. Services are delivered as physical health or custodial, rather than psychiatric, care.

The corollary is the underutilization of the formal mental health system by the aged. Although the aged are frequent users of general hospital, physician, and nursing home services, they use formal mental health providers at a far lower rate than their numbers in the population and their prevalence of mental illness would predict (Shapiro et al., 1984). Much underutilization is the consequence of the system of funding for mental health services (see chapter 5), but additional factors are involved. An understanding of this underutilization is essential to the description of the formal service delivery system for the mentally ill elderly.

Community Mental Health

Community care for mentally ill elders is largely delivered by nonpsychiatric physicians rather than by formal mental health providers. Factors such as family support, geographical location, transportation, and physical ability to access community services all contribute to the ability of the aged to use such services (Kramer, Taube, & Redick, 1973). However, many of the problems relate to the nature of, or to the lack of, community services.

Community care and other community resources have always been inadequate to care for the mentally ill aged, especially in the wake of deinstitutionalization (Anderson, 1984; Butler & Lewis, 1977; Koran, 1981;

Morrissey & Goldman, 1984; Okin, 1978; Ozarin, 1976; Sharfstein, 1982). For many, care is simply not available: "Many patients who have been institutionalized for years now find themselves living in low-cost rooming houses, rocking in front of television sets, and wandering the streets" (Okin, 1978, p. 1356). Further, the community care that was established as deinstitutionalization took place was not directly substitutable for government inpatient hospitalization: "Although community mental health programs were established to supplant the traditional state mental hospital, both their ideology and their most common services are not directed at the needs of those who have traditionally resided in state psychiatric institutions" (Kirk and Therrien, 1975, p. 210).

Although the community mental health movement had fairly clear goals and some specification of methods, recent unpredicted trends have resulted from concerns other than those of the community mental health movement (for example, cost constraint) and were unintended consequences of policy. Because "the dollars did not follow the patient" (Rubin, 1982), and because state mental hospitals continued to exist without great cuts in their expenses, community programs added new costs onto those of institutions (Deiker, 1986; Estes & Harrington, 1981). States have tended to be reluctant to pick up the added costs necessary to fund an adequate system of community care. Gruenberg and Archer (1979) speak of an "abandonment of responsibility" that characterized deinstitutionalization after about 1970. They see this period as characterized by a "trend to transfer financial responsibility for the chronically mentally ill patient from state mental departments to the social welfare system" (Gruenberg & Archer, 1979, p. 498).

As a result, the chronically mentally ill who have been "returned to the community" tend not to be of the community, rather in continued segregation from it (Morrissey & Goldman, 1984; Reich, 1973). Although many patients discharged from mental hospitals returned to families and other social supports (Solomon, Gordon, & Davis, 1986), Kirk and Therrien (1975) had earlier criticized the "community" to which patients were to be returned as being in fact the catchment area, which may contain diverse communities unready to accept returned mental patients.

Although there may theoretically be sufficient services for deinstitutionalized patients, these services, including inpatient beds, may not offer the levels of care needed by those who are discharged (Lawton, Lipton, Fulcomer, & Kleban, 1977). For some who are chronically mentally ill, community-based care is inadequate, no matter how good or available it may be (Gruenberg & Archer, 1979). Lamb (1981, 1984) argues that continued segregation from the community is a necessity for many discharged patients. The concern here is, however, with those who could be helped by community care if it were available.

Private Care Provision in the Community

Research is sparse on the utilization of private mental health services—office-based psychiatrists and other mental health professionals seen on a basis other than in community centers or hospital outpatient clinics. Service utilization is typically reported in some combination of outpatient clinics, day-care services, community mental health centers, halfway houses, and psychiatric services in hospitals and nursing homes (Kramer et al., 1973).

Studies that report on specific use of private mental health professionals by the aged confirm the well-known fact of underutilization of such services by older populations. Reported rates range from 0.0 percent to 3.2 percent of sample populations (Cypress, 1978; German, Shapiro, & Skinner, 1985; Horgan, 1985; Kramer et al., 1973; Wan & Arling, 1983). In one study of community-resident aged, less than 10 percent reported ever having seen a psychiatrist or psychologist in their lifetimes (Waxman, Carner, & Blum, 1983). The aged have the lowest rate of utilization of office-based psychiatrists, only about 2 visits per 100, compared to 7 for the population as a whole (Cypress, 1978). The reasons for such underutilization of private mental health services by the aged have been widely discussed. The most common finding is that older people see their general physician for any problem, be it physical or mental, and thus receive mental health care, if any, from a primary care physician.

One study reported that 3.2 percent of respondents aged 65 or older consulted mental health specialists for mental problems, compared to 16.3 percent who went to general medical providers for similar problems (Horgan, 1985). According to Schurman, Mitchell, and Kramer (1984), almost half of mental health visits to physicians are to nonpsychiatric, usually primary care physicians. This is especially pronounced among the aged, about 80 percent of whose visits are to nonpsychiatric physicians, compared to about 40 percent for younger patients. Nonpsychiatric visits may often be due to the unavailability of sufficient trained mental health providers, but the great majority of visits result from physical rather than psychological symptoms. Although many of these visits are related to medical conditions that generate emotional reactions in patients, many such visits result in psychiatric diagnoses, particularly of neurotic disorders and depression. Such findings warrant careful consideration to determine both the reasons for such practices and their consequences for effective mental health care of the community elderly.

The consequences of the underutilization of mental health providers can be serious. Non–mental health providers are often not equipped to provide needed services, and in fact are often equipped neither to accurately diagnose psychiatric problems nor to adequately refer patients to mental health care (Goldberg, Wallace, Rothney, & Wartman, 1984). Deinstitutionalized patients may not have adequate access to medical and other nonpsychiatric care in the community—much reinstitutionalization results from medical problems and lack of social supports (Harris, Bergman, & Bachrach, 1986).

Sometimes only the physical illness is treated, with the expectation that psychological symptoms will subside. Such an approach not only denigrates the importance of psychological symptoms, but can lead to the development of polypharmacy problems, as aged patients return to their physicians, often reporting different forms of the same psychological distress and are again treated for an assumed physical malady.

The co-incidence of physical and mental illness in later life is well documented (see chapter 2). Symptoms of mental illness are often attributed to a co-occurring physical illness, by general physicians as well as by the patients themselves (Fox, 1984; German et al., 1985). Such misdiagnosis is encouraged by health care reimbursement mechanisms (see chapter 5).

The aged typically use general physicians for mental health care because of long-term, trusting relationships. Many elders also feel stigmatized by seeing, or even feeling the need to see, mental health specialists (Fox, 1984; German et al., 1985; VanderBos, Stapp, & Kilburg, 1981). Such fear of stigma is particularly salient for the current generation of elderly because they grew up in an era of trusted family doctors who provided all services for all family members. For this cohort, mental illness carried societal as well as personal stigma. Because of the consequent attitudes among the aged, simply prescription that they see mental health professionals will not increase such utilization.

The physician is on the other side of this care relationship. As noted, the physician is as likely as the patient to attribute psychological symptoms to physical problems. This is exacerbated by the lack of adequate training to discriminate between the two so as to accurately recognize and diagnose mental illness (VanderBos et al., 1981).

Many physicians also believe that any mental distress experienced by the aged is relatively minor, not warranting referral to a specialist. One study (Kucharski, White, & Schratz, 1979) found that physicians who read vignettes about presenting problems wherein only the ages of patients differed (over or under age 60), referred younger patients more often than older patients for psychiatric treatment. This is apparently not an uncommon occurrence (see Ginsberg & Goldstein, 1974; Popkin, Mackenzie, & Callies, 1984).

Psychologists and psychiatrists, as well as general physicians, appear to share the bias when confronted by elderly patients. A study using stratified random sampling of members of the American Psychological Association revealed that only 2.7 percent of the members saw patients aged 65 or older; 69.2 percent had never seen an elderly patient; and only 0.4 percent described themselves as specializing in gerontology or geriatrics (VanderBos et al., 1981).

Community Programs

Community programs have been criticized for focusing on populations with the least serious problems, and largely ignoring the elderly and the chronically mentally ill (Ahr & Holcomb, 1985; Greenblatt & Glazier, 1975; Kirk & Therrien, 1975; Lamb, 1981; Okin, 1978, 1984; Rose, 1979), while trying "to be all things to all people" (Borus, 1978, p. 1029). Knight (1986) supplies limited evidence, however, that mental health workers have more positive attitudes than does the community in general toward the aged, that their attitudes are not related to their work with the aged, and that the characteristics of the provider site are the important predictors of amount of contact of mental health workers with the aged.

The evidence is that CMHCs have not entirely ignored the chronically mentally ill (Goldman, Regier, Taube, Redick, & Bass, 1980). There have been some initiatives specifically aimed at the chronically mentally ill, such as the Community Support Services models (Stroul, 1986). Tessler, Bernstein, Rosen, and Goldman (1982) found, however, that community support programs serve chronic patients, but not the aged. The CMHC has been of relatively little importance to the aged because of their low utilization of its services (Flemming, Buchanan, Santos, & Rickards, 1984a; General Accounting Office [GAO], 1982). In spite of repeated clear congressional mandates for federally funded centers to provide specialized services for the aged (GAO, 1982), CMHCs have failed to serve as an important base for mental health care for the aged. Community services like those provided by CMHCs can, however, reach the aged when outreach and specialized services are important components of center design and functioning (Selan & Gold, 1980).

Some centers are adopting services that can lower access barriers for the aged, and appear to be increasing their elderly clientele. In a survey conducted at the University of California, San Francisco (Swan & Bergthold, 1987), 101 CMHCs in 9 metropolitan areas were interviewed by telephone. Respondents were chosen from among those who served at least some aged clients each month. The 99 CMHCs serving the aged reported that the aged constituted about 22 percent of their clientele, on the average. Fifteen of these centers reported over half of their clientele to be 65 years of age or older.

On a number of dimensions, CMHCs with higher percentages of aged clients differed from those with fewer aged clients. Overall, 72 percent of the CMHCs in the sample reported being affected by Medicare DRG reimbursement to hospitals. Such reports were significantly related to the percentage of aged clientele, CMHCs with more aged clients being more likely to report DRG effects. About 36 percent of responding CMHCs reported having important formal relationships with Area Agencies on Aging. Again, the existence of such relationships was significantly related to higher proportions of aged clientele. Even within the mental health system, the aged may be more likely than younger persons to see nonpsychiatric physicians. Very few centers (17 percent) reported the employment of physicians other than psychiatrists; but again such employment was significantly greater the higher the proportion of aged clients (6 of 15 CMHCs with more than half of their clients aged reported the employment of nonpsychiatric physicians).

Horgan (1986) shows that of those who must pay out-of-pocket for at least part of their care, the aged use fewer ambulatory mental health services than do the middle-aged; whereas such an effect is not found among those who do not pay anything out-of-pocket for such services. This can be taken to suggest that first-party payment (out-of-pocket payment, including deductibles and copayments) may explain part of the underutilization of ambulatory mental health services by the aged (but not necessarily the lower likelihood of any use of such services). It may be that emphasis on first-party payment disproportionately discourages use by the aged, so that CMHC emphases on such payment may further discourage use by the aged. However, Horgan's analysis was designed to measure age differences within coverage groups, rather than coverage differences within age groups.

Home Health Care for the Mentally Ill

Although there is little literature on home health care for the mentally ill, it is clear that home health services can be important for the mentally ill elderly. In-home diagnosis and referral has promise for improving or stabilizing such cases, even among those with dementia (Wasson et al., 1984). In-home psychiatric care has been more successful (Wasson et al., 1984) than outpatient referrals, suggesting that mental health care might be usefully included among home health services, especially given the underutilization by the aged of mental health services outside of the home (Shapiro et al., 1984; Waxman, Carner, & Klein, 1984). Home health care is not equally accessible to all who need it, however, because of financing and geographical patterns of service availability (Oktay & Palley, 1982).

Funding of Community Care

Mental health care in the community has been molded by reimbursement policy (see chapter 5). Federal funding originally encouraged the creation of a system of community mental health centers, but withdrawal of support diminished the ability of centers to serve their original clientele, or to survive at all (Sharfstein, 1978; Weiner, Woy, Sharfstein, & Bass, 1979). When the federal seed money ran out, CMHC responses included increased third-party reimbursement and increased reliance on state and alternate federal funds (Weiner et al., 1979). The former response raised the possibility of deemphasis of certain types of clients (for example, low-income) and services (for example, preventive or high-cost). Centers opting for the latter response experienced less growth than did those opting for increased third-party reimbursement (Weiner et al., 1979). These CMHCs were also more subject to the uncertainties of state (and alternate federal) funding policies, especially the cuts of the 1980s.

The Medicare requirement that mental health services be given under medical supervision excludes providers such as CMHCs, and the services that they provide (GAO, 1982). Freestanding CMHCs cannot receive direct Medicare reimbursement (Flemming et al., 1984a); CMHCs are covered by Medicaid in some states but not in others (GAO, 1982).

Policy for Community Mental Health Care

A survey of state mental health directors (Ahr & Holcomb, 1985) found a consensus that the major issue was the provision of community mental health services to the chronically mentally ill. Opinion differed, however, on the desirability of relating institutionalization to community services. Concern for geriatric care was fairly low, that for youth and adolescents clearly being higher. Funding and reimbursement issues were also rated as important.

A consensus on the importance of community care for the chronic mentally ill is reflected in greater attention to such services by CMHCs. The fact remains, however, that CMHCs tend to underserve older clients (Flemming et al., 1984a; GAO, 1982). Moreover, the emphasis on the chronic mentally ill may have compromised services for the aged—in particular, bringing about a reduction in the numbers of centers with specialized geriatric programs (Flemming et al., 1984a; Okin, 1984). Initiatives aimed at the chronically mentally ill, such as the Community Support Program of NIMH, do not tend to emphasize services for the aged. For example, although the Community Support Services model was designed for all those over age 18, most programs have fairly young clientele (Stroul, 1986).

The nature and extent of the mental health problems of the aged are still not well understood. Most CMHCs do not perform local needs assessments, particularly for the elderly, and there are no generally accepted standards as to what specialized mental health services should be provided to the aged (GAO, 1982). The General Accounting Office defined "the essential elements of a basic program for community mental health services for the elderly" as: psychogeriatric assessment; outreach; crisis/emergency/short-term inpatient care; day care/treatment; specialized outpatient treatment; case management; "a range of institutional care, sheltered living and social support services"; family counseling; and consultation and education (GAO, 1982, pp. 13–16). Some of the community services in the GAO list (counseling, education) are among those that CMHCs are tending to drop (Okin, 1984).

Often, the nature of the legal provisions regarding mental illness are not understood in state agencies. One study found "a lack of uniform knowledge about and interest in outpatient commitment by mental health directors and attorneys general" (Miller, 1985, p. 266). Conflicting and ambiguous court decisions on regulations and laws add to this lack of uniform knowledge (Goldman, Feder, & Scanlon, 1986).

Mental Hospitalization

What happens to older people with mental illness? Relatively few are in mental hospitals (Goldman, Adams, & Taube, 1983), and they are underrepresented in other mental treatment programs as well (Shapiro et al., 1984). The aged were formerly heavily represented in mental health inpatient facilities (Johnson & Grant, 1985), and some of the aged remain in state and county mental hospitals. In 1979, 39 percent of patients who had been in such hospitals for at least a year were over age 65, accounting for 23 percent of the year-end census of such hospitals (Taube, Thompson, Rosenstein, Rosen, & Goldman, 1983). Most states have retained some level of publicly financed mental health hospitalization for the aged (Taube et al., 1983). Nevertheless, deinstitutionalization has radically changed the care of the mentally ill aged (Barter, 1983; Koran, 1981).

Prior to the middle of this century, the state mental hospital evolved as the locus of government-funded mental health care in the United States (see Gruenberg & Archer, 1979; Morrissey & Goldman, 1984; Rose, 1979). Since the 1950s, however, deinstitutionalization has transformed mental health care (Manderscheid, Witkin, Rosenstein, & Bass, 1984; Morrissey & Goldman, 1984). State mental hospital populations declined from a high of 559,000 in 1955 to 139,000 in 1980 (Goldman, Taube, Regier, & Witkin, 1983). Between 1955 and 1977, mental health patient care episodes fell by 30 percent in state mental hospitals, while outpatient episodes increased 280 percent (Goldman, Taube, Regier & Witkin, 1983; Sharfstein, 1982). During the same period, the number of state mental hospital beds declined by 70 percent (Sharfstein, 1982). Between 1969 and 1978 alone, state mental hospital inpatient days declined 60 percent (Kiesler & Sibulkin, 1983). In the 1970s, the numbers of public mental hospitals undertaking capital projects declined greatly, with only a small increase in total capital expenditures due to increases in costs of individual projects, while the numbers of private hospitals undertaking such projects remained fairly constant (Checker, 1986).

Continued Institutionalization:
Short-Term General Hospitals

Deinstitutionalization did not eliminate inpatient psychiatric care (Goldman, Adams, & Taube, 1983; Okin, 1982; Pardes, 1981; Sigel, 1984). Decreases in state mental hospital populations were accompanied by increases of inpatients in general hospitals, board-and-care facilities, and nursing homes. Lower usage of state and county mental hospitals was matched by greater usage of general hospitals for psychiatric care: "Patient care data indicate that while the number of resident patients has decreased and the average length of stay has shortened, the rate of psychiatric hospitalization in the country has remained roughly constant" (Pardes, 1981, p. 779). Kiesler (1982) argues that, counting general hospital care, overall mental hospitalization may in fact be increasing. Inpatient admission and readmission rates are high among those in community treatment (Schoonover & Bassuk, 1983). Although it seems clear that readmission rates have increased for state and county mental hospitals, it is not clear that they have increased greatly for mental hospitalization in general (Kiesler, 1982). Although mental disorders account for a smaller proportion of all inpatient days than previously, they still account for about a fourth of inpatient hospital days (Kiesler, 1982). In sum, while outpatient care has greatly expanded, inpatient mental health care has itself remained stable or grown slightly (Goldman, Adams, & Taube, 1983).

Most psychiatric inpatient care in general hospitals (the great majority as late as 1978) takes place outside of designated psychiatric inpatient units (Bachrach, 1981). Much care is received from nonpsychiatric physicians, despite a high prevalence of psychiatric symptoms among general hospital inpatients. Nonpsychiatric physicians tend to underuse psychiatric liaison services in hospitals, particularly in the case of older patients (Craig, 1982).

Psychiatric care in general hospitals differs according to whether or not there are psychiatric inpatient units. Patients with primary psychiatric diagnoses in hospitals with psychiatric units are more likely to receive psychotherapy, shock therapy, and rehabilitation therapies than are those in hospitals without such units. Patients receiving such therapies are also likely to receive a greater variety of services in hospitals with psychiatric units (Wallen, 1985). However, types of diagnoses also differ according to whether a hospital has an inpatient psychiatric unit. Hospitals with units have more patients with diagnoses of psychosis; those without have higher proportions of patients diagnosed with alcoholism and organic brain syndrome (Wallen, 1985). This may account for some of the differences in treatment rates.

In hospitals with inpatient psychiatric units, medical or surgical ward patients who have behavioral disorders or are otherwise disruptive to their own medical treatment can be transferred to the psychiatric unit, allowing either continued medical treatment there or sufficient stabilization to allow transfer back to the medical or surgical ward for treatment (Weimer & Fenn, 1982). Where they exist, combined medical–psychiatric inpatient units are especially adapted to the treatment of patients with coexistent medical and psychiatric disorders (Hoffman, 1984).

Hospitals can apply for waivers from Medicare DRG reimbursement to psychiatric units, thus exempting psychiatric care to the aged in such units from the effects of DRG reimbursement. The waivering of its psychiatric unit, however, may induce a hospital to alter its practices regarding that unit—for example, to increase diagnoses that place patients in that unit in order to avoid DRG reimbursement limits. Before the implementation of DRGs, psychiatric patients in general hospitals with psychiatric units had average lengths of stay double those for all general hospital psychiatric patients (Wallen, 1985). Reductions in lengths of stay outside of psychiatric units since the implementation of DRGs may have increased this difference.

Some investigators (Flamm, 1981; Keill, 1981) argue that, especially because of its accessibility and medical support services, the general hospital is and should be the core of the mental health system. The further question is whether general hospitals should accept involuntary patients or by contrast have only open units with voluntary patients. In spite of caveats as to how such a policy should be implemented, some observers (Leeman, Sederer, Rogoff, Berger, & Merrifield, 1981) conclude that general hospitals should be central to the treatment of involuntary patients, but that separate open and locked units should be available (Merrifield in Leeman et al., 1981).

Schoonover and Bassuk (1983) note, however, that most general hospitals do not offer a full range of treatment options and services. They argue that general hospitals will have to change considerably if they are to avoid repeating the failures of state hospitals (and see Sederer in Leeman et al., 1981). The adequacy of general hospital mental health care is especially important for the aged, who are more likely to turn to medical than to mental health providers for help with mental problems. Of particular concern is the issue of whether smaller, short-stay hospitals might not become "inundated" with the mentally ill, reducing quality of care and individualized care (see Sederer in Leeman et al., 1981). Given the short-stay character of general hospital care, discharge planning and referral to posthospital care are especially important for the mentally ill (Burda, 1986; Flamm, 1981).

Mental Hospitals after Deinstitutionalization

The state mental hospitals have not disappeared. The decline in state mental hospital populations has now ended (Taube et al., 1983). The number of state mental hospitals was about the same in 1980 as in 1955 (Sharfstein, 1982; Thompson, Bass, & Witkin, 1982), and admissions to state mental hospitals have increased (Miller, 1981). Direct nationwide expenditures for mental health care in state mental hospitals in 1980 ($3.5 billion) were still about as large as those for inpatient psychiatric care in general hospitals ($3.6 billion) (Frank & Kamlet, 1985). State mental hospitals still provide the majority of days of inpatient psychiatric care (Goldman, Adams, & Taube, 1983; National Institute of Mental Health, 1984).

State facility function and patient case mix have changed, however (Ozarin, 1976; Thompson et al., 1982). In a study of the California state mental hospital population in the early 1980s, DeRisi and Vega (1983) found that the patients, because of their youth, physical health, and violent nature, were unsuitable for placement in nursing homes. These characteristics, along with their dependence and lack of resources, also made such patients unsuitable for return to the community: "California's state hospital system now treats a population that is primarily of low socioeconomic status, almost half of whom have recently engaged in dangerous behavior and one-third of whom are still considered dangerous" (DeRisi & Vega, 1983, p. 143). Similar patterns have been found in other states (Ames, 1983; Craig & Laska, 1983; Miller, 1981).

These changes were accompanied by a drop in average lengths of stay (Goldman, Adams, & Taube, 1983) as many more short-stay patients were served (DeRisi & Vega, 1983; Gruenberg & Archer, 1979; Kirk & Therrien, 1975). Long-stay patients still exist in state hospitals (Taube et al., 1983), but now share the facilities with greater numbers of short-stay patients. Patients discharged after a short stay may put pressure on community-based service providers (Flemming et al., 1984b; Gruenberg & Archer, 1979) and also have high rates of rehospitalization (Gruenberg & Archer, 1979). "Currently, the state mental hospital operates like two separate but functionally related inpatient facilities: a custodial institution for long-stay patients and an acute hospital for short-stay and intermediate-stay patients" (Goldman, Taube, Regier, & Witkin 1983, p. 297).

These changes make it clear that the mental hospital has not so much lost its function as that it has largely lost any functions of caring for the aged. Forensic, chronically mentally ill, or otherwise disruptive younger patients are served by state mental hospitals. It is of dubious desirability to place older patients in institutions serving such functions.

Trends in Institutionalization

There may be a trend back toward institutionalization in the near future, based on cuts in government financing, particularly Medicaid coverage of mental health services (Beigel, 1982; Morrissey & Goldman, 1984; Okin, 1982; Sharfstein, Frank, & Kessler, 1984). Any such move would be further motivated by the problems of dealing with those who in the past would have been institutionalized (DeRisi & Vega, 1983; Taube et al., 1983): "The simple fact is that there is often no place in our system for patients who are seriously ill and in desperate need of treatment" (Bachrach, 1986, p. 470).

Continued institutionalization and reinstitutionalization can be seen as threats to the mental health system as a whole, because of trade-offs between institutional and noninstitutional funding (see Smith, 1984; Talbott, 1985; Windle & Scully, 1976). For a state to decrease the number of beds in its mental hospitals is not necessarily to reduce the amount it budgets for these hospitals (Gruenberg & Archer, 1979). Inpatient treatment consumes a share of mental health funds far out of proportion to the number of recipients served (Goodrick, 1984). It appears that the "dollars have not followed the patients" to community settings, rather that they have remained in institutional settings in the form of higher costs (Okin, 1982; Rubin, 1982).

Institutional versus noninstitutional care cannot be seen as an either–or question (Rubin, 1981; Spiro, 1982). Many observers argue that the state hospital will remain, serving an "irreducible minimum" of chronic patients (Ames, 1983; Craig & Laska, 1983; Goodrick, 1984; Gruenberg & Archer, 1979; Kaiser & Townsend, 1981; Okin, 1982; Shadish & Bootzin, 1981; Sigel, 1984; Stotsky & Stotsky, 1983). Taube et al. (1983) note that long-stay patients (those staying at least 1 year) account for about 65 percent of state mental hospital inpatient days, even though they constitute only about one-fifth of the patients resident in the hospitals during a year. Bachrach (1986), while agreeing that the state mental hospital will continue to exist and will be an important part of the service system for the chronically mentally ill, cautions that its place in the system varies from state to state and from community to community. Reinstitutionalization in mental hospitals that do not serve the aged may threaten the funding for more beneficial community care.

It is debated whether the state mental hospital is the appropriate locus of institutionalization. Some argue that these facilities serve unique and important functions (Ames, 1983; Kaiser & Townsend, 1981; Sigel, 1984; Winslow, 1982) that could be enhanced in a more adequate system of psychiatric care (Miller, 1981). Others find state mental hospitals to be inappropriate (Okin, 1983; Talbott, 1985), even though they will likely continue to be used for some types of patients (Okin, 1982). Talbott argues that any return to institutionalization in state hospitals would be "anachronistic," characterizing any such trend as "scientifically unsupportable, clinically unconscionable, and economically unfeasible" (Talbott, 1985, p. 48). This is particularly true for the elderly.

The Role of Nursing Homes

The development of Medicaid payment for nursing care and the consequent expansion of nursing facilities and beds were major factors in the deinstitutionalization from government mental hospitals (Goldman, Adams, & Taube, 1983; Koran, 1981; Rose, 1979; Spiro, 1982). The nursing home replaced the state mental hospital as the locus of care for the mentally ill aged (Goldman, Adams, & Taube, 1983; Manderscheid et al., 1984; Ozarin, 1976; Rose, 1979; Rovner & Rabins, 1985; Shadish & Bootzin, 1981; Teeter, Garetz, Miller, & Heiland, 1976). The aged have not been deinstitutionalized. "As reflected in the numbers of patients placed and the dollars spent, nursing homes are the centerpiece of a de facto mental health policy of institutionalization" (Shadish & Bootzin, 1981, p. 488).

Many nursing home residents are mentally ill (Koran, 1981; Ragier, Goldberg, & Taube, 1978; Rovner & Rabins, 1985). The mentally ill aged are especially likely to be found in skilled nursing facilities (SNFs); intermediate care facilities (ICFs) have higher proportions of younger residents who are mentally ill (Schmidt, Reinhardt, Kane, & Olsen, 1977; Shadish & Bootzin, 1981). There is some evidence, however, that mental hospitals do not discharge their more severe cases to nursing homes (Dittmar & Franklin, 1980a).

Because of Medicaid reimbursement practices (Elpers & Crowell, 1982; GAO, 1982), because of the undesirable characteristics of many mentally ill patients, and because of negative community attitudes (GAO, 1982), nursing homes tend to limit numbers of residents diagnosed as mentally ill, or avoid them altogether (Koran, 1981).

The Medicaid reimbursement limits are particularly important. Nursing homes can lose their eligibility for Medicaid reimbursement if more than 50 percent of their patients have primary mental health diagnoses, so "homes have incentives to deemphasize the mental problems of patients" (GAO, 1982, p. 23). Such nursing homes, and others that can be defined as primarily treating mental illness can be redefined for Medicaid certification as "institutions for mental disease." These restrictions have been upheld by the courts (Connecticut v. Heckler, 1985). Although state Medicaid programs can choose to reimburse institutions for mental disease, nursing homes can be put at a disadvantage if they are so classified because they can no longer receive Medicaid reimbursement for those between the ages of 21 and 65; and in any case, some states do not allow such reimbursement to nursing homes even for the aged. In consequence, nursing homes have incentives to avoid the aged who are primarily diagnosed as mentally ill, and especially to avoid the provision of mental health treatment, even where the state does allow for such Medicaid reimbursement.

The aged mentally ill in nursing homes differ in the etiology of problems. The General Accounting Office noted three categories: (1) older chronic mentally ill, many of whom had been in state hospitals; (2) those who entered the facilities on the basis of their mental disorders, often with concurrent physical health problems; and (3) those who developed mental illness while resident in nursing homes (GAO, 1982). Over half of nursing home patients with mental disorders alone, over two-thirds with both physical and mental disorders, and over 90 percent with "senility" are aged 65 or over (Goldman et al., 1986). Goldman et al. (1986) find that the group of older nursing home residents with senility are more dependent and need more assistance with activities of daily living than younger patients. Younger mentally ill nursing home residents without senility are less dependent, but need specialized care related to their specific disorders and retained capacities.

There is evidence of substantial psychiatric misdiagnosis in nursing homes (Barnes & Raskind, 1980; GAO, 1982; Schmidt et al., 1977; Stotsky & Stotsky, 1983). Teeter et al. (1976) found that 61 percent of cases with serious, diagnosable mental illness went undiagnosed by the facilities in their sample.

Miller and Elliott found that 64 percent of all primary diagnoses in their nursing home sample were inaccurate, the most common error being the failure to identify chronic functional psychiatric illness, and 84 percent of errors involving "the common failure to identify disabling neurologic disease or disabling psychiatric illness or combinations thereof" (Miller & Elliott, 1976, pp. 113–114). Nursing home psychiatric record keeping was also found inadequate (Teeter et al., 1976). In consequence, some observers (GAO, 1982; Rovner & Rabins, 1985; Shadish & Bootzin, 1981) argue that mental health morbidity among the aged in nursing homes is much higher than reflected in official records.

Precise figures are not available on mental health morbidity in nursing homes (GAO, 1982; Shadish & Bootzin, 1981). Better data on mental illness among the aged in nursing homes will be available in the future from the NIMH Ecological Catchment Area studies, which include large samples of the institutionalized elderly (Eaton et al., 1984). Pending these data, the best estimates range from around 30 percent (Ahr & Holcomb, 1985; Rovner & Rabins, 1985) to 85 percent (Carling, 1981; Rovner & Rabins, 1985; Teeter et al., 1976). In part, the disagreement stems from differences in how to characterize "senility" (Carling, 1981; Koran, 1976). There is some evidence that the prevalence of "mental status problems" are higher in freestanding than in hospital-based skilled nursing facilities (Wiener, Liu, & Scnieber, 1985).

Reimbursement systems had much to do with the shift to placement of the aged in nursing homes (Spiro, 1982). Although per diem costs are much lower for nursing homes than for state mental hospitals, nursing home care may not be more cost-effective. Because of a tendency to longer stays, costs may not be lower per episode or per patient. Further, higher expenditures for alternatives to nursing homes might buy more care—"programs of active treatment will be far more expensive than custodial care" (Rubin, 1982, p. 751). Rubin (1982) argues that even if the average costs of care are lower in nursing homes than in state hospitals, the marginal costs to the states may not be lower because of the large fixed costs that states continue to pay for their hospitals.

Mental Health Care in Nursing Homes

Few nursing homes are equipped to provide mental health care, and most provide none (Department of Health and Human Services [DHHS], 1980; GAO, 1982; Talbott, 1985). Goldman et al. note that "Medicare and Medicaid policy discourages nursing homes from developing programs targeted to mentally ill residents" (Goldman, Pincus, Taube, & Regier, 1984, p. 461). Nursing homes were originally designed to care for the aged and infirm, not for the mentally ill (Carling, 1981), and do not provide as many services as do specialized mental health facilities (Spiro, 1982). Patients with "greater psychiatric disturbance" are more likely than other patients to make unsuccessful adjustments to the nursing home (Stotsky, 1967). The nursing home, as a medical setting, often seeks medical solutions for "social psychological problems" (Wack & Rodin, 1978).

The aged mentally ill in nursing homes need services that go beyond nursing care, ranging from extra supervision (GAO, 1982) and psychological assessment (Lebray, 1979) to comprehensive psychiatric services (Carling, 1981; Held, Ransohoff, & Goehner, 1984). Mentally ill residents vary widely in the services and levels of care required. They tend to need less aid in activities of daily living but to present greater behavioral problems than do residents with physical disorders alone (Goldman et al., 1986).

These needs of the mentally ill are often not met in nursing homes. In a sample of skilled nursing facilities, Zimmer, Watson, and Treat (1984) found that only 15 percent of patients with "serious behavioral problems" received psychiatric consultation. In 1977, only about a third of mentally ill nursing home residents received psychological therapy, while only about 7 percent received psychotherapy, and a similar percentage received reality orientation (Goldman et al., 1986). Especially likely to go untreated are residents with potentially reversible dementias (Sabin, Vitug, & Mark, 1982). Such patients are particularly likely to be elderly. Though diagnoses of specific dementias are possible in the nursing home setting, nonspecific diagnoses and non-diagnoses are common (Barnes & Raskind, 1980).

Nursing home staff are seldom qualified to deliver mental health care (Carling, 1981; DHHS, 1980; Stotsky & Stotsky, 1983), and may show negative attitudes toward mentally ill residents (Rovner & Rabins, 1985; Teeter et al., 1976). The importance of staff attitudes is emphasized by a study of nursing home patients who had been discharged from mental hospitals. Findings indicated that "specific environmental factors have as much influence on residents' integration as do residents' level of physical and psychosocial functioning," of particular importance being "the manner in which staff interact with residents" (Kruzich, 1986, p. 12).

There is widespread use of psychotropic medications in nursing homes. In 1977, about three-fourths of the mentally ill in nursing homes received at least one medication for their disorders (Goldman et al., 1986). There is evidence, however, that such medications are used inappropriately (Schmidt et al., 1977; Teeter et al., 1976; Waxman, Klein, & Carner, 1985), often to keep patients docile rather than as part of a mental health treatment plan (Schmidt et al., 1977). In one study, less than 60 percent of SNF patients with serious behavioral problems were found to receive psychoactive drugs on a regular basis (Zimmer et al., 1984).

In sum, nursing homes in the United States do not offer adequate mental health care, certainly not at a level necessary for rehabilitation (Carling, 1981; DHHS, 1980). This is especially unfortunate in the case of patients with "potentially reversible conditions," who may amount to one-fourth of mentally impaired nursing home residents (Rovner & Rabins, 1985, p. 119). Some findings suggest that nursing home patients have poorer prognoses than mental hospital patients with similar initial conditions (Spiro, 1982); other findings suggest that mental hospital patients discharged to nursing homes do as well as those retained by the hospitals (Dittmar & Franklin, 1980b).

Mental health programs have been neglected in nursing homes mostly for reasons of reimbursement (Fink, 1982; Weiss & Dubin, 1982). This is true even though the costs are relatively small (Stotsky, 1972).

Some nursing home programs promise treatment and rehabilitation for nursing home patients with mental and behavioral problems (Kane, Jorgensen, Teteberg, & Kuwahara, 1976; Lieff & Brown, 1981). Such approaches as reality orientation, milieu therapy, remotivation therapy, and behavior modification are effective in the nursing home setting (Johnson & Grant, 1985). Partial hospitalization has the potential of bringing adequate mental health care to nursing home residents (Bobrove, Carner, Simon, Gabriel, & Altshuler, 1983), and is cost-effective (Weiss & Dubin, 1982). Nursing homes can usefully employ mental health specialists in the training of other nursing home personnel and in program development (Lebray, 1979).

Psychiatric nursing homes exist and can, at state discretion, receive Medicaid reimbursement. In California, locked SNFs (Lamb, 1982) provide therapy, education, and structured activities in a secure facility. Patients are either voluntary commitments or are under conservatorship. Lamb argues that such a facility "fulfills the function of the state hospital for patients who would be among its more difficult charges," but is preferable to "the large state hospital where the treatment is inadequate or impersonal and fosters a life of institutional regression" (Lamb, 1982, p. 7).

It has been argued that nursing homes are necessary adjuncts to the mental health system, offering care to chronic patients (usually aged) who would not otherwise be served, and especially providing custodial care to mental health patients (Shadish & Bootzin, 1981). We must conclude, however, that the nursing home in its present form is not appropriate when mental health services beyond simple nursing and custodial care are needed (Carling, 1981; Koran, 1981; Schmidt et al., 1977). As Carling notes: "There seems to be a growing consensus that we have failed to incorporate nursing homes into the mental health system in any meaningful way" (Carling, 1981, p. 579). This has been further exacerbated by recent court decisions upholding the Health Care Financing Administration (HCFA) restrictions on Medicaid funding for care in "nursing homes" that in fact engage primarily in treating those with mental diseases (Toff & Scallet, 1986).

Nursing Home Reimbursement Issues

Funding of nursing home care for the aged follows patterns different from those for other types of care. As noted in chapter 5, nursing home care is heavily funded by Medicaid, in contrast to hospital and physician services, which depend largely on Medicare. The latter are more heavily dependent on Medicare than are nursing home expenditures on Medicaid, and are more dependent on government in general than is nursing home care. Because little support for nursing home care is forthcoming from private insurance, reimbursement for nursing home care is a greater (and growing) burden on the consumer than are hospital and physician services.

States have discretion in Medicaid programs to reimburse institutions for mental disease (IMDs) for care delivered to those aged 65 or over and to those under 21. Such care may be delivered in mental hospitals, psychiatric SNFs, or psychiatric ICFs. Most states allow for some such Medicaid reimbursement, but in few states are there many Medicaid recipients in IMDs (Swan, 1987). There is some evidence that IMD use under the Medicaid program occurs primarily where access to nursing home beds is particularly difficult (Swan, 1987). The allowance of state supplements to Medicaid funding for care in psychiatric skilled nursing facilities (which are IMDs) is limited to those patients with the possibility of rehabilitation, thus excluding many of the mentally ill aged (see chapter 5). Such funding programs do, however, promise some mental health treatment in nursing homes to those of the mentally ill aged who can profit from rehabilitation.

Some states have covered care (including care of those between the ages of 21 and 65) in "nursing homes" that were in fact facilities engaged primarily in treating the mentally ill. However, this practice is not accepted by federal Medicaid regulations, which exclude Medicaid nursing home funding to facilities that primarily treat those with mental diseases. This disallowance has been upheld by the Supreme Court (Connecticut v. Heckler, 1985). The effects of such rulings are to further discourage nursing homes from offering psychiatric care, or even accepting patients with mental health diagnoses; to prevent state governments from using what is sometimes a more appropriate approach than either placement in state mental hospitals or deinstitutionalization; and to place state Medicaid programs in jeopardy of substantial repayments to the federal government for cases found to be improper payments to IMDs (Toff & Scallet, 1986). The decisions uphold an interpretation that mental health care is primarily a state responsibility, with very narrowly defined exceptions (Connecticut v. Heckler, 1985). Although one such exception is the allowance of Medicaid reimbursement for care in IMDs in the cases of elderly patients, the restrictions in fact discourage nursing home participation in the mental health treatment of even the aged.

Such rulings, and attendant fiscal risks, may motivate states to narrowly define mental health care, thereby abandoning responsibility for many who need care (especially in the case of behavioral disorders with organic origin). In consequence, the rigid definition of federal responsibility threatens those IMDs (and nursing homes that skirt close to the definition of IMD) serving those under 65, and state reactions may threaten IMDs serving those over 65.

In addition to the effects of government policy, other factors influence nursing home utilization, including use by the mentally ill. For example, the availability of nursing home beds varies widely among the states, and in turn affects nursing home utilization (Harrington & Swan, in press).

The great expansion in outpatient mental health care has in large part involved patients and types of patients who did not previously receive mental health care, institutional or not, or at least who would have been treated elsewhere than in state hospitals (Kirk & Therrien, 1975). Some doubt that deinstitutionalization has in fact occurred, seeing rather a shift to nursing homes and general hospitals (DeRisi & Vega, 1983; Goldman, Adams, & Taube, 1983; Shadish & Bootzin, 1981). At least in this respect, however, government mental hospitals have been supplanted: "Of all the organized health care settings, only the nursing home can be demonstrated clearly to have become a substitute for the long-term custodial care function of the state and county mental hospital" (Goldman, Adams, & Taube, 1983, p. 132). This is but a different form of institutionalization.

As noted in chapter 5, Medicaid reimbursement encourages institutionalization and has shaped the development of the nursing home industry as the substitute for state mental hospital institutionalization for the elderly. Further, Medicaid is a program with much state discretion, so that Medicaid coverage of nursing home care is a patchwork of benefits, eligibility rules, service limits, and reimbursement policies (DHHS, 1980; Rubin, 1981).

Of great potential importance to the care of the mentally ill would be further initiatives to allow Medicaid coverage of psychiatric services delivered in SNFs. The California use of state mental health monies to fund psychiatric adult day care in SNFs might also be emulated. It is not at all clear, however, that many states will extend Medicaid coverage of care in SNFs and ICFs for mental disease.

Proposals Regarding System Components

The nonsystem of care for the elderly with mental health problems contains both institutional and noninstitutional components, both of which must be addressed. In the institution, the major considerations are the assurance of the availability of mental health treatment, efforts at rehabilitation and cure where such are possible, and reimbursement mechanisms that would support these efforts. In the community, the major considerations are mental health services that actually reach the elderly who might benefit from them, the provision of types of services and service locations that will benefit the aged, the prevention or delay of institutionalization, and reimbursement mechanisms that would support such efforts. In both settings, there must be concern with who provides the care, and with the training and knowledge of such caregivers. Because of the fragmented nature of mental health services for the aged, much consideration should be given to the integration and coordination of services.

Community Mental Health

Suggestions for improving community mental health care for the aged, or for any other group, generally begin with the advocacy of increased commitment of resources to such care. There is no argument here against such a prescription, but it is difficult to imagine that great amounts of additional funding will be forthcoming in the immediate future. Further, the underutilization by the elderly of existing community mental health services suggests that any new commitment of resources is unlikely to be concentrated on services to the aged. The concern here will, therefore, be on improvements in community mental health services to the aged that do not entail massive commitments of resources or expansion of the system.

Two approaches present themselves. One is to accept the current use patterns and emphasize the delivery of mental health services through the medical providers to whom the mentally ill aged now go for care. The other is to change community mental health, increasing its emphasis on the aged, and making it more responsive to their needs. Posed against the former option is the possibility that current use patterns are cohort-based; future cohorts of the elderly may have very different attitudes and patterns of utilization, perhaps being much more open to the use of community mental health services— provided they exist. Current use patterns should be considered, however, and any strategy for the provision of community mental health services to the aged should take into account that many of the mentally ill elderly do now and may continue to go for care to their private physicians, to community hospitals, and to nursing homes.

Focusing on the existing community mental health sector, there are a number of approaches that seem promising. Some CMHCs specialize in psychogeriatric services. Such specialization may make such centers more approachable for the aged, but it may also make community mental health care less geographically accessible to the aged. In some cities, the existence of the psychogeriatric CMHC means that other centers tend not to treat aged clients. Provision of adequate transportation is a partial response to this quandary, but it is not clear that many of the aged with mental health problems will be willing to travel long distances to psychogeriatric services, no matter how adequate the means of transport.

Another approach is to bring mental health care to the home. In-home psychiatric care, in some cases in-home psychogeriatric care (beyond crisis intervention), is apparently increasingly available. Expansion of such care is strongly recommended. As with other in-home care, such services will most likely be reserved largely for those with severe problems.

Less resource-intensive, more support-oriented services are also called for. The 1982 GAO reporting of needed services remains applicable. One of the assumptions of a community approach to mental health care for the aged is that the living situation of the older patient is conducive to the use of community services. Providers must not only be aware of their own side of the care relationship, in terms of providing the services most appropriate for older patients, but must also be sensitive to the context in which these services fit from the consumer's point of view. Support of both the provider and the user is necessary for effective high-quality mental health care for the aged.

Institutional Services

Although some of the mentally ill elderly remain in state mental hospitals, it is clear that the major institutional providers are now and will likely continue to be general hospitals and nursing homes. Medicare DRG reimbursement makes it likely that general hospital care will continue to evolve away from the direction of an adequate system of mental health care for the aged. An adequate response would, therefore, be contingent on the recognition within Medicare and other funding programs of the need for such hospital-based services as observation for medical conditions possibly underlying behavioral problems; care for those with coincident mental and physical disorders, which may greatly complicate and prolong treatment; mental disorders, particularly depression and disorientation, that follow on, or derive from, medical treatment, including from early discharge from hospitals of patients who do not feel ready to cope with their physical limitations at home.

Recommendations regarding nursing home care also depend on changes in funding systems. The single most important change would be the assumption of Medicaid and Medicare responsibility for the funding of mental health services in the nursing home. So long as the provision of adequate mental health services puts a nursing home at risk of losing Medicaid reimbursement, and puts states at risk of assuming the costs of such care, adequate treatment of the mentally impaired in nursing homes will not be generally feasible.

Integration and Coordination
of Services and Providers

At the systems level, linkages between mental health and aging systems are needed at both state and local levels. Coordination would benefit from the linkage activities noted in chapter 7. It is clear, however, that linkages must also be improved with the systems of medical care provision.

A model for integrative health service delivery might be derived by consideration of successful practices of the health maintenance organization (HMO). Within such organizations, three programmatic arrangements deserve attention: mental health education of primary physicians; consulting programs between medical and mental health providers; and team approaches to patient care (Coleman & Patrick, 1976). Educational programs cannot make primary care physicians specialists in mental illness, but can increase physician sensitivity to emotional and behavioral problems. Consulting programs, though difficult in general hospital settings due to the diffusion of responsibility for patients, have been creatively addressed in HMOs. Such programs provide general practitioners with access to psychiatric assistance that would not otherwise be available. Team approaches have been widely heralded as the most effective method of treating elderly patients (Lewinsohn, Teri, & Hautzinger, 1984; Portnoi & Shriber, 1980; Wasylenki, Harrison, Britnell, & Hood, 1984). In this model, mental health practitioners form a part of a primary care team, and are thus included from the beginning in patient evaluation and treatment. This allows for the provision of care to the aged neither by the general physician nor by the mental health professional alone, so that concomitant physical and mental symptoms can be effectively addressed.

Finally, service integration and coordination are largely dependent on reimbursement mechanisms. Chapter 5 discusses how funding has shaped the current fragmented system. As suggested there, integrated funding streams are essential to the creation of a coordinated system of care.

New Psychogeriatric Service Types and Practitioners

New types of care are particularly necessary in nursing homes. Such care might use services such as reality orientation, remotivation therapy, milieu therapy, behavior modification, adult day care, and partial hospitalization. Development of reimbursement mechanisms would be a major problem, as would the development of screening and monitoring systems to assure cost constraint. Special treatment funding under California's MediCal program is an example of a start on such an approach, but that program is limited to treatment of short-term patients in locked SNFs—the need is for psychiatric care for chronic patients as well, and in all levels of nursing home care.

Likewise, there is a need for psychiatric ombudspersons in nursing homes. Ombudspersons could advocate accurate mental health diagnoses and proper use of psychotropic drugs, could recognize symptoms of mental illness in the elderly, and could advocate the targeting of mental health care to nursing home residents likely to profit from it. This would presuppose the development of reimbursement mechanisms for such services.

The provision of new services in nursing homes might necessitate the development of psychiatric nurse practitioners. Such professionals might work for nursing homes, necessitating adequate funding for facilities providing their services. Or they might work out of CMHCs and service the aged in nursing homes. This would entail the establishment of adequate training, implementation by CMHCs, and the development of funding arrangements.

References

Ahr, P.R., & Holcomb, W.R. (1985). State mental health directors' priorities for mental health care. *Hospital and Community Psychiatry, 36*, 39–45.

Ames, D. (1983). The limits of general hospital care: A continuing role for state hospitals. *Hospital and Community Psychiatry, 34*, 145–149.

Anderson, W.T. (1984). Thousands released; Few treatment facilities. *California Journal, 15*, 215–218.

Bachrach, L.L. (1981). The effects of deinstitutionalization on general hospital psychiatry. *Hospital and Community Psychiatry, 32*, 786–790.

Bachrach, L.L. (1986). The future of the state mental hospital. *Hospital and Community Psychiatry, 37*, 467–474.

Barnes, R.F., & Raskind, M.A. (1980). DSM-III criteria and the clinical diagnosis of dementia: A nursing home study. *Journal of Gerontology, 36*, 20–27.

Barter, J.T. (1983). California—transformation of mental health care: 1957–1982. In J.A. Talbott (Ed.), *Unified mental health systems: Utopia unrealized* (pp. 7–18). San Francisco, CA: Jossey-Bass.

Beigel, A. (1982). Community mental health centers: A look ahead. *Hospital and Community Psychiatry, 33*, 741–745.

Bobrove, P., Carner, E.A., Simon, D., Gabriel, E., & Altshuler, L. (1983). A partial hospitalization program for nursing home residents. *Hospital and Community Psychiatry, 34*, 553–555.

Borus, J. (1978). Issues critical to the survival of community mental health. *American Journal of Psychiatry, 135*, 1029–1035.

Burda, D. (1986). Follow-up care for chronic mentally ill: Whose job? *Hospitals, 60*, 106.

Butler, R.N., & Lewis, M.I. (1977). *Aging and mental health: Positive psychosocial approaches*. St. Louis, MO: C.V. Mosby.

Carling, P.J. (1981). Nursing homes and chronic mental patients: A second opinion. *Schizophrenia Bulletin, 7*, 574–579.

Checker, A. (1986). Capital projects funding for psychiatric hospitals, 1972–1981. *Hospital and Community Psychiatry, 37*, 380–385.

Coleman, J.V., & Patrick, B.L. (1976). Integrating mental health services into primary medical care. *Medical Care, 14*, 654–661.

Connecticut Department of Income Maintenance v. Margaret M. Heckler, Department of Health and Human Services, 105S.Ct. 2210 (1985).

Craig, T.J. (1982). An epidemiologic study of a psychiatric liaison service. *General Hospital Psychiatry, 4*, 131–137.

Craig, T.J., & Laska, E.M. (1983). Deinstitutionalization and the survival of the state hospital. *Hospital and Community Psychiatry, 34*, 616–622.

Cypress, B.K. (1978). *Office visits to psychiatrists: National Ambulatory Medical Care Survey, United States, 1975–76* (Advance Data from Vital & Health Statistics of the National Center for Health Statistics, No. 38). Washington, DC: Government Printing Office.

Deiker, T. (1986). How to ensure that the money follows the patient: A strategy for funding community services. *Hospital and Community Psychiatry, 37*, 256–260.

Department of Health and Human Services. Steering Committee on the Chronically Mentally Ill. (1980). *A national plan for the chronically mentally ill.* Washington, DC: Government Printing Office.

DeRisi, W., & Vega, W.A. (1983). The impact of deinstitutionalization on California's state hospital population. *Hospital and Community Psychiatry, 34*, 140–145.

Dittmar, N.D., & Franklin, J.L. (1980a). State hospital patients discharged to nursing homes: Are hospitals dumping their more difficult patients? *Hospital and Community Psychiatry, 31*, 251–254.

Dittmar, N.D., & Franklin, J.L. (1980b). State hospital patients discharged to nursing homes: How are they doing? *Hospital and Community Psychiatry, 31*, 255–258.

Eaton, W.W., Holzer, C.E., Von Korff, M., Anthony, J.C., Helzer, J.E., George, L., Burnam, M.A., Boyd, J.H., Kessler, L.G., & Locke, B.Z. (1984). The design of the epidemiologic catchment area surveys. *Archives of General Psychiatry, 41*, 942–948.

Elpers, J., & Crowell, G. (1982). How many beds? An overview of resource planning. *Hospital and Community Psychiatry, 33*, 755–761.

Estes, C.L., & Harrington, C.A. (1981). Fiscal crisis, deinstitutionalization, and the elderly. *American Behavioral Scientist, 24*, 811–826.

Fink, E.B. (1982). Encouraging third-party coverage of partial hospitals. *Hospital and Community Psychiatry, 33*, 38–41.

Flamm, G.H. (1981). General hospital psychiatry: Structure or concept? *General Hospital Psychiatry, 3*, 315–319.

Flemming, A.S., Buchanan, J.G., Santos, J.F., & Rickards, L.D. (1984a). *Mental health services for the elderly: Report on a survey of community mental health centers: Vol. 1.* Washington, DC: Action Committee to Implement the Mental Health Recommendations of the 1981 White House Conference on Aging.

Flemming, A.S., Buchanan, J.G., Santos, J.F., & Rickards, L.D. (1984b). *Mental health services for the elderly: Report on a survey of community mental health centers: Vol. 2.* Washington, DC: Action Committee to Implement the Mental Health Recommendations of the 1981 White House Conference on Aging.

Fox, J.W. (1984). Sex, marital status and age as social selection factors in recent psychiatric treatment. *Journal of Health and Social Behavior, 25*, 394–405.

Frank, R.G., & Kamlet, M.S. (1985). Direct costs and expenditures for mental health care in the United States in 1980. *Hospital and Community Psychiatry, 36*, 165–168.

General Accounting Office. (1982). *The elderly remain in need of mental health services* (Publication #GAO/HRD-82-112). Gaithersburg, MD: Author.

German, P.S., Shapiro, S., & Skinner, E.A. (1985). Mental health of the elderly. *Journal of the American Geriatrics Society, 33*, 246–252.

Ginsberg, A., & Goldstein, S. (1974). Age bias in referral for psychological consultation. *Journal of Gerontology, 29*, 410–415.

Goldberg, R.J., Wallace, S., Rothney, J., & Wartman, S. (1984). Medical clinic referrals to psychiatric social work: Review of 100 cases. *General Hospital Psychiatry, 6*, 147–152.

Goldman, H.H., Adams, N.H., & Taube, C.A. (1983). Deinstitutionalization: The data demythologized. *Hospital and Community Psychiatry, 34*, 129–134.

Goldman, H.H., Feder, J., & Scanlon, W. (1986). Chronic mental patients in nursing homes: Reexamining data from the National Nursing Home Survey. *Hospital and Community Psychiatry, 37*, 269–272.

Goldman, H.H., Pincus, H.A., Taube, C.A. & Regier, D.A. (1984). Prospective payment for psychiatric hospitalization: Questions and issues. *Hospital and Community Psychiatry, 35*, 460–464.

Goldman, H.H., Regier, D.A., Taube, C.A., Redick, R.W., & Bass, R.D. (1980). Community mental health centers and the treatment of severe mental disorder. *American Journal of Psychiatry, 137*, 83–86.

Goldman, H.H., Taube, C.A., Regier, D.A., & Witkin, M. (1983). The multiple functions of the state mental hospital. *American Journal of Psychiatry, 140*, 296–300.

Goodrick, D. (1984). *Survival of public inpatient mental health systems: Strategies for constructive change* (NASMHPD state report presented at the National Conference of State Legislatures program, "State Mental Hospitals: Their Future Role in the Wake of Deinstitutionalization," Boston, MA, July 25). Washington, DC: National Association of State Mental Health Program Directors.

Greenblatt, M., & Glazier, E. (1975). The phasing out of mental hospitals in the United States. *American Journal of Psychiatry, 132*, 1135–1140.

Gruenberg, E.M., & Archer, J. (1979). Abandonment of responsibility for the seriously mentally ill. *Milbank Memorial Fund Quarterly, 57*, 485–506.

Harrington, C.A., & Swan, J.H. (in press). State Medicaid nursing home policies, utilization, and expenditures. *Inquiry.*

Harris, M., Bergman, H.C., & Bachrach, L.L. (1986). Psychiatric and nonpsychiatric indicators for rehospitalization in a chronic patient population. *Hospital and Community Psychiatry, 37*, 630–631.

Held, M., Ransohoff, P.M., & Goehner, P. (1984). A comprehensive treatment program for severely impaired geriatric patients. *Hospital and Community Psychiatry, 35*, 156–160.

Hoffman, R.S. (1984). Operation of a medical-psychiatric unit in a general hospital setting. *General Hospital Psychiatry, 6*, 93–99.

Horgan, C.M. (1985). Specialty and general ambulatory mental health services. *Archives of General Psychiatry, 42*, 565–572.

Horgan, C.M. (1986). The demand for ambulatory mental health services from specialty providers. *Health Services Research, 21*, 291–318.

Johnson, C.L., & Grant, L.A. (1985). *The nursing home in American society.* Baltimore, MD: Johns Hopkins University Press.

Kaiser, J., & Townsend, E.J. (1981). A community support system's use of state hospitalization: Is it still necessary? *Hospital and Community Psychiatry, 32*, 625–628.

Kane, R.L., Jorgensen, L.A., Teteberg, B., & Kuwahara, J. (1976). Is good nursing home care feasible? *Journal of the American Medical Association, 235*, 516–519.

Keill, S.L. (1981). The general hospital as the core of the mental health services system. *Hospital and Community Psychiatry, 32*, 776–778.

Kiesler, C.A. (1982). Public and professional myths about mental hospitalization: An empirical reassessment of policy-related beliefs. *American Psychologist, 37*, 1323–1339.

Kiesler, C.A., & Sibulkin, A.E. (1983). Proportion of inpatient days for mental disorders: 1969–1978. *Hospital and Community Psychiatry, 34*, 606–611.

Kirk, S.A., & Therrien, M.E. (1975). Community mental health myths and the fate of former hospitalized patients. *Psychiatry, 38*, 209–217.

Knight, B. (1986). Therapists' attitudes as explanation of underservice of elderly in mental health: Testing an old hypothesis. *International Journal of Aging and Human Development, 22*, 261–269.

Koran, L.M. (1976). Mental health services in the public and private sectors. *American Journal of Psychiatry, 135*, 1052–1057.

Koran, L.M. (1981). Mental health services. In M.I. Roemer (Ed.), *Health care delivery in the United States* (pp. 235–271). New York: Springer.

Kramer, M., Taube, C.A., Redick, R.W. (1973). Patterns of use of psychiatric facilities by the aged: Past, present, and future. In C. Eisdorfer & M.P. Lawton (Eds.), *The psychology of adult development and aging*. Washington, DC: American Psychological Association.

Kruzich, J.M. (1986). The chronically mentally ill in nursing homes: Issues in policy and practice. *Health and Social Work, 11*, 5–14.

Kucharski, L.T., White, R.M., Schratz, M. (1979). Age bias, referral for psychological assistance and the private physician. *Journal of Gerontology, 34*, 423–428.

Lamb, H.R. (1981). What did we really expect from deinstitutionalization? *Hospital and Community Psychiatry, 32*, 105–109.

Lamb, H.R. (1982). *Treating the long-term mentally ill.* San Francisco, CA: Jossey-Bass.

Lamb, H.R. (1984). Deinstitutionalization and the homeless mentally ill. *Hospital and Community Psychiatry, 35*, 899–907.

Lawton, M.P., Lipton, M.B., Fulcomer, M.C., & Kleban, M.H. (1977). Planning for a mental hospital phasedown. *American Journal of Psychiatry, 134*, 1386–1390.

Lebray, P.R. (1979). Geropsychiatry in long-term care settings. *Professional Psychology, 10*, 475–484.

Leeman, C.P., Sederer, L.I., Rogoff, J., Berger, H.S., & Merrifield, J. (1981). Should general hospitals accept involuntary psychiatric patients? A panel discussion. *General Hospital Psychiatry, 3*, 245–253.

Lewinsohn, P.M., Teri, L., Hautzinger, M. (1984). Training clinical psychologists for work with older adults: A working model. *Professional Psychology, 15*, 187–202.

Lieff, J.D., & Brown, R.A. (1981). A psychogeriatric nursing home resocialization program. *Hospital and Community Psychiatry, 32*, 862–865.

Manderscheid, R.W., Witkin, M.J., Rosenstein, M.J., & Bass, R.D. (1984). A review of trends in mental health services. *Hospital and Community Psychiatry, 35*, 673–674.

Miller, M.B., & Elliott, D.F. (1976). Errors and omissions in diagnostic records on admission of patients to a nursing home. *Journal of the American Geriatrics Society, 24*, 108–116.

Miller, R.D. (1981). Beyond the old state hospital: New opportunities ahead. *Hospital and Community Psychiatry, 32*, 27–31.

Miller, R.D. (1985). Commitment to outpatient treatment: A national survey. *Hospital and Community Psychiatry, 36*, 265–267.

Morrissey, J.P., & Goldman, H.H. (1984). Cycles of reform in the care of the chronically mentally ill. *Hospital and Community Psychiatry, 35*, 785–793.

National Institute of Mental Health. (1984). *Distribution of psychiatric beds, United States and each state, 1982* (Mental Health Statistical Note No. 167). Rockville, MD: Author.

Okin, R.L. (1978). The future of state mental health programs for the chronic psychiatric patient in the community. *American Journal of Psychiatry, 135,* 1355–1358.

Okin, R.L. (1982). State hospitals in the 1980s. *Hospital and Community Psychiatry, 33,* 717–721.

Okin, R.L. (1983). The future of state hospitals: Should there be one? *American Journal of Psychiatry, 140,* 577–581.

Okin, R.L. (1984). How community mental health centers are coping. *Hospital and Community Psychiatry, 35,* 1118–1125.

Oktay, J., & Palley, H.A. (1982). Home health and in-home service programs for the chronically-limited elderly: Some equity and adequacy considerations. *Home Health Care Services Quarterly, 2*(4), 5–28.

Ozarin, L.D. (1976). Community alternatives to institutional care. *American Journal of Psychiatry, 133,* 69–72.

Pardes, H.E. (1981). Mental health–general health interaction: Opportunities and responsibilities. *Hospital and Community Psychiatry, 32,* 779–782.

Popkin, M.K., Mackenzie, T.B., & Callies, A.L. (1984). Psychiatric consultation to geriatric medically ill patients in a university hospital. *Archives of General Psychiatry, 41,* 703–707.

Portnoi, V.A., & Shriber, L.S. (1980). Management of the mental health of ambulatory elderly patients. *Journal of the American Geriatrics Society, 28,* 325–330.

Regier, D.A., Goldberg, I.D., & Taube, C.A. (1979). The de facto U.S. mental health services system. *Archives of General Psychiatry, 35,* 685–693.

Reich, R. (1973). Care of the chronically mentally ill—a national disgrace. *American Journal of Psychiatry, 130,* 911–912.

Rose, S.M. (1979). Deciphering deinstitutionalization: Complexities in policy and program analysis. *Milbank Memorial Fund Quarterly, 57,* 429–460.

Rovner, B.W., & Rabins, P.V. (1985). Mental illness among nursing home patients. *Hospital and Community Psychiatry, 36,* 119–128.

Rubin, J. (1981). The national plan for the chronically mentally ill: A review of financing proposals. *Hospital and Community Psychiatry, 32,* 704–713.

Rubin, J. (1982). Cost measurement and cost data in mental health settings. *Hospital and Community Psychiatry, 33,* 750–754.

Sabin, T.D., Vitug, A.J., & Mark, V.H. (1982). Are nursing home diagnosis and treatment inadequate? *Journal of the American Medical Association, 248,* 321–322.

Schmidt, L.J., Reinhardt, A.M., Kane, R.L., & Olsen, D.M. (1977). The mentally ill in nursing homes. *Archives of General Psychiatry, 34,* 687–691.

Schoonover, S.C., & Bassuk, E.L. (1983). Deinstitutionalization and the private general hospital inpatient unit: Implications for clinical care. *Hospital and Community Psychiatry, 34,* 135–139.

Schurman, R., Mitchell, J.B., & Kramer, P.D. (1984). *The hidden mental health network: Provision of mental health services by non-psychiatrist physicians* (ODAM Report No. 5-84). Rockville, MD: Department of Health and Human Services, Bureau of Health Professions, Office of Data Analysis and Management.

Selan, B.H., & Gold, C.A. (1980). The late life counseling service: A program for the elderly. *Hospital and Community Psychiatry, 31,* 403–406.

Shadish, W.R., & Bootzin, R.R. (1981). Nursing homes and chronic mental patients. *Schizophrenia Bulletin, 7*, 488–498.

Shapiro, S., Skinner, E.A., Kessler, L.G., Von Korff, M., German, P.S., Tischler, G.L., Leaf, P.J., Benham, L., Cottler, L., & Regier, D.A. (1984). Utilization of health and mental health services: Three epidemiological catchment area sites. *Archives of General Psychiatry, 41*, 971–978.

Sharfstein, S.S. (1978). Will community mental health survive in the 1980s? *American Journal of Psychiatry, 135*, 1363–1365.

Sharfstein, S.S. (1982). Medicaid cutbacks and block grants: Crisis or opportunity for community mental health? *American Journal of Psychiatry, 139*, 466–470.

Sharfstein, S.S., Frank, R.G., & Kessler, L.G. (1984). State Medicaid limitations for mental health services. *Hospital and Community Psychiatry, 35*, 213–215.

Sigel, G.S. (1984). In defense of state hospitals. *Hospital and Community Psychiatry, 35*, 1234–1236.

Smith, C.J. (1984). Geographic patterns of funding for community mental health centers. *Hospital and Community Psychiatry, 35*, 1133–1140.

Solomon, P., Gordon, B., & Davis, J.M. (1986). Reconceptualizing assumptions about community mental health. *Hospital and Community Psychiatry, 37*, 708–712.

Spiro, H.R. (1982). Reforming the state hospital in a unified care system. *Hospital and Community Psychiatry, 33*, 722–728.

Stotsky, B.A. (1967). A controlled study of factors in the successful adjustment of mental patients in nursing homes. *American Journal of Psychiatry, 124*, 1243–1251.

Stotsky, B.A. (1972). Social and clinical issues in geriatric psychiatry. *American Journal of Psychiatry, 129*, 117–126.

Stotsky, B.A., & Stotsky, E.S. (1983). Nursing homes: Improving a flawed community facility. *Hospital and Community Psychiatry, 34*, 238–242.

Stroul, B.A. (1986). *Models of community support services: Approaches to helping persons with long-term mental illness.* Boston, MA: Center for Psychiatric Rehabilitation, Boston University.

Swan, J.H. (1987). The substitution of nursing home for inpatient psychiatric care. *Community Mental Health Journal, 23*, 13–18.

Swan, J.H., & Bergthold, L. (1987). *Community mental health centers in a DRG environment* (Working Paper, DRG Impact Study). San Francisco, CA: Institute for Health & Aging, University of California.

Talbott, J.A. (1985). The fate of the public psychiatric system. *Hospital and Community Psychiatry, 36*, 46–50.

Taube, C.A., Thompson, J.W., Rosenstein, M.J., Rosen, B.M., & Goldman, H.H. (1983). The "chronic" mental hospital patient. *Hospital and Community Psychiatry, 34*, 611–615.

Teeter, R.B., Garetz, F.K., Miller, W.R., & Heiland, W.F. (1976). Psychiatric disturbances of aged patients in skilled nursing homes. *American Journal of Psychiatry, 133*, 1430–1434.

Tessler, R.C., Bernstein, A.G., Rosen, B.M. & Goldman, H.H. (1982). The chronically mentally ill in community support systems. *Hospital and Community Psychiatry, 33*, 208–211.

Thompson, J.W., Bass, R.D., & Witkin, M.J. (1982). Fifty years of psychiatric services: 1940–1990. *Hospital and Community Psychiatry, 33*, 711–717.

Toff, G.E., & Scallet, L.J. (1986). Report on issues of policy: The mentally ill in nursing homes (State Health Reports on Mental Health, Alcoholism, and Drug Abuse). Washington, DC: Intergovernmental Health Policy Project.

VanderBos, G.R., Stapp, J., & Kilburg, R.R. (1981). Health services providers in psychology. *American Psychologist, 36*, 1395–1418.

Wack, J., & Rodin, J. (1978). Nursing homes for the aged: The human consequences of legislation-shaped environments. *Journal of Social Issues, 34*(4), 6–21.

Wallen, J. (1985). *Use of short-term general hospitals by patients with psychiatric diagnoses* (Hospital Cost and Utilization Project, Research Note 8, Hospital Studies Program. DHHS Publication No. [PHS] 86-3395). Washington, DC: National Center for Health Services Research and Health Care Technology Assessment.

Wan, T.T.H., & Arling, G. (1983). Differential use of health services among disabled elderly. *Research on Aging, 5*, 411–431.

Wasson, W., Ripeckyj, A., Lazarus, L.W., Kupferer, S., Barry, S., & Force, F. (1984). Home evaluation of psychiatrically impaired elderly: Process and outcome. *Gerontologist, 24*, 238–242.

Wasylenki, D.A., Harrison, M.K., Britnell, J., & Hood, J. (1984). A community-based psychogeriatric service. *Journal of the American Geriatrics Society, 32*, 213–218.

Waxman, H.M., Carner, E.A., & Blum, A. (1983). Depressive symptoms and health service utilization among the community elderly. *Journal of the American Geriatrics Society, 31*, 417–420.

Waxman, H.M., Carner, E.A., & Klein, M. (1984). Underutilization of mental health professionals by community elderly. *Gerontologist, 24*, 23–30.

Waxman, H.M., Klein, M., & Carner, E.A. (1985). Drug misuse in nursing homes: An institutional addiction. *Hospital and Community Psychiatry, 36*, 886–887.

Weimer, S.R., & Fenn, H.H. (1982). Patient transfers from medical and surgical settings to psychiatric inpatient wards. *General Hospital Psychiatry, 4*, 179–185.

Weiner, R.S., Woy, J.R., Sharfstein, S.S., & Bass, R.D. (1979). Community mental health centers and the "seed money" concept: Effects of terminating federal funds. *Community Mental Health Journal, 15*, 129–138.

Weiss, K.J., & Dubin, W.R. (1982). Partial hospitalization: State of the art. *Hospital and Community Psychiatry, 33*, 923–928.

Wiener, J., Liu, K., & Scnieber, G. (1985, Nov. 19). *Case-mix differences between hospital-based and freestanding skilled nursing facilities: A review of the evidence.* Paper presented at the annual meeting of the American Public Health Association, Washington, DC.

Windle, C., & Scully, D. (1976). Community mental health centers and the decreasing use of state mental hospitals. *Community Mental Health Journal, 12*, 239–243.

5
Reimbursement and Funding Systems

James H. Swan
Lenore E. Gerard

Mental health care, like other health and social services, depends on funding. Policies established by government and private actors determine the size of mental health funding streams, and reimbursement systems channel the flow. In the United States, funding policies have often had unfortunate effects on the mental health system—generally favoring inpatient over outpatient care; direct over indirect services; medically oriented over psychologically oriented care; acute over chronic care; and more-restrictive over less-restrictive alternatives. The resulting system is fragmented, uncoordinated, inequitable, and incapable of implementing needed programs and services (Department of Health and Human Services [DHHS], 1980; Mechanic, 1978; Talbott, 1985).

Current fiscal restraints and cutbacks especially threaten the mental health system. Government initiatives such as block grants and deregulation have further fragmented an already uncoordinated mental health system (Beigel, 1982). Cutbacks also extend to private insurance benefits for mental health care (Sharfstein, Eist, Sack, Kaiser, & Shadoan, 1984).

Nongovernmental systems alone are unable to serve the mentally ill elderly. Many needed services are provided only as a result of government programs and would not be provided in the private sector without government intervention. Nongovernmental practices sometimes add to system problems. For example, proprietary providers have incentives to accept and retain only patients for whom they can expect adequate payment (Eisenberg, 1984; Sigel, 1984). Some providers, such as general hospitals, dump unprofitable patients onto public programs. While "skimming the cream" of reimbursable patients, such providers leave the more costly cases for government programs (Eisenberg, 1984; Goldman, Pincus, Taube, & Regier, 1984; Sigel, 1984). Private insurance avoids coverage of unprofitable conditions and people.

Government funding programs have been particularly important in shaping the mental health system (Katz & Cancro, 1982; Stotsky & Stotsky, 1983). Higher proportions of funding have come from government for mental health than for other forms of health care (Sharfstein, 1978a). High levels of government involvement stem from the reluctance of private insurers to cover mental health care (Hall, 1974; Sharfstein, 1978a); from the tendency to severely limit mental health benefits when coverage is offered; and from lack of private insurance coverage of lower-income populations (Muller & Schoenberg, 1974).

As noted in chapter 4, reimbursement programs, particularly those that funded alternate types of care, promoted deinstitutionalization from state mental hospitals and reinstitutionalization in nursing homes. These moves resulted in the substitution of federal for state funding. Nursing home costs were lower per diem than mental hospital care. However, longer average nursing home stays may keep such moves from being cost effective. Moreover, part of the per diem differential is based on the receipt by patients of less active treatment in nursing homes than in mental hospitals. It is clear, however, that states participated in the shift of aged patients to nursing homes in order to promote cost savings in their programs—federal match to state Medicaid payments was a strong incentive to switch from state-funded mental hospitals (Sharfstein, 1982). The question now is what is happening in mental health reimbursement in the wake of deinstitutionalization under current conditions of fiscal restraint and changes in reimbursement and provision systems.

Major Government Funding Programs

Federal reimbursement programs grew along with deinstitutionalization, as states attempted to shift the mental health funding burden onto the federal government (Goldman, Adams, & Taube, 1983). The provisions of federal programs have created problems for the mental health system, particularly fragmentation. Katz and Cancro note that "this situation has been perpetuated by reimbursement formulas that reward short-term inpatient treatment and penalize other services" (Katz & Cancro, 1982, p. 730). Much government support for mental health care involves reimbursement for care by nongovernmental providers, including community mental health centers (CMHCs) and other community providers (Koran, 1976).

An understanding of changes in government funding requires consideration of several major government programs. Most federal mental health programs are funded by Medicare and Medicaid, particularly the latter (Sharfstein, 1982). Other federal mental health support is derived from programs such as Supplemental Security Income (SSI), Social Security Disability Income (SSDI), community mental health, the Veterans Administration, social services, and the Civilian Health and Medical Program of the Uniformed Services (CHAMPUS) (Morrissey & Goldman, 1984; Rubin, 1981).

State governments vary greatly in their mental health funding. State support has traditionally centered on state mental hospitals, but state funding of other services has been substantial, amounting to 29 percent of the revenues administered through state departments of mental health (National Association of State Mental Health Directors [NASMHD], 1984, 1985). State funding in support of CMHCs has recently been increased (Smith, 1984). Local government has also been a major supporter of mental health care (Katz & Cancro, 1982). In total, state and local government account for about 83 percent of public mental health expenditures, compared to about 13 percent by the federal government (National Institute of Mental Health [NIMH], 1985).

Medicare

In 1981, only about 13 percent of federal mental health funding came from Medicare (NIMH, 1985). From the start, Medicare severely restricted its mental health coverage (Goldstein & Rice, 1971; Hall, 1974). Medicare has a 190-day lifetime limit on inpatient psychiatric care, 150 days for any one benefit period (Koran, 1981). However, Medicare has no such limitation on psychiatric care in general hospitals, the benefits being the same as for medical care. Even Medicare's more generous coverage of psychiatric care in general hospitals is now subject to restrictions and distortions due to diagnosis-related group (DRG) reimbursement to such hospitals. Agencies for the care and treatment of mental diseases are excluded from Medicare reimbursement for the delivery of posthospital skilled nursing facility (SNF) care (Scheffler, 1985).

Medicare restricts outpatient mental health services to $250 per patient per year, with a 50-percent coinsurance rate (DHHS, 1980), thereby making mental health care costly or unavailable to many, as well as "discouraging participation by psychiatrists in the treatment of patients in nursing homes or in clinics" (Stotsky & Stotsky, 1983, p. 241). Medicare requirements that mental health services be given under medical supervision exclude some types of providers and services (General Accounting Office [GAO], 1982). Freestanding CMHCs cannot receive direct Medicare reimbursement (Flemming, Buchanan, Santos, & Rickards, 1984). Agencies for the treatment of mental disease are also excluded from Medicare home health care reimbursement (Scheffler, 1985).

These restrictions reinforce the tendency of the aged to receive care for mental disorders from medical providers, often under medical diagnosis. Thus, most care for the mentally disordered aged is delivered by general hospitals and nursing homes.

Even though much of the care of the aged with mental disorders is provided in nursing homes, Medicare restrictions on nursing home care result in a very small proportion of such care being funded by the program. Nursing home coverage is restricted to SNF care following acute hospitalization, is limited to 100 days per episode, and is highly subject to disallowance of claims (Cohen, Holahan, & Liu, 1986). Medicare coverage of such care is threatened by the voluntary decertification of SNFs, a trend that is likely to accelerate in the future due to freezes on Medicare reimbursement rates and other cost containment measures (American Association of Homes for the Aged [AAHA] & American Health Care Association [AHCA], 1985).

Finally, Medicare always placed much of the burden on its beneficiaries in the form of coinsurance and copayment requirements. Recent changes in the Medicare program will place higher burdens on patients, making mental health care less accessible through Medicare (Katz & Cancro, 1982).

Medicaid

Medicaid has always been more generous than Medicare with regard to mental health benefits (Hall, 1974). By 1981 it accounted for about two-thirds of federal funding for mental health (NIMH, 1985). There are problems for the mental health system in Medicaid's policies, however. Medicaid reimbursement encourages institutionalization (Cohen et al., 1986; Estes & Harrington, 1981; Sharfstein, 1982; Stotsky & Stotsky, 1983). Higher spend-down levels for institutionalized than for noninstitutionalized patients, and policies regarding the determination of institutional versus noninstitutional medical expenses for spend-down purposes, impart a strong incentive to institutionalization under Medicaid (Cohen et al., 1986). Medicaid has funded the development of the nursing home industry as a substitute for state mental hospitals, especially for the aged (Gruenberg & Archer, 1979; Koran, 1981; Stotsky & Stotsky, 1983). Because Medicaid has paid for nearly half of all nursing home care in the United States, its policies continue to shape the industry (GAO, 1982).

Medicaid is a program with much state discretion, so that its coverage of mental health care, as well as nursing home care, is a patchwork of benefits, eligibility rules, service limits, and reimbursement policies (DHHS, 1980; Rubin, 1981). For example, CMHCs are covered by Medicaid in some states but not in others (GAO, 1982); and care in SNFs and intermediate care facilities (ICFs) for the care of mental diseases or in mental hospitals is a state option for coverage under Medicaid (Scheffler, 1985).

Medicaid money is not earmarked for psychiatric care. Stotsky and Stotsky note that "no analysis has ever indicated that mental health budgets in the 50 states have increased in proportion to the amount of Medicaid reimbursement" (Stotsky & Stotsky, 1983, p. 240).

Medicaid coverage was cut in the early 1980s, especially by new length-of-stay limits and by reimbursement rate limits for inpatient psychiatric care (Sharfstein, Frank, & Kessler, 1984). Such cuts throw the burden of caring for the indigent mentally ill back on state and local governments and limit the access of the poor to mental health care. In 1983 and 1984, however, there was some expansion of program eligibility, perhaps somewhat offsetting earlier cuts and putting an end to the earlier trend toward reduction (Intergovernmental Health Policy Project [IHPP] & National Governors' Association [NGA], 1984). Cuts in federal funding have negative effects on patients as well as on state governments. For example, Frank and Lave (1985) found that Medicare limits on days of inpatient psychiatric coverage per admission resulted in greater probability of transfers to state mental hospitals. Thus, in addition to leading to some reinstitutionalization, failure of federal programs to cover care clearly places greater burdens on state resources.

Supplemental Security Income

Supplemental Security Income (SSI) is a welfare program, important in that it often defines the mentally ill as disabled (DHHS, 1980; Rubin, 1981) and consequently funds many of the mentally ill. SSI eligibility also establishes a basis for Medicaid eligibility, although some states do not allow Medicaid eligibility to all SSI cash recipients (Newcomer, 1985). The aged are categorically eligible for SSI (they must also meet needs tests), but there is sometimes an advantage in becoming eligible on the basis of disability. Younger mentally ill persons are also eligible, so the categorically disabled are age-heterogeneous. In recent years, however, SSI disability reviews have excluded many from eligibility, thus denying income and linked benefits to many low-income, including mentally ill, people.

Reimbursement and Mode of Care Provision

Reimbursement, in shaping the mental health care system, has molded its components. Both the reimbursement systems and their effects differ by mode of provision. This section considers community mental health care, nursing home care, and inpatient hospital care.

Community Mental Health

Community mental health care has been molded by its funding. Federal funds encouraged the creation of a system of community mental health centers (CMHCs), although patterns of development differed according to state and local policy (Smith, 1984). Federal support originally took the form of "seed money" so that support dwindled over time, with negative implications for the ability of centers to serve those they had originally set out to serve (Morrissey & Goldman, 1984; Sharfstein, 1978b; Weiner, Woy, Sharfstein, & Bass, 1979). Some of the loss in federal support was made up by increases in third-party reimbursement (Weiner et al., 1979; Winslow, 1982), but limits in federal programs, particularly in Medicare, have now restricted such funding opportunities.

Recent cutbacks in federal support of CMHCs and the placing of their funding into the Alcohol, Drug Abuse, and Mental Health Services (ADMS) block grant (Okin, 1984) have further threatened community mental health care.

Centers may be faced with the choice of either emphasizing traditional mental health services to the exclusion of other services or retaining a full range of comprehensive community services, to the detriment of their resource bases (Woy, 1981). Centers have oriented care to the chronically and severely mentally ill (Jerrell & Larsen, 1985). Requirements that CMHCs provide services specific to the aged were dropped under the block grant; and centers that serve the elderly are more likely to have suffered under block grant funding (Flemming et al., 1984).

Any failure of community mental health to deal with the chronic mentally ill stemmed in part from divorcing federally funded CMHCs from state-funded, state-run mental health systems (Okin, 1978). Recently, block grants and the switch to state support have changed the focus of the CMHCs (Okin, 1984) and have established new mandates (Pardes, 1982). It is not clear, however, that these changes will improve the delivery of mental health care to the aged, particularly if new priorities create service competition between the aged and the chronically mentally ill (Roybal, 1984).

Nursing Homes

Funding of nursing home care for the aged follows different patterns than that for other types of care. Data from Waldo and Lazenby (1984) are illustrative. Medicaid paid for approximately 42 percent of nursing home expenditures in 1984, as compared to 5 percent of hospital expenditures and 2 percent of physician reimbursement. Little nursing home funding comes from Medicare (2 percent in 1984). Hospital (75 percent) and physician (58 percent) funding depend more heavily on Medicare than does nursing home payment on Medicaid. Other government sources provide only 4 percent of nursing home payment, so nursing home care is not as heavily government-dependent as are hospital and physician care; higher proportions of nursing home payments are made by the private sector. Because private insurance pays for only 1 percent of nursing home care, compared to 8 percent of hospital and 14 percent of physician costs, nursing home care is a heavy burden on the consumer. About 50 percent was paid out-of-pocket in 1984, compared to 3 percent of hospital and 26 percent of physician payments. Thus, as well as being more Medicaid-dependent and less Medicare-dependent, payment for nursing home care is a greater (and growing) burden on the consumer than are hospital and physician services. This is in spite of the increasing cost sharing required in the Medicare program for hospital, physician, and other services it reimburses.

Recent projections of total nursing home expenditures confirm the growing consumer burden. In 1983, a total of $28.8 billion was spent on nursing home care, of which half was paid directly by the consumer. The Health Care Financing Administration estimates that total spending for nursing home care will rise to $55.1 billion in 1990, and the proportion paid directly by the consumer will rise to 53 percent (Arnett, Cowell, Davidoff, & Freeland, 1985).

Inpatient Hospital Care

Mental hospitals owned by chains may be more expensive than nonprofit hospitals for a number of reasons: higher charges and collections; greater use of ancillaries; dumping and skimming to shift costs onto government and nonprofit providers; and not fairly sharing in the funding of professional education (Eisenberg, 1984). Private general hospital costs may appear lower than state hospital costs because the former accept only partial responsibility for patients, assuming that government will be responsible for the remainder of the care needed by patients, especially through state and local government hospitals (Sigel, 1984).

State Funding. State support has traditionally centered on state mental hospitals. The states have funded a substantial proportion of mental hospital care, approximately 66 percent of the revenues administered through state departments of mental health being used for this purpose (NASMHD, 1984). State mental hospitals still provide the majority of days of inpatient psychiatric care (Goldman et al., 1983; National Institute of Mental Health, 1984). Direct expenditure for state hospital mental health care was about $3.5 billion in 1980, about as large as the $3.6 billion for inpatient psychiatric care in general hospitals (Frank & Kamlet, 1985). Although deinstitutionalization may have saved state money that would otherwise have supported hospitalization (Rose, 1979), state mental hospital budgets have not necessarily been cut when numbers of beds have decreased (Gruenberg & Archer, 1979).

Medicare Coverage. Medicare does not have generous inpatient psychiatric coverage. Coinsurance and copayment provisions exacerbate the problem. Its severe limits on inpatient psychiatric care, combined with the lack of such limits on medical care, constitute a major reason that a large proportion of mental health care for the aged is delivered in general hospitals (Koran, 1981; Stotsky & Stotsky, 1983).

Medicare mental health coverage in general hospitals also leaves much to be desired. Those patients already in psychiatric hospitals when they become eligible for Medicare have reduced eligibility for mental health care even in general hospitals (Scheffler, 1985).

Further, Medicare prospective payment to general hospitals is less suited to mental than to medical care (Goldman et al., 1984; Morrissey & Goldman, 1984; Taube, Lee, & Forthofer, 1984; Widem, Pincus, Godman, & Jencks, 1984). The 15 psychiatric DRGs do not predict utilization well (Taube et al., 1984) and put hospitals at greater financial risk. Psychiatric diagnoses may nevertheless be favored in some cases because the lengths of stay under psychiatric DRGs are fairly long and because many hospitals have waivers for their psychiatric units.

The use of DRG reimbursement limits the ability to admit patients for diagnostic procedures when medical conditions are suspected to underlie behavioral problems. The DRG approach may not be appropriate to psychiatry, especially insofar as psychiatric length of stay is a function of symptomatology, ability to function, and social supports, rather than of diagnosis (see Mezzich & Coffman, 1985). Finally, Medicare may not adequately reimburse care under medical DRGs for patients with secondary psychiatric diagnoses when the latter increase costs and necessary lengths of stay; and psychiatric DRGs might not adequately reimburse for necessary medical treatment.

General hospitals can apply for the exemption of their psychiatric wards from DRG reimbursement, but they are not always given such waivers (Taube et al., 1984), in part because of the requirement that these psychiatric units meet the same conditions for Medicare participation as do psychiatric hospitals (Taube et al., 1984). This requirement may be inappropriate, because of the varied functions and case mixes served by general hospital units (Spiro, 1982). Further, much psychiatric inpatient care in general hospitals (the great majority as late as 1978) takes place outside of designated psychiatric inpatient units (Bachrach, 1981), and so is subject to DRG reimbursement.

Medicaid Coverage. Reimbursement for inpatient psychiatric care for the aged is small in comparison to nursing home payments. Total inpatient care in institutions for mental disease (including both mental hospitals and psychiatric nursing homes) under Medicaid accounted for 3 percent of 1983 Medicaid program expenditures (Doty, Liu, & Weiner, 1985), an amount only one-twentieth the size of Medicaid nonpsychiatric nursing home payments.

Some states have covered care for large numbers of the mentally ill under Medicaid nursing home coverage. The federal government has, however, maintained a strict exclusion of Medicaid nursing home funding to facilities that primarily treat those with mental diseases (institutions of mental disease or IMDs), arguing that such care is a state responsibility. This disallowance has been upheld by the courts, particularly the Supreme Court in Connecticut v. Heckler (1985). States may optionally cover care to those aged 65 and older, and those under age 21, in IMDs. However, some states do not allow such coverage at all, and in no state do Medicaid expenditures for IMD care begin to approach those for nursing home care.

In California, extra Medicaid reimbursement is allowed for psychiatric treatment in a locked skilled nursing facility (L-SNF), a nursing home with locked wards. This supplement is added to the SNF rate, providing higher payment for certified patients. This supplement is not allowed for those determined to be chronic patients, however; and the state has rigorously monitored cases to determine whether they should be ruled chronic and made ineligible for the special funding. Locked SNFs have an incentive to discharge patients decertified for the special funding, in order to free beds for eligible (that is, higher reimbursement) patients. Thus, the L-SNF cannot promise long-term placement for the chronic patient, as did the old state mental hospital.

In California, counties may use state-source mental health funding to provide subacute psychiatric day treatment in L-SNFs. Such funding is an add-on to, and can amount to twice, the Medicaid per diem rate. This funding is reserved for treatable patients judged to have the possibility of rehabilitation. Such funding may help prevent some patients from becoming, but does not directly aid those who are, chronic patients.

Private Health Insurance

Most private health insurance in the United States is acquired indirectly as an employment-related benefit, rather than directly from a private health insurance carrier (Cafferata, 1984; Dicker, 1983; Farley, 1985). Because the majority of the aged are retired, employment-related coverage is less likely, although there is some evidence that as many as 30 percent of retirees in the mid-1970s had the option of continuing their private group plan insurance (Skolnick, 1976). Whether current retirees still have this option, and if so, whether they can afford to continue a work-based plan, is not known.

The share of personal health expenditures paid by private insurance has increased as a percentage of nongovernmental payments, from 44 percent in 1977 to 52 percent in 1984 (Gibson, 1979; Levit, Lazenby, Waldo, & Davidoff, 1985). Private insurance paid $2.9 billion in 1977 for health services used by the noninstitutionalized elderly (Cafferata, 1984).

Coverage of Mental Health Conditions

There are substantial differences in coverage for mental health conditions as compared to general medical conditions. Recent national survey data indicate that private insurance for mental health conditions "was typically more restrictive than for general medical conditions. Not only were mental health conditions sometimes specifically excluded, but even where coverage was provided, it often stipulated lower benefits than for general medical care" (Farley, 1986, p. 16).

Farley's data show that private health insurance benefits are distributed differently for adults aged 25 to 54 than for those aged 55 to 64. The latter age group is more likely to hold nongroup insurance and the associated lower level of service coverage and benefits. This is attributed to the declining rates of employment and the relatively large proportion of nonworking women. As a result, this age group tends to have fewer benefits for most types of services, including mental health care, as well as less generous inpatient mental health benefits (Farley, 1986).

The expanded role of short-term general hospitals in the delivery of psychiatric inpatient care in the past several decades is largely due to the increased coverage of inpatient care for acute psychiatric episodes by many commercial carriers and Blue Cross (Wallen, 1985). Some have noted, however, that private-insurance mental health coverage is still quite limited even for the working population; little more than half of those under age 65 with private insurance have such coverage (Sharfstein, Eist, Sack, Kaiser, & Shandoan, 1984).

For the retired population 65 years of age or older, private insurance is even less likely to be available for psychiatric care. Due to superannuation policies and retirement decisions, most of the aged do not have the option of obtaining coverage for psychiatric care through the employment-related insurance system. Further, for an individual diagnosed as chronically mentally ill, it is very unlikely that there is any opportunity for private insurance.

Over the past decade, the private sector has developed the "Medi-gap" market to supplement Medicare benefits. In 1980, nearly 16 million elderly Medicare beneficiaries had at least one supplemental policy (Garfinkel & Terrell, 1983). Most of this market is directed to supplemental coverage for hospital and in-hospital physician services. Most supplemental policies do not pay for nursing home care, homemaking services, prescription drugs, eyeglasses, or dental services (McCall, Rice, & Hall, 1983). Given the limitations of the Medi-gap market, it is unlikely that mental health or psychiatric services are often included. Moreover, unfair trade practices, fraud, and the inadequacy of the Medi-gap private insurance market have been sources of concern for consumers and state and federal policymakers.

Schlesinger, Mumford, Glass, Patrick, and Sharfstein (1983) present data suggesting that greater numbers of mental health visits for patients with chronic medical conditions lead to lower subsequent overall costs through the reduction of subsequent inpatient costs. They interpret this to suggest that the allowance of unlimited mental health visits might reduce insurer net costs despite the increased costs of mental health treatment for some types of insurees.

Health Maintenance Organizations

In addition to traditional third-party insurance plans, health maintenance organizations (HMOs) have been promoted as a less costly alternative to fee-for-service arrangements. Most HMOs provide mental health coverage, often because of state and federal requirements (Lubotsky & Glasser, 1980). As with other insurance coverage, mental health visits under HMOs appear to decrease the subsequent costs for other services (Goldensohn & Fink, 1979).

In today's changing policy environment, however, the question of coverage for mental health and psychiatric care in private and federally funded HMOs is unsettled. Federal requirements that HMOs include short-term outpatient services are limited. Moreover, there is considerable doubt as to the adequacy of these HMO plans, their coverage tending to be limited in terms of inpatient days (about 30 per year) and outpatient visits (about 20 per year) (Lubotsky & Glasser, 1980). Talbott and Sharfstein observed that "to date, health maintenance organizations (HMOs) have not delivered adequate treatment and care for the severely or chronically mentally ill" (Talbott & Sharfstein, 1986, p. 1128).

Coverage of Care in Nursing Homes

Because nursing homes are the single largest source of care for the mentally ill (Intergovernment Health Policy Project [IHPP], 1986), and large numbers of mentally ill elderly are resident in nursing homes, private insurance in long term care is potentially important. However, insurance companies have been resistant to providing long term care insurance, and the little coverage that exists often excludes care resulting from mental illness (Cohen et al., 1986). Currently, private long term care insurance is the source of payment for only 1 percent of total nursing home expenditures in the United States (Cohen et al, 1986).

Recent national survey data indicate that in "contrast to the almost universal and generally comprehensive coverage of hospital inpatient stays, benefits for care in skilled nursing facilities (SNFs) were available to only 48.7 percent of the privately insured" (Farley, 1986, p. 12). Many elderly are not covered beyond Medicare's benefits for skilled nursing facilities—only 40 percent of Medicare beneficiaries had private insurance coverage for such care in 1977 (Cafferata, 1985). Of these, only 16 percent were fully covered for up to a year, although such coverage was higher among older beneficiaries (about 19 percent among those aged 75 or over). This coverage was particularly low among those with low income (about 9 percent covered). Thus, most were not covered, and those most in need of coverage were even less likely to have it.

Although some sectors of the private insurance industry have begun to offer long term care insurance, the benefit package is quite restrictive in terms of eligibility and coverage. More importantly, the policy debate with regard to the need for long term care insurance is framed predominantly in terms of reimbursement for medical, not mental, conditions. The exclusion of mental health coverage from private long term care insurance plans leaves the responsibility to the public sector, more by default than design. A recent study analyzing financing of long term care for the mentally ill concluded that the "characteristics of existing policies indicate that private insurance is currently not a major mechanism for financing the long term care requirements of people with mental health problems" (Cohen et al., 1986, p. 46). This omission assures the reinforcement of the existing tendency of the mental disorders of the aged to receive physical health diagnoses, and of the aged with mental disorders to receive care from medical providers.

Cost Containment

Several approaches have been tried to cut the costs of mental health care to government as well as to private payers. Historically, deinstitutionalization is the best-known and most far-reaching of these initiatives. In the current political and fiscal environment, however, cost containment is emphasized to a much greater extent than in the past; and this promises to continue for the foreseeable future. Mental health cost constraint takes various forms: deinstitutionalization (Gruenberg & Archer, 1979); implementation of new reimbursement methods (Morrissey & Goldman, 1984); replacing grants-in-aid with block grants (Beigel, 1982; Estes & Wood, 1984; Okin, 1984); and contracting out services and management (Held, Ransohoff, & Goehner, 1984; Levenson, 1983).

Whether or not recent changes constrain costs, they may have negative implications for the mentally ill (Estes & Wood, 1984; Gruenberg & Archer, 1979; Rose, 1979). Reimbursement changes aimed solely at cost containment present clear dangers to the adequacy of mental health care (Talbott, 1985).

Cutbacks

The care that has been financed through both public and private sources is itself at risk of severe limitation and cutback. Restraints and cutbacks result from general economic and political developments, in addition to responses to rapid increases in health care costs (Estes, Gerard, Zones, & Swan, 1984), including the costs of mental health care (Rose, 1979; Thompson, Bass, & Witkin, 1982). Cuts in government reimbursement programs threaten a return to a two-tiered system of care in which poor patients are treated in state mental hospitals or not at all (Sharfstein, Frank, & Kessler, 1984).

Deinstitutionalization

The deinstitutionalization from state mental hospitals is now largely a historical initiative, although still occurring to some extent in a few states. As noted above, deinstitutionalization may or may not have reduced state funding of mental health care. In any case, the changes have placed increasing budget power in the hands of the federal government, thus making mental health care increasingly vulnerable to cutbacks at the federal level (Rose, 1979). The changes may also have meant that states have failed to continue fulfilling their responsibilities to the mentally ill, in effect dumping the mentally ill onto federal programs and/or from state mental health systems to state social welfare systems (Gruenberg & Archer, 1979).

Use of Low-Cost Alternatives

Presumed low-cost alternatives may not prove cost-effective (Arnhoff, 1975; GAO, 1982; Koran, 1981; Mattes, 1982). Mattes (1982) points out that the lower costs of some alternative mental health care initiatives may derive largely from such factors as staff initiative and enthusiasm, which may wane over time, resulting in less efficiency and higher costs.

There is some evidence that alternative mental health programs have lower costs than institutionalization. In a secondary analysis of data from 10 experimental studies, Kiesler (1982) found alternate care programs to be less costly and consistently as good as or better than mental hospital care. Test and Stein (1980) found that such factors as the burden on the family, arrests, suicide attempts, and use of emergency rooms were not higher under an alternative to mental hospitalization. Benefits were judged to outweigh costs, and patients tended to show more improvement in the alternative program (Weisbrod, Test, & Stein, 1980). Bond (1984) reported results of one study and secondary data analysis from two others showing psychosocial rehabilitation in the community to result in lower costs than did mental hospitalization, taking into account all costs of care, rehospitalization, and earnings. Deiker (1986) found not only that community residential care had substantially lower costs than hospitalization, but that the transition from hospital to residential care could be managed within the resources that would otherwise have been expended for further hospitalization. Such findings offer evidence that some alternatives to institutionalization are effective, are cost-efficient, and may not have higher associated indirect societal costs.

Home care appears to be less costly than nursing home care, except in cases of severe disability (Comptroller General, 1977). Some (Gaumer et al., 1986; Pegels, 1980) report evidence that institutionalization can be prevented or delayed by in-home care. It is not clear, however, that increased use of in-home care results in savings to government, especially if control is not maintained over service expansion (Pegels, 1980). Mundinger (1983) notes that home care poses reimbursement risks not encountered with institutional care in that, once certified for Medicare reimbursement, home health agencies can rapidly expand services by hiring new personnel. Thus, home health costs may escalate more rapidly than institutional expenditures.

Sharfstein, Taube, and Goldberg (1977) note the difficulty of comparing private- to public-sector costs because of differences in reporting, case mixes, staffing, reliance on varied provider settings (so that costs are spread among different providers), and therapy modality. Nevertheless, Sharfstein and associates conclude that "certainly there is nothing in the data we have presented to suggest that the per-patient cost in private practice is less than that in CMHCs; indeed, one might be tempted to conclude that if anything the reverse is true" (Sharfstein et al., 1977, p. 31).

Cost comparisons are also difficult across service and facility types. Different providers deal with different case mixes and with different problems through different modalities (Sharfstein et al., 1977). Thus, presumed low-cost alternatives may not be cost-effective, and it is hard to show that they are (Arnhoff, 1975; Koran, 1981; Mattes, 1982; Weissert, Wan, & Livieratos, 1980).

The use of low-cost alternatives also may not reduce use of nor expenditure for high-cost alternatives (Kirk & Therrien, 1975; Okin, 1978). State hospital costs increased in the wake of deinstitutionalization (Okin, 1978). New alternatives sometimes create new demand among those who have not been served by older systems (Kirk & Therrien, 1975; Thompson et al., 1982). Moreover, higher-cost short-term treatment may be more cost-effective than lower-unit-cost long term care (Elpers & Crowell, 1982). Despite valid arguments that new systems and services for a new clientele are in themselves beneficial, such outcomes do not constitute cost constraint.

Changes in Reimbursement Methods

Changes in reimbursement systems are often justified as reforms that eliminate waste. The essence of such changes is, however, the reduction of costs, whether from the elimination of waste or of needed services. Of particular importance have been the development and implementation of methods of prospective reimbursement.

Prospective reimbursement is clearly the chosen means of cost containment in government programs. The Social Security Amendments of 1983 established prospective reimbursement for inpatient hospital services based on 467 diagnosis-related groups (DRGs). Patients are classified into groups based on their diagnoses (International Classification of Diseases [ICD] codes)—"the presence of a surgical procedure, patient age, presence or absence of significant comorbidities or complications, and other relevant criteria" (Office of Technology Assessment [OTA], 1985, p. B-1). At present, DRGs are based in part on hospital-specific and area-specific factors, but the plan is to move to a national rate system.

Of the 467 DRGs, 15 are mental health DRGs (Taube et al., 1984). The mental health DRGs apply only to general hospital inpatients who are in nonpsychiatric units or psychiatric units that are not exempted from DRG reimbursement.

Medicare DRGs raise a number of issues of adequacy of care (see also chapter 4). The use of DRGs has apparently lowered the average length of stay in acute hospitals, but concern has been raised that this has resulted in the shifting of cost and illness burdens to posthospital long term care service systems (Chelimsky, 1985). Premature hospital discharges may return patients to the community in poorer health, creating greater demands on community care systems, inappropriate placements, denial of needed benefits and coverage, and increases in postdischarge care costs (Chelimsky, 1985; Lave, 1985; Rupp, Steinwachs, & Salkever, 1984). Reimbursement using a DRG system may be inevitable for mental health, but if so, a number of issues will have to be confronted, including a better system of dealing with outliers; accounting for the costs of special psychiatric treatments; allowing for different treatment practices outside the psychiatric unit that affect the types of patients and costs inside the unit; and a more adequate approach to the chronically mentally ill, perhaps involving capitation programs (Jencks, Goldman, & McGuire, 1985). One approach would be to incorporate a rating of severity of illness into the classification methods of a DRG system (Mezzich & Sharfstein, 1985).

Prospective payment has also become the rule in Medicaid nursing home reimbursement. Despite state policy discretion, there is a national trend: by 1986 only 5 states retained retrospective reimbursement for skilled nursing facilities (SNFs), down from 18 in 1978; only 3 of these states paid intermediate care facilities (ICFs) retrospectively, compared to 14 in 1978 (Swan, Fox, & Estes, 1986). Of 45 states with some form of prospective SNF reimbursement in 1986, 28 had facility-specific methods, which pay prospectively but at rates based on facility costs. Six states had class-based systems, whereby rates are set for groups of facilities. And 11 states had combination systems that set rates in advance but routinely allowed upward adjustments afterward based on costs. Prospective nursing home reimbursement has been shown to lead to both lower increases in Medicaid reimbursement rates and to constraints on Medicaid nursing home expenditures (Harrington & Swan, in press).

Many states are adopting prospective Medicaid payment for hospitals, some based on DRG methods (IHPP & NGA, 1984). Some states are experimenting with prospective reimbursement for other services, including home health. Current Medicaid home health reimbursement methods vary: Medicare principle; Medicare principle with cap; maximum allowance schedule; fee-for-service; fee schedule; flat rate; and varied prospective systems based on negotiated fees, agency-specific rates determined by formula, determinations by rate-setting commissions, or state government rate determinations (Williams, Kominski, Down, & Soper, 1984). Various prospective systems have been proposed for home health: capitation, payment by episode of care, by episode by type of patient, by month, and per visit by type of visit.

Cost Constraint in Perspective

Whether a given approach to payment, such as prospective reimbursement, contains costs is a complex issue. The scope of the examination of costs is particularly important—costs to whom, and what types of costs. Although such approaches as prospective reimbursement appear to constrain specific program costs (Harrington & Swan, 1984; Kirk & Therrien, 1975; Rupp et al., 1984; Widem et al., 1984), the calculation of overall costs to individuals, to government, and to society as a whole is far more complicated (Gruenberg & Archer, 1979; Kirk & Therrien, 1975; Morrissey & Goldman, 1984; Rice, Hodgson, & Kopstein, 1985; Rose, 1979; Weisbrod et al., 1980; Winslow, 1982). Schlesinger, Dorwart, and Pulice (1986) report that competitive contracting for mental health care by a state government resulted in lower quality and higher costs.

No policy is going to greatly cut costs while simultaneously improving care and/or quality of life. Gruenberg and Archer argue that neither purpose has been served: "When mental health policy makers compete with budget directors to hold down governmental costs, we get patient abandonment, not cost savings" (Gruenberg & Archer, 1979, p. 502).

Policy Implications

Changes in Medicaid reimbursement for nursing homes will likely occur. Although most states have already switched to prospective reimbursement methodology for Medicaid, there are many differences among such systems. A likely future change is the adoption of reimbursement systems based on case mix—an alternative being studied, for example, in Connecticut (IHPP & NGA, 1984). There is increasing allowance of Medicaid SNF reimbursement for hospital swing beds when patients are awaiting SNF placement, as well as reimbursement of SNF care in hospitals in locations where no SNF facilities are available (see IHPP & NGA, 1984). This is important to psychiatric patients, who are particularly difficult for hospitals to place in nursing homes.

Of great potential for the care of the mentally ill would be the allowance of Medicaid coverage for psychiatric services delivered in SNFs. The California use of state mental health monies to fund psychiatric adult day care in SNFs might be emulated. It is not clear, however, whether many states will extend Medicaid coverage of care in SNFs and ICFs for mental disease.

Unified Funding Streams

The fragmented nature of mental health funding for the aged and others has often been noted and various calls made for uniform funding. The frequency and futility of such calls do not undermine their validity. A start might be made within the state—for example, coordination between the mental health agency and the Medicaid agency regarding Medicaid reimbursement of psychiatric services. The ultimate response must, however, be at the federal level, particularly in federal reimbursement programs.

Conclusions

Trends in mental health care have fragmented mental health systems, and have proven contradictory: the rapid growth of community mental health and its current cutback, and changes; deinstitutionalization and the possible reinstitutionalization of mental health care; the growth of large federal payment programs and the current cutbacks; and the movement of the aged with mental disorders into nursing homes coupled with current concern about nursing home costs. Although the community mental health movement had clear goals and some specification of methods, these trends toward fragmentation were for the most part unpredicted; they largely resulted from concerns other than community mental health movement concerns (for example, cost constraint); and were by and large unintended consequences of policy. Current changes are likely to create further unintended and unplanned consequences for mental health. Even without further cuts to the mental health system, there is currently little chance at the federal or state level to introduce any new approaches entailing new funding.

Adequate mental health services for the aged will require changes in reimbursement systems as well as greater resources. Changes currently transpiring involve not only cuts in funding but also many changes in reimbursement that are detrimental to the aged. The provision of adequate mental health care for the elderly will require not only changes in funding streams, but in many cases, a reversal of the current direction of flow.

References

American Association of Homes for the Aged & American Health Care Association (AAHA & AHCA). (1985). *Data prepared for House Select Committee on Aging on the impact of cost containment on access to skilled nursing facility services.* Washington, DC: Author.

Arnett, R.H., Cowell, C.S., Davidoff, L.M., Freeland, M.S. (1985). Health spending trends in the 1980s: Adjusting to financial incentives. *Health Care Financing Review, 6*(3), 1–26.

Arnhoff, F.N. (1975). Social consequences of policy toward mental illness. *Science, 188,* 1277–1281.

Bachrach, L.L. (1981). The effects of deinstitutionalization on general hospital psychiatry. *Hospital and Community Psychiatry, 32,* 786–790.

Beigel, A. (1982). Community mental health centers: A look ahead. *Hospital and Community Psychiatry, 33,* 741–745.

Bond, G.R. (1984). An economic analysis of psychosocial rehabilitation. *Hospital and Community Psychiatry, 35,* 356–362.

Cafferata, G.L. (1984). *Private health insurance coverage of the Medicare population* (NCHSR Data Preview No. 18). Baltimore, MD: National Center for Health Services Research.

Cafferata, G.L. (1985). The elderly's private insurance coverage of nursing home care. *American Journal of Public Health, 75,* 655–656.

Chelimsky, E. (1985). *Evaluating the effects of Medicare prospective payment on post-hospital care* (General Accounting Office, Program Evaluation and Methodology Division, report to the United States Senate Special Committee on Aging, November 12). Washington, DC: General Accounting Office.

Cohen, J., Holahan, J., & Liu, K. (1986). *Financing long-term care for the mentally ill: Issues and options.* Washington, DC: Urban Institute.

Comptroller General. (1977). *Home health—the need for a national policy to better provide for the elderly: Report to the Congress* (HRD-78-19). Washington, DC: General Accounting Office.

Connecticut Department of Income Maintenance v. Margaret M. Heckler, Department of Health and Human Services, 105S.Ct. 2210 (1985).

Deiker, T. (1986). How to ensure that the money follows the patient: A strategy for funding community services. *Hospital and Community Psychiatry, 37,* 256–260.

Department of Health and Human Services (DHHS). Steering Committee on the Chronically Mentally Ill. (1980). *Toward a national plan for the chronically mentally ill.* Washington, DC: Government Printing Office.

Dicker, M. (1983). Health care coverage and insurance premiums of families: United States, 1980 (NCHS Preliminary Data Report No. 3). Baltimore, MD: National Center for Health Statistics.

Doty, P., Liu, K., & Weiner, J. (1985). An overview of long-term care. *Health Care Financing Review, 6*(3), 69–78.

Eisenberg, L. (1984). The case against for-profit hospitals. *Hospital and Community Psychiatry, 35,* 1009–1013.

Elpers, J., & Crowell, G. (1982). How many beds? An overview of resource planning. *Hospital and Community Psychiatry, 33,* 755–761.

Estes, C., Gerard, L.E., Zones, J.S., & Swan, J.H. (1984). *Political economy, health, and aging.* Boston, MA: Little, Brown.

Estes, C.L., Harrington, C. (1981). Fiscal crisis, deinstitutionalization, and the elderly. *American Behavioral Scientist, 24,* 811–826.

Estes, C.L., & Wood, J. (1984). A preliminary assessment of the impact of block grants on community mental health centers. *Hospital and Community Psychiatry, 35,* 1125–1129.

Farley, P.J. (1985). *Private insurance and public programs: Coverage of health services* (NCHSR Data Preview No. 20). Baltimore, MD: National Center for Health Services Research.

Farley, P.J. (1986). *Private health insurance in the United States* (NCHSR Data Preview No. 23). Baltimore, MD: National Center for Health Services Research.

Flemming, A.S., Buchanan, J.G., Santos, J.F., & Rickards, L.D. (1984). *Mental health services for the elderly: Report on a survey of community mental health centers: Vol. 1.* Washington, DC: Action Committee to Implement the Mental Health Recommendations of the 1981 White House Conference on Aging.

Frank, R.G., & Kamlet, M.S. (1985). Direct costs and expenditures for mental health care in the United States in 1980. *Hospital and Community Psychiatry, 36,* 165–168.

Frank, R.G., & Lave, J.R. (1985). The impact of Medicaid benefit design on length of hospital stay and patient transfers. *Hospital and Community Psychiatry, 36* 749–753.

Garfinkel, S., & Terrell, S. (1983). *The use of private insurance plans by the aged Medicare population.* Baltimore, MD: Health Care Financing Administration.

Gaumer, G.L., Birnbaum, H., Pratter, F., Burke, R., Franklin, S., & Ellington-Otto, K. (1986). Impact of the New York long-term home health care program. *Medical Care, 24,* 641–653.

General Accounting Office (GAO). (1982). *The elderly remain in need of mental health services* (Publication No. GAO/HRD-82-112). Gaithersburg, MD: Author.

Gibson, R.M. (1979). National health expenditures, 1978. *Health Care Financing Review, 1*(1), 1–34.

Goldensohn, S.S., & Fink, R. (1979). Mental health services for Medicaid enrollees in a prepaid group practice plan. *American Journal of Psychiatry, 136*, 160–164.

Goldman, H.H., Adams, N.H., & Taube, C.A. (1983). Deinstitutionalization: The data demythologized. *Hospital and Community Psychiatry, 34*, 129–134.

Goldman, H.H., Pincus, H.A., Taube, C.A., & Regier, D.A. (1984). Prospective payment for psychiatric hospitalization: Questions and issues. *Hospital and Community Psychiatry, 35*, 460–464.

Goldstein, M., & Rice, D.P. (1971). *Financing mental health care under Medicare and Medicaid* (DHEW Research Report No. 37). Washington, DC: Government Printing Office.

Gruenberg, E.M., & Archer, J. (1979). Abandonment of responsibility for the seriously mentally ill. *Milbank Memorial Fund Quarterly, 57*, 485–506.

Hall, C.P. (1974). Financing mental health services through insurance. *American Journal of Psychiatry, 131*, 1079–1088.

Harrington, C., & Swan, J.H. (1984). Medicaid nursing home reimbursement policies, rates, and expenditures. *Health Care Financing Review, 6*(1), 39–49.

Harrington, C., & Swan, J.H. (in press). State Medicaid nursing home policies, utilization, and expenditures. *Inquiry*.

Held, M., Ransohoff, P.M., & Goehner, P. (1984). A comprehensive treatment program for severely impaired geriatric patients. *Hospital and Community Psychiatry, 35*, 156–160.

Intergovernmental Health Policy Project (IHPP). (1986). Report on issues of policy: The mentally ill in nursing homes. *State Health Reports* (25), 1–14.

Intergovernmental Health Policy Project (IHPP) & National Governors' Association (NGA). (1984). *Recent and proposed changes in state Medicaid programs: A fifty state survey.* Washington, DC: Author.

Jencks, S.F., Goldman, H.H., & McGuire, T.G. (1985). Challenges in bringing exempt psychiatric services under a prospective payment system. *Hospital and Community Psychiatry, 36*, 764–769.

Jerrell, J.M., & Larsen, J.K. (1985). How community mental health centers deal with cutbacks and competition. *Hospital and Community Psychiatry, 36*, 1169–1174.

Katz, S.E., & Cancro, R. (1982). The metamorphosis of the county psychiatric service. *Hospital and Community Psychiatry, 33*, 728–731.

Kiesler, C.A. (1982). Public and professional myths about mental hospitalization: An empirical reassessment of policy-related beliefs. *American Psychologist, 37*, 1323–1339.

Kirk, S.A., & Therrien, M.E. (1975). Community mental health myths and the fate of former hospitalized patients. *Psychiatry, 38*, 209–217.

Koran, L.M. (1976). Mental health services in the public and private sectors. *American Journal of Psychiatry, 135*, 1052–1057.

Koran, L.M. (1981). Mental health services. In M.I. Roemer (Ed.), *Health care delivery in the United States* (pp. 235–271). New York: Springer.

Lave, J.R. (1985). Prospective payment—how will it affect hospital quality of care? *Generations, 9*(4), 19–22.

Levenson, A.I. (1983). Issues surrounding the ownership of private psychiatric hospitals by investor-owned hospital chains. *Hospital and Community Psychiatry, 34,* 1127–1131.

Levit, K.R., Lazenby, H., Waldo, D.R., & Davidoff, L.M. (1985). National health expenditures, 1984. *Health Care Financing Review, 7*(1), 1–36.

Lubotsky, B., Glasser, J.H. (1980). Mental health coverage within prepaid health plans. *Administration in Mental Health, 7,* 271–281.

Mattes, J.A. (1982). The optimal length of hospitalization for psychiatric patients: A review of the literature. *Hospital and Community Psychiatry, 33,* 824–828.

McCall, N., Rice, T., & Hall, A. (1983). *Medigap—study of comparative effectiveness of various state regulations.* Menlo Park, CA: SRI International.

Mechanic, D. (1978). Considerations in the design of mental health benefits under national health insurance. *American Journal of Public Health, 68,* 482–488.

Mezzich, J.E., & Coffman, G.A. (1985). Factors influencing length of hospital stay. *Hospital and Community Psychiatry, 36,* 1262–1264.

Mezzich, J.E., & Sharfstein, S.S. (1985). Severity of illness and diagnostic formulation: Classifying patients for prospective payment systems. *Hospital and Community Psychiatry, 36,* 770–772.

Morrissey, J.P., & Goldman, H.H. (1984). Cycles of reform in the care of the chronically mentally ill. *Hospital and Community Psychiatry, 35,* 785–793.

Muller, C., & Schoenberg, M. (1974). Insurance for mental health: A viewpoint on its scope. *Archives of General Psychiatry, 31,* 871–878.

Mundinger, M.O. (1983). *Home care controversy: Too little, too late, too costly.* Rockville, MD: Aspen.

National Association of State Mental Health Directors (NASMHD). (1984). *Final report—funding sources and expenditures for state mental health agencies: Revenue–expenditure study results.* Washington, DC: Author.

National Association of State Mental Health Directors (NASMHD). (1985). *Funding sources and expenditures of state mental health agencies: Revenue/expenditure study results, fiscal year 1983* (updated final report). Washington, DC: Author.

National Institute of Mental Health (NIMH). (1984). *State and county mental hospitals, United States: 1980–81 and 1981–82* (Mental Health Statistical Note No. 166). Washington, DC: Author.

National Institute of Mental Health (NINH). (1985, May 28–31). *Resource reference directory.* Prepared for National Conference on Mental Health Statistics, San Francisco, CA.

Newcomer, R.J. (1985). State Medicaid policy choices in a period of fiscal austerity. In C.L. Estes, P.R. Lee, R.J. Newcomer, & Associates, *Correlates of long term care expenditure and services utilization in 50 states* (Final report to the National Center for Health Services Research). San Francisco, CA: Institute for Health & Aging, University of California.

Office of Technology Assessment (OTA). (1985). *First report on the Prospective Payment Assessment Commission (ProPAC).* Washington, DC: Author.

Okin, R.L. (1978). The future of state mental health programs for the chronic psychiatric patient in the community. *American Journal of Psychiatry, 135,* 1355–1358.

Okin, R.L. (1984). How community mental health centers are coping. *Hospital and Community Psychiatry, 35,* 1118–1125.

Pardes, H.E. (1982). Budget, policy changes: NIMH in transition. *Hospital and Community Psychiatry, 33*, 525–526.

Pegels, C.C. (1980). Institutional vs. noninstitutional care for the elderly. *Journal of Health Politics, Policy, and Law, 5*, 205–212.

Rice, D.P., Hodgson, T.A., & Kopstein, A.N. (1985). The economic cost of illness: A replication and update. *Health Care Financing Review, 7*(1), 61–80.

Rose, S.M. (1979). Deciphering deinstitutionalization: Complexities in policy and program analysis. *Milbank Memorial Fund Quarterly, 57*, 429–460.

Roybal, E.R. (1984). Federal involvement in mental health care for the aged: Past and future directions. *American Psychologist, 39*, 163–166.

Rubin, J. (1981). The national plan for the chronically mentally ill: A review of financing proposals. *Hospital and Community Psychiatry, 32*, 704–713.

Rupp, A., Steinwachs, D.M., & Salkever, D.S. (1984). The effect of hospital payment methods on the pattern and cost of mental health care. *Hospital and Community Psychiatry, 35*, 456–459.

Scheffler, R.M. (1985). Mental health services: New policies and estimates. *Generations, 9*(4), 33–35.

Schlesinger, H.J., Mumford, E., Glass, G.V., Patrick, C., & Sharfstein, S.S. (1983). Mental health treatment and medical care utilization in a fee-for-service system: Outpatient mental health treatment following the onset of a chronic disease. *American Journal of Public Health, 73*, 422–429.

Schlesinger, M., Dorwart, R.A., & Pulice, R.T. (1986). Competitive bidding and states' purchase of services: The case of mental health care in Massachusetts. *Journal of Policy Analysis and Management, 5*, 245–263.

Sharfstein, S.S. (1978a). Third-party payers: To pay or not to pay. *American Journal of Psychiatry, 135*, 1185–1188.

Sharfstein, S.S. (1978b). Will community mental health survive in the 1980s? *American Journal of Psychiatry, 135*, 1363–1365.

Sharfstein, S.S. (1982). Medicaid cutbacks and block grants: Crisis or opportunity for community mental health? *American Journal of Psychiatry, 139*, 466–470.

Sharfstein, S.S., Eist, H., Sack, L., Kaiser, I.H., & Shadoan, R.A. (1984). The impact of third-party payment cutbacks on the private practice of psychiatry: Three surveys. *Hospital and Community Psychiatry, 35*, 478–481.

Sharfstein, S.S., Frank, R.G., & Kessler, L.G. (1984). State Medicaid limitations for mental health services. *Hospital and Community Psychiatry, 35*, 213–215.

Sharfstein, S.S., Taube, C.A., & Goldberg, I.D. (1977). Problems in analyzing the comparative costs of private versus public psychiatric care. *American Journal of Psychiatry, 134*, 129–132.

Sigel, G.S. (1984). In defense of state hospitals. *Hospital and Community Psychiatry, 35*, 1234–1236.

Skolnick, A. (1976). Twenty-five years of employee benefit plans. *Social Security Bulletin, 39*(9), 3–21.

Smith, C.J. (1984). Geographic patterns of funding for community mental health centers. *Hospital and Community Psychiatry, 35*, 1133–1140.

Spiro, H.R. (1982). Reforming the state hospital in a unified care system. *Hospital and Community Psychiatry, 33*, 722–728.

Stotsky, B.A., & Stotsky, E.S. (1983). Nursing homes: Improving a flawed community facility. *Hospital and Community Psychiatry, 34*, 238–242.

Swan, J.H., Fox, P.J., & Estes, C.L. (1986). Community mental health services and the elderly: Retrenchment or expansion? *Community Mental Health Journal, 22*, 275–285.

Talbott, J.A. (1985). The fate of the public psychiatric system. *Hospital and Community Psychiatry, 36*, 46–50.

Talbott, J.A., & Sharfstein, S.S. (1986). A proposal for future funding of chronic and episodic mental illness. *Hospital and Community Psychiatry, 37*, 1126–1130.

Taube, C., Lee, E.S., & Forthofer, R.N. (1984). Diagnosis-related groups for mental disorders, alcoholism, and drug abuse: Evaluation and alternatives. *Hospital and Community Psychiatry, 35*, 452–455.

Test, M.A., & Stein, L.I. (1980). Alternative to mental hospital treatment: Pt. 3. Social cost. *Archives of General Psychiatry, 37*, 409–412.

Thompson, J.W., Bass, R.D., & Witkin, M.J. (1982). Fifty years of psychiatric services: 1940–1990. *Hospital and Community Psychiatry, 33*, 711–717.

Waldo, D.R., & Lazenby, H.C. (1984). Demographic characteristics and health care use and expenditures by the aged in the United States: 1977–1984. *Health Care Financing Review, 6*(1), 1–29.

Wallen, J. (1985). *Use of short-term general hospitals by patients with psychiatric diagnoses* (Hospital Cost and Utilization Project, Research Note 8, Hospital Studies Program. DHHS Publication No. [PHS] 86-3395). Washington, DC: National Center for Health Services Research and Health Care Technology Assessment.

Weiner, R.S., Woy, J.R., Sharfstein, S.S., & Bass, R.D. (1979). Community mental health centers and the "seed money" concept: Effects of terminating federal funds. *Community Mental Health Journal, 15*, 129–138.

Weisbrod, B.A., Test, M.A., & Stein, L.I. (1980). Alternative to mental hospital treatment: Pt. 2. Economic benefit–cost analysis. *Archives of General Psychiatry, 37*, 400–405.

Weissert, W.G., Wan, T.H., & Livieratos, B.B. (1980). *Effects and costs of day care and homemaker services for the chronically ill: A randomized experiment* (NCHSR Research Report Series, DHEW Publication No. [PHS] 79-3258). Hyattsville, MD: National Center for Health Services Research.

Widem, P., Pincus, H.A., Godman, H.H., & Jencks, S. (1984). Prospective payment for psychiatric hospitalization: Context and background. *Hospital and Community Psychiatry, 35*, 447–451.

Williams, S.V., Kominski, G.F., Down, B.E., & Soper, K.A. (1984). Methodological limitations in case mix hospital reimbursement, with a proposal for change. *Inquiry, 21*, 17–31.

Winslow, W.W. (1982). Changing trends in CMHCs: Keys to survival in the eighties. *Hospital and Community Psychiatry, 33*, 273–277.

Woy, J.R. (1981). Community mental health centers: Movement away from the model. *Community Mental Health Journal, 17*, 265–276.

Williams, S.V., Kominski, G.F., Down, B.E., & Soper, K.A. (1984). Methodological limitations in case mix hospital reimbursement, with a proposal for change. *Inquiry, 21*, 17–31.

Winslow, W.W. (1982). Changing trends in CMHCs: Keys to survival in the eighties. *Hospital and Community Psychiatry, 33*, 273–277.

Woy, J.R. (1981). Community mental health centers: Movement away from the model. *Community Mental Health Journal, 17*, 265–276.

6

Self-Help Groups and the Elderly: An Overview

Morton A. Lieberman

What are self-help groups? How do they work? What forces in modern society influence their development? How extensive are their services, and what do we know about their effectiveness? How can such groups be of maximum benefit to the elderly and their caregivers?

The label self-help group (SHG) is applied to a vast range of activities. It is commonly applied to support systems; social movements; spiritual movements and secular religious systems of consumer participation; supplementary communities; expressive–social influence groups; and organizations of those facing discrimination (Killilea, 1976). Homogeneous therapeutic groups are sometimes labeled self-help groups. Theoretical as well as empirical distinctions exist between professionally led groups and SHGs. These groups are composed of members who share a common condition, situation, heritage, symptom, or experience. They are largely self-governing and emphasize self-reliance. SHGs generally offer a face-to-face fellowship network, available and accessible without charge. They tend to be self-supporting rather than dependent on external funding.

SHGs involve an estimated 12 to 14 million adults. They address nearly every known disease and problem. SHGs include many that address problems common among the elderly, such as the aftereffects of cardiovascular disease, widowhood and other life changes, Alzheimer's disease, and mental illness.

Although evaluative research on SHGs has not been very sophisticated to date, findings suggest that SHGs can be as efficacious as professional services, and are certainly less expensive. However, knowledge gained from the current limited research representing a few types of SHGs cannot be generalized to all SHG activities.

SHGs of special relevance to the health care system have been classified by Levy (1979):

This study was supported in part by an NIMH Research Career Investigator Award, People Changing Groups (5K05MH2034-2-11). The author is indebted to Mary E. McCall, who provided invaluable assistance in developing and collating the information about self-help groups for the elderly and in providing insights on implementation.

1. Behavioral control or conduct reorganization groups (such as Alcoholics Anonymous, Gamblers Anonymous, Overeaters Anonymous, and Parents Anonymous) have as their *sole* purpose helping members control their common problematic behavior.

2. Stress-coping and support groups (such as Al-Anon, Compassionate Friends, Emotions Anonymous, Make Today Count, Parents without Partners, THEOS, and Recovery, Inc.), aim to ameliorate the stress through mutual support and the sharing of coping strategies and advice. There is no attempt to change their members' status, which is taken as fixed.

3. Survival-oriented groups (such as women's consciousness-raising groups and gay rights organizations) are composed of people whom society has either stigmatized or discriminated against. These groups help their members maintain or enhance their self-esteem through mutual support and consciousness-raising. They also attempt to better their lot by eliminating discrimination.

4. Personal growth and self-actualization groups (such as Integrity Groups), in contrast, are made up of members who do not share a core problem that brings them together. Instead, there is the shared belief that together they can help each other improve the quality of their lives.

How Self-Help Groups Work

Psychotherapy researchers have studied and theorized for over 30 years about the transactions associated with change, and a number of experiences and events ("curative factors") are thought to be directly associated with change. Although there has been no dearth of speculation on how SHGs function (Dean, 1971; Gartner & Riessman, 1977; Hurvitz, 1976; Katz, 1970; Robinson & Henry, 1977; Trice & Roman, 1970), much of this literature is anecdotal. Nevertheless, several formal studies of therapeutic factors in SHGs have been conducted.

Lieberman and Borman (1979) compared the responses on a change-mechanism questionnaire by several thousand people in a variety of groups. Using a comparative framework, the investigators found that all types of helping groups (both professional and SHG) are collections of fellow sufferers in high states of personal need. All groups require some aspect of the personal, often painful, affliction to be shared in public. No matter what the kind of group, participants uniformly indicate that the ability of such groups to provide for normalization (universalization) and support is central. Levy (1979) compared a small sample of groups and found that the common core across all groups was an emphasis on empathy, mutual affirmation, explanation, sharing, morale-building, self-disclosure, positive reinforcement, personal goal-setting, and catharsis.

Despite these common elements, examination of different types of SHG emphasizes unique mechanisms. Lieberman (1983) examined the relationship between change processes in two bereavement groups—THEOS and Compassionate Friends—and found that in each group a particular mechanism was associated with relief from feelings of grief and loss. Despite a common core in all group settings, there are major differences in the mechanisms that the participants find useful. Professional groups differ more from SHGs than do the SHGs among themselves.

Antze (1976) elaborates a different framework for understanding SHG processes and emphasizes the persuasive function of SHGs, theorizing that some of their special characteristics lead to high persuasiveness. He sees SHGs as fixed communities of belief, in which the sharing of an experience through the stories told by members becomes an object lesson and a means of indoctrination. Antze suggests that each type of SHG has a specific ideology, closely linked to the underlying psychological problem associated with the affliction.

Lieberman and Videka-Sherman (1986) suggest another perspective on SHG change: inducing processes. They analyzed spousal bereavement SHGs from the point of view of social support and social network theory. The emphasis on linkages with similar sufferers leads to the creation of new social networks, which were found to be linked to positive outcomes.

Self-Help Groups Compared to Professionally Led Groups

Self-help and professional approaches differ considerably as to the processes by which groups work. SHG process differs significantly from that of professionally conducted therapy. It is therefore useful to conceptually contrast SHGs to professionally led groups.

The psychological distance between members and leaders in SHGs is small compared to the psychological distance between patients and therapists. Professional helping groups of almost all theoretical persuasions view the group as a small social world reflecting in miniature all the dimensions of the larger social environment. It is this aspect of the group—its reflection of the interpersonal and symbolic issues that confront individuals in the larger society—that is most highly prized as the way groups induce change. SHGs, by contrast, do not emphasize analysis of the interpersonal transactions of members as a basic tool of change.

Another distinguishing characteristic of the SHG is its continued insistence on the possession of a common problem. In contrast, professionally conducted helping groups may work on a variety of problems presented by the members.

Lieberman and Bliwise (1985) illustrate the consequences of such distinctions in their study of SAGE (Senior Actualization and Growth Explorations), a group program developed initially by professionals for the well elderly. An earlier study (Lieberman & Bliwise, 1979) found SAGE to be effective. Over the years, the program developed into a SHG. The 1985 study, based on random assignment of participants into professionally led groups and those led by the elderly using SAGE techniques, suggested that the SHGs using the SAGE procedures were less successful than those conducted by professionals.

This study illustrates the limits of transferring techniques used effectively by professionals to the development of SHGs. Unlike the vast majority of SHGs, SAGE's helping methods did not grow out of a particularistic view of the affliction, the product of a long series of "empirical trials" codified into an ideology. This distinction is salient for SHGs among the elderly and their caregivers. The label "self-help" has often been applied to activities that are professionally structured, involving populations with similar problems or afflictions. Less numerous are SHGs that have processes of providing service developed by the afflicted themselves. The distinction is not between professional involvement and the total absence of professionals—the critical test is that of the origins of the helping model.

Origins

Although the use by health practitioners of groups to aid people in distress is of relatively recent origin, small groups have always served as important healing agents. Group forces have been used to inspire hope, increase morale, offer strong emotional support, induce serenity and confidence, or counteract psychic and bodily ills.

Several views have been offered for their growth and development. The most common explanatory model emphasizes a functionalist framework, whereby new institutions arise in society when there are meaningful and recognized needs that are not being met by existing institutions. The inadequate professional response to problems of alcoholism is proffered as the classical example. A second explanation emphasizes alternate pathways to obtaining services that are already available. Here the emphasis is not on the unmet need but on the form through which the service is offered. A third view suggests that the growth and development of the SHG is best explained by the need for affiliation and community with others in similar conditions. Although the emphasis is on unmet needs, they are a different kind than those addressed by the group's overt purpose.

Scope

Reliable information on growth, magnitude, and prevalence has been difficult to obtain until quite recently. Gussow and Tracy's (1976) study indicates a yearly

3 percent growth rate in numbers of chapters for nationally organized groups. Their data do not, however, address the diversity of loosely affiliated or nonaffiliated local groups.

Relatively new institutions, self-help clearing houses provide information on the magnitude of SHGs. The Self-Help Center of Evanston, Illinois, for example, publishes a listing of SHGs active within the Chicago metropolitan area, listing 320 organizations in its 1981–1982 directory. These SHGs range from well-established national groups, such as AA, to single chapter groups, such as the All-but-Dissertation SHG. The breadth and diversity of problems these groups address are indeed astonishing. Almost all chronic diseases are represented, as are psychiatric conditions such as agoraphobia, depression, and anxiety disorders. Also included are a variety of neurological diseases, eating disorders, and a multitude of serious emotional crises brought on by expected as well as unexpected life events—retirement, widowhood, loss of a child, birth of twins, illnesses or handicaps of children, unemployment, suicide by a family-member, and divorce.

Results from a recent national survey provide prevalence information. Mellinger and Balter (1983) report findings on a 1-year utilization rate from a probability sample of over 3,000 households. In 1 year, 5.6 percent of all individuals consulted mental health professionals, 5 percent turned to clergy or pastoral sources, and 5.8 percent utilized SHGs. These findings support the estimates that from 12 to 14 million adults utilize SHGs and suggest that mutual aid groups are a major source of help for a variety of physical and emotional difficulties.

Effectiveness of Self-Help Groups

SHGs will merit the serious attention of the helping professions to the extent to which their "services" can be shown to be effective. Empirical research on outcomes is limited and covers a narrow band of activities. Studies of behavioral deviations—alcoholism, overeating, and drug abuse—predominate. Studies of groups that deal with life transitions, crises, or diseases are rare. Clinical–descriptive studies are far more numerous than more rigorous quasi-experimental or experimental designs.

The most widely studied SHG is Alcoholics Anonymous (AA). Some studies evaluate AA alone (Bohince & Orensteen, 1950; Henry & Robinson, 1978); others examine the contribution of AA as one of several interventions (Kish & Hermann, 1971; McCance & McCance, 1969; Pattison, Headley, Glesser, & Gottschalk, 1968; Robson, Paulus, & Clarke, 1965; Rohan, 1970; Rossi, 1970; Tomsovic, 1970). Large-scale studies based upon cross-sectional surveys are represented by Bailey and Leech (1965), who obtained questionnaire responses from over 1,000 persons; by Edwards, Hensman, Hawker, and

Williamson (1967), who reported on 306 respondents; and the AA survey of 11,355 respondents. Such cross-sectional findings suggest that, at any time, from a third to a half of AA participants have been sober less than 1 year. Studies evaluating AA as one element in the treatment program suggest that those alcoholics do better who attend AA in addition to other treatment modalities.

SHGs for eating disorders are rapidly expanding, with estimates of upwards of a half million members in the United States for one such group, Take Off Pounds Sensibly (TOPS). Stunkard, Levine, and Fox (1970) suggest that the effectiveness of TOPS is limited. In contrast, a recent study by Grimsmo, Helgesen, and Borchgrevink (1981), reporting on a Norwegian prospective study of over 10,000 SHG participants, found significant and meaningful weight-reduction outcomes.

Outcome studies are less plentiful of SHGs other than behavioral-disorder groups. Much of this research has been conducted by the author and his colleagues, who over the past 7 years have examined eight different SHGs: women's consciousness-raising groups; Mended Hearts, a medical SHG concerned with individuals who have had open-heart surgery; NAIM and THEOS, both directed toward widows and widowers; Compassionate Friends, a SHG for parents who have suffered the death of a child; mothers' groups and mothers of twins groups, both addressing the emotional problems of motherhood; and SAGE, a group for those over age 65. The outcome question was addressed by surveys of both participants and nonparticipants ($N = 5,000$). For follow-up, members and nonmembers were assessed at least twice at yearly intervals; in the bereavement groups, 4-year follow-ups were also used.

Overall, the results of these studies are encouraging (Lieberman & Bond, 1976; Lieberman & Borman, 1981; Lieberman, Solow, Bond, & Reibstein, 1979; Lieberman & Videka-Sherman, 1986; Videka-Sherman, & Lieberman, 1985). Measurable improvement was found in levels of depression and self-esteem among women who joined consciousness-raising groups. The spousally bereaved who participated in SHGs showed a marked improvement in levels of depression, well-being, self-esteem, and life satisfaction, in comparison to controls. Among the members of Mended Hearts, the large subgroup that had retired as a consequence of surgery showed significantly improved scores on mental health indicators. Among parents who had lost children, there was improvement (relative to a control group) in coping strategies and in measures of existential concerns, but no significant improvement, after 1 year of participation, in mental health or social functioning. The results for first-time mothers were more ambiguous; there were no substantial data that participation in such groups substantially improved women's psychological or social functioning. Mothers of twins, however, showed some improvement in their social functioning.

In recent years, there has been a rapid increase in the number and diversity of programs developed to provide help to caregivers for Alzheimer's patients. Some of these programs represent SHGs as defined in this chapter; others are homogeneous therapy groups (Weiner, 1986). Other programs resemble a particular kind of SHG that has a primary focus on advocacy, whether expressed through the development of funding sources to attack a disease (for example, Huntington's chorea), or through advocacy to change social policy (such as Mothers Against Drunk Driving). Other programs have developed innovative technologies for linking people to one another through telephone exchanges. It is beyond the scope of this chapter to evaluate the variety of programs directed toward Alzheimer's caretakers. It suffices to say that some programs form and function like SHGs with the means of control and the basis of control and ownership, as well as the helping strategies, resembling SHGs.

The recent review by Ory et al. (1985) provides ample evidence that despite the proliferation of mutual-aid groups for family caregivers, little is known about their effectiveness. Most of the published evaluative research is on homogeneous therapy groups, professionally directed groups in which all the members share a common problem. Research findings suggest that membership in such "support" groups strengthens the emotional well-being and morale of caregivers for Alzheimer's patients (Barnes, Raskind, Scott, & Murphy, 1981). Lazarus, Stafford, Cooper, Cohler, and Dysken (1981) concluded that discussion groups provide both educational and supportive functions to relatives of Alzheimer's patients. Glasser and Wexler (1985) found in their evaluation of caregiver educational support groups that members benefit most from acquiring knowledge of the problems they might expect in the future. Medical information on dementia syndromes and the sharing of management skills were also highly rated.

The most extensive information on self-help groups for caretakers comes from the report on SHGs established through the educational and logistic efforts of the Duke University Center. George and Gwyther (1985) report on the Duke University Family Support Program, presenting cross-sectional findings comparing members and nonmembers of support groups, as well as analyses of pretest and posttest measures with a smaller sample. The results suggest that SHG participation significantly increases the knowledge of the variety of community services available but has little impact on increasing the use of such community services. Findings also support the view that loneliness and feelings of isolation are lessened by participation in SHGs.

The data presently represent an early stage of research. Member satisfaction and attitude change are characteristic findings. Data are not yet available regarding such issues as how SHG participation affects the levels of stress and well-being of caregivers, alters the behavior of patients, or delays institutionalization.

Utilization by the Elderly

The elderly appear to be underrepresented to about the same extent in self-help groups as they are in other psychological services. Lieberman and Borman

(1979) found that widows over age 60 represent 20 percent of membership in national widowhood SHGs, less than expected using demographic projections on widowhood. Participants over age 60 in Mended Hearts, a group dealing with the emotional and physical consequences of open-heart surgery, represent 40 percent of the membership, likewise less than expected based on the demographics of open-heart surgery. In contrast, Borkman's (1982) review of the published literature suggests that for such problem areas as alcoholism, elderly participation accurately reflects the frequency of the disorder.

Secondary analysis of the Mellinger and Balter (1983) data provides estimates of utilization, as well as some information on social and psychological factors linked to SHG participation. In 1979 approximately 20 percent of the population under age 65 was involved in some form of psychosocial treatment, while of those aged 65 to 79 about 9 percent were so involved—a 55 percent difference (see table 6–1). The overall drop-off rate between mid-life (ages 50–64) and elderly persons for all forms of psychosocial treatment other than SHGs was 30 percent; the rate for the clergy was 25 percent; but the drop-off rate for SHGs was 72 percent. This indicates that although the use of psychosocial treatments generally declines with age, the drop-off is even greater for SHGs.

What factors explain the sharp decrease by the aged in the utilization of SHGs? Previous research (Lieberman & Borman, 1979) shows that analyses of specific samples of participants and nonparticipants in SHGs (equating for availability) did not yield substantial, robust findings on the characteristics of members of such groups. Those who utilize SHGs were found on the average to be more likely to use other helping resources and to be somewhat more socially active than their matched nonparticipants.

The Mellinger–Balter survey data have been used to examine the relationship between participation in SHGs compared to utilization of professional

Table 6–1
Rate of Utilization by Age: National Survey Information
(3,000 + Households)

	Age				
	18–24	*25–34*	*35–49*	*50–64*	*65–79*
Behavioral SHG	02%[a]	28%	33%	33%	05%
Support SHG	14%	40%	42%	05%	0%
Growth SHG	30%	30%	18%	18%	09%
Professional psychotherapy	22%	26%	21%	21%	09%

Source: Data derived from Mellinger & Balter, 1983.

Note: Based on prevalence—1979; 5.8%—SHG; 5.6%—Mental health profession; 5.0%—Clergy.

[a]Percentage based on total number in population participating in behavioral self-help groups. Similar procedure used for support and growth SHG as well as psychotherapy.

psychosocial treatment. The questions asked were: Is there a linkage between social support availability and participation? What effect do health problems have on the utilization of SHGs? What effect does life stress have? To what degree do psychic distress and role impairment due to emotional causes link to utilization of SHGs? The analysis contrasts self-help and psychosocial treatment by age.

The results of this analysis indicate that both instrumental and emotional support decrease with age. Numbers reporting lack of social support increase with age. As anticipated, there is no support for the argument that the elderly have other resources in lieu of professional help and of SHGs.

Serious role impairment is related to the use of professional mental health services but not to that of SHGs. Similarly, use of psychosocial therapy is linked to the existence of health problems. Persons with more severe health problems were more likely to use professional help, but not SHGs. These factors, however, do not explain the decreasing use with age of both psychosocial therapy and SHGs.

Life stress (using a measure of number of negative events) is related to the use of SHGs, but even more strongly related to the use of professional help. As anticipated, life stress (as measured) decreases with age. This suggests that one reason for lower utilization of SHGs by the aged is a lower incidence of the types of events that precipitate the use of such groups by younger populations. However, the moderate decline with age in the report of life-stressing events cannot explain the sharp drop-off in the use of SHGs.

Overall, the analysis of this survey does not reveal a convincing explanation for the decline in use of SHGs by the aged. Other factors must play a role in such utilization patterns. Perhaps the view of SHGs by the elderly can be best summarized by the question: How can other troubled or sick people help me? Likewise, the elderly may have a greater cultural investment in professional over nonprofessional, and medical over mental health, help. The values, beliefs, and views of the helping process that characterized the current generation of elderly may not fit comfortably into the basic self-help paradigm.

Some SHGs may erect barriers, particularly through their procedures for attracting members. Lieberman and Borman (1979) found, however, that the recruitment procedures used by several SHGs did not appear to systematically exclude the elderly. This is an issue that demands further inquiry, for which adequate data are not currently available.

Theoretical Implications

There are special theoretical concerns beyond service underutilization that warrant the attention of gerontologists. The homogeneity of the affliction, problem, or issue facing the participants is of paramount importance for SHGs. A SHG for those who have had open-heart surgery illustrated this principle when the issue of bypass surgery versus valve replacement as a membership requirement became emotionally charged. Although such a distinction might seem odd to an outsider, it reflects an important and basic requirement of SHG formation: instant and early identification among members.

Age alone does not appear to be a valid criterion for homogeneous group composition. Except among groups organized to advocate changes in the larger society, it is unlikely that SHGs for mutual aid and self-improvement could be organized on the basis of age alone. The requirement is a perceived similarity based on disease or affliction, status, crises, or life transitions. Groups focused on retirement, unemployment, grandparents who have suffered the death of a child, grandparents of the divorced, and other life situations can be salient for the aged. Whether the elderly would do better in age-heterogeneous groups if the basis of identification were established cannot presently be ascertained.

The important point is that mutual, immediate, and psychologically salient identification must be present. Caregivers of family members with Alzheimer's disease and related disorders, for example, have a readily identifiable issue. Despite the identity of caregiving issues, however, it is unlikely that caregivers for those with a diversity of afflictions would generate groups based on general issues of caretaking.

Recent emphasis in many social science journals and applied programs on the beneficial effects of social support underscores the need for conceptual clarity when examining SHGs. Researchers on social support have frequently recommended implementation in SHGs of social support knowledge. Certainly, SHGs meet some of the basic requirements elucidated by social support researchers: They offer supportive networks of people who are organized to exchange emotional support, information, and instrumental services. They seem on the surface to meet all the conditions necessary for increasing the quality of support from informal networks. Although SHGs are not part of the kin-kith of the person's ordinary social structure, they are specialized, bounded systems created to offer services, thereby resembling other specialized societal structures for the provision of help.

Recent research, however (Lieberman, 1986) alerts investigators to the conceptual pitfalls of translating the impacts of SHGs into evidence of the beneficial effects of social support. This research demonstrates that relationships are formed in all groups: people talk to one another, often about emotionally important and sensitive issues; the exchange of important information about the affliction is more often than not a permanent pattern of these groups; people are frequently exposed to information about coping strategies; and in most SHGs, members are provided with conditions for acceptance and enhancement of self-esteem. It is thus not an issue whether "socially supportive" transactions occur both during formal meetings and in time between meetings.

The occurrence of socially supportive transactions does not translate into evidence that they are the necessary and sufficient conditions for the helpfulness of SHGs. Two recent studies (Lieberman & Videka-Sherman, 1986; Videka-Sherman & Lieberman, 1985) used identical study methods to examine the bereaved. Cohorts of bereaved members of SHGs were compared to matched bereaved parents and spousally bereaved persons who had access to such groups but chose not to join. All samples were followed for 1 year on outcome measures assessing a variety of mental health, social functioning, and health factors. Analysis of the spousally bereaved cohort indicates that the development of new linkages with other widows or widowers in which mutual exchange occurred was a necessary condition for significant change. The participants in these groups who experienced a diversity of therapeutic mechanisms, such as abreaction, advice, and inculcation of hope, but who did not form new social-exchange relationships, did not significantly improve. When identical measures were used among bereaved parents, however, those who established significant and important exchange relationships were no more likely to improve than those who did not do so.

These two studies illustrate the pitfalls of a facile conceptual generalization that does a disservice to our understanding of the specificity of SHGs. On the one hand, such structures need to be differentiated from a variety of other small face-to-face groups that have formed part of the professional community for a half century; but on the other hand, SHGs also need to be distinguished conceptually from informal social networks. SHGs are complex entities, involving processes to some extent akin to group therapy, experiences that are thought by many to be therapeutic in nature, such as inculcation of hope, development of understanding, and the experience of being loved. SHGs are also cognitive restructuring systems, possessing elaborate ideologies about the core cause and source of difficulty and the way individuals need to think about their dilemmas in order to get help. SHGs are also social linkage systems, in which people form relationships that provide social support. The belief, on the one hand, that SHGs are like other helping systems and, on the other, that they are so similar to one another that studying one SHG provides information about others, vitiates our ability to understand both the promise and the limits of SHGs, and the means by which we may encourage them for targeted populations.

Implementation

SHGs, like other service structures, require societal legitimization, in which professionals can play a critical role. Health care providers frequently transfer legitimization to SHGs. Other traditional systems, such as religious institutions, sanctioned by society to serve the bereaved, are frequently the prime legitimizers of bereavement SHGs. Some political movements can perform a similar function—for example, the National Organization for Women provides a basis of legitimization for women's consciousness-raising groups. Specific government and foundation-funded projects have attempted to generate SHGs among the elderly using social service or hospital affiliation as a base. For example, Duke University lends legitimacy to a large project for Alzheimer's caregivers. Gerontologists can play an important role in aiding SHGs by giving them legitimacy. Without such legitimacy, self-help groups look inward, lack vitality, and often disappear within a few years.

The ultimate test of the utility of professional influence is empirical. Not all professional involvement in self-help revolves around the transfer of professional helping models. The Duke University Alzheimer's Caregiver Project (George & Gwyther, 1985) is a good example of how volunteers and professionals can be linked together to generate and maintain groups. Published data from such projects are currently insufficient to determine the long-range outcome of this kind of group after professional stimulation and maintenance is withdrawn. Another model, currently beginning at the Self-Help Center at the University of California, Los Angeles, involves programmed learning tapes that will provide structure for interaction and group formation. This model does not involve commitment to permanency on the part of professionals.

What enables most SHGs to flourish and maintain themselves over time is a set of shared ideas. Professionals must be sensitive to these ideas, which address the nature, cause, and cure of afflictions or problems. Such ideas are often diametrically opposed to a professional view of the nature of the problem, and most particularly of the procedures for helping.

New SHGs often "spin off" from older ones, well-established groups such as Alcoholics Anonymous being copied by groups with a variety of other afflictions. Such an approach has had limited success. Because the ideology, strategy, and structure of AA address special issues of alcoholism, they may have little relevance to other problems. The groups that appear to have been successful in borrowing current ideologies and structures have modified them. Some self-help clearing houses have assisted with the spread and maintenance of SHGs by providing consultation from one SHG to another. A study of the history of many SHGs (Lieberman & Borman, 1979) clearly suggests the central role of professionals in many such organizations.

There are many models, and successful models recognize the distinction between professional involvement and professional direct service—it is the latter that inhibits the development of SHGs. A clear understanding of the kinds of institutions being developed is needed to avoid the common mistake of co-opting terms with current value (such as "self-help"), while continuing to provide service in traditional ways. SHGs are useful on pragmatic grounds in that they offer an alternative to professional services. The issue is not which is better, but the value of encouraging diversity in service.

Critics blame SHGs for direct and indirect "harm" to participants, who may receive bad services, or not receive needed services because of being diverted into SHGs. The author's studies suggest, however, that such occurrences are relatively trivial and infrequent. Of greater concern is the possibility that encouragement of the SHG might divert resources from the development and funding of essential services that society as a whole should provide.

In conclusion, SHGs merit the attention and interest of health professionals, because SHGs provide a forum for meaningful discovery, and constitute a living laboratory in which to examine change processes. The author's research has repeatedly shown impressive findings that SHGs produce measurable positive change using processes distinct from those commonly employed in psychotherapy. Because the possibly significant SHG role in prevention has not been studied, further research is needed. Investigations of SHGs can lead to genuine discoveries of alternative change models and thus broaden the available therapeutic base.

References

Antze, P. (1976). The role of ideologies in peer psychotherapy organizations. *Journal of Applied Behavioral Science, 12,* 323–346.

Bailey, M.B., & Leech, B. (1965). *Alcoholics Anonymous, pathway to recovery: A study of 1,058 members of the AA fellowship in New York City.* New York: The National Council on Alcoholism.

Barnes, R.G., Raskind, M.A., Scott, M., & Murphy, C. (1981). Problems of families caring for Alzheimer patients: Use of a support group. *Journal of American Geriatrics Society, 19,*80–85.

Bohince, E.A., & Orensteen, A.C. (1950). *An evaluation of the services and program of the Minneapolis Chapter of Alcoholics Anonymous.* Unpublished master's thesis, University of Minneapolis, Minneapolis, MN.

Borkman, T. (1982). Where are older persons in mutual self-help groups? In A. Kolker & P.I. Ahmed (Eds.), *Aging* (pp. 257–284). New York, NY: Elsevier Biomedical.

Dean, S.R. (1971). Self-help group psychotherapy: Mental patients rediscover will power. *International Journal of Social Psychiatry, 17,* 72–78.

Edwards, G., Hensman, C., Hawker, A., & Williamson, V. (1967). Alcoholics Anonymous: The anatomy of a self-help group. *Social Psychiatry, 1,* 195–204.

Gartner, A., & Riessman, F. (1977). Self-help models and consumer intensive health practice. *American Journal of Public Health, 66,* 783–784.

George, L.K., & Gwyther, L.P. (1985). *Family caregivers of Alzheimer patients: Correlator of burden and the impact of self-help groups.* Unpublished manuscript. Center for the Study of Aging and Human Development, Duke University, Durham, NC.

Glasser, G., & Wexler, D. (1985). Participants evaluation of educational/support groups for families of patients with Alzheimer's disease and other dementias. *The Gerontologist, 25,* 232–236.

Grimsmo, A., Helgensen, G., & Borchgrevink, C. (1981). Short-term effects of lay groups on weight reduction. *British Medical Journal, 283,* 1093–1095.

Gussow, R., & Tracy, M. (1976). Self-help groups. *Journal of Applied Behavioral Sciences, 12,* 265–282.

Henry, S., & Robinson, F. (1978). The dangers of self-help groups. *New Society, 22*, 654–656.

Hurvitz, N. (1976). The origins of the peer self-help psychotherapy group movement. *Journal of Applied Behavioral Science, 12*, 283–294.

Katz, A.H. (1970). Self-help organizations and volunteer participation in social welfare. *Social Work, 15*, 51–60.

Killilea, M. (1976). Mutual help organizations: Interpretations in the literature. In G. Caplan & M. Killilea (Eds.)., *Support systems and mutual help* (pp. 37–93). New York: Grune and Stratton.

Kish, G.B., & Hermann, H.T. (1971). The Fort Meade Alcoholism Treatment Program: A follow-up study. *Quarterly Journal of Studies on Alcohol, 32*, 628–635.

Lazarus, L.W., Stafford, B., Cooper, K., Cohler, B., & Dysken, M. (1981). A pilot study of an Alzheimer patients' relatives discussion group. *The Gerontologist, 21*, 353–357.

Levy, L.H. (1976). Self-help groups: Types and psychological processes. *Journal of Applied Behavioral Science, 12*, 310–322.

Lieberman, M.A. (1983). Comparative analyses of change mechanisms in groups. In H.H. Blumberg, V. Kent, & M. Davies (Eds.), *Small groups* (pp. 239–252). London: Wiley Press.

Lieberman, M.A. (1986). Social supports: The consequences of psychologizing. *Journal of Consulting and Clinical Psychology, 54*, 461–465.

Lieberman, M.A., & Bliwise, N. (Gourash). (1979). Evaluating the effects of change groups on the elderly: The impact of SAGE. *International Journal of Group Psychotherapy, 29*, 283–304.

Lieberman, M.A., & Bliwise, N.G. (1985). Comparisons among peer and professionally directed groups for the elderly: Implications for the development of self-help groups. *International Journal of Group Therapy, 35*, 155–174.

Lieberman, M.A., & Bond, G.R. (1976). The problem of being a woman: A survey of 1,700 women in consciousness-raising groups. *Journal of Applied Behavioral Sciences, 12*, 363–379.

Lieberman, M.A., & Borman, L.D. (1979). *Self-help groups for coping with crises: Origins, members, processes, and impact.* San Francisco, CA: Jossey-Bass.

Lieberman, M.A., & Borman, L.D. (1981, July). The impact of self-help groups on widows' mental health. *The National Research and Information Center's National Reporter, 4*, 7.

Lieberman, M.A., Solow, N., Bond, G.R., & Reibstein, J. (1979). The psychotherapeutic impact of women's consciousness-raising groups. *Archives of General Psychiatry, 36*, 161–168.

Lieberman, M.A., & Videka-Sherman, L. (1986). The impact of self-help groups on the mental health of widows and widowers. *American Journal of Orthopsychiatry, 56*, 435–449.

McCance, C., & McCance, P.R. (1969). Alcoholism in North East Scotland: Its treatment and outcome. *British Journal of Psychiatry, 115*, 189–198.

Mellinger, G., & Balter, M. (1983). *Institute for Research in Social Behavior (IRSB) report* (Collaborative project). Oakland, CA: IRSB & National Institute of Mental Health.

Ory, M.G., Williams, T.F., Emir, M., Leibowitz, B., Robins, P., Salloway, J., Sluss-Radbaugh, T., Wolff, E., & Zarit, S. (1985). Families, supports and Alzheimer's disease. *Research on Aging, 7*, 623–644.

Pattison, E.M., Headley, E.B., Glesser, G.C., & Gottschalk, L.A. (1968). Abstinence and abnormal drinking: An assessment of changes in drinking patterns in alcoholics after treatment. *Quarterly Journal of Studies on Alcohol, 29*, 610–633.

Robinson, D., & Henry, S. (1977). *Self-help and health.* London: Martin Robertson.

Robson, R.A.H., Paulus, I., & Clarke, G.C. (1965). An evaluation of the effect of a clinic treatment programme on the rehabilitation of alcoholic patients. *Quarterly Journal of Studies on Alcohol, 26*, 264–278.

Rohan, W.P. (1970). A follow-up study of problem drinkers. *Diseases of the Nervous System, 31*, 259–265.

Rossi, J.J. (1970). A holistic treatment program for alcoholism rehabilitation. *Medical Ecology and Clinical Research, 3*, 6–16.

Stunkard, A., Levine, H., & Fox, S. (1970). The management of obesity: Patient self-help and medical treatment. *Archives of Internal Medicine, 125*, 1067–1072.

Tomsovic, M. (1970). A follow-up study of discharged alcoholics. *Hospital and Community Psychiatry, 21* 94–97.

Trice, H.M., & Roman, P.M. (1970). Delabeling, relabeling and Alcoholics Anonymous. *Social Problems, 17*, 538–546.

Videka-Sherman, L., & Lieberman, M. (1985). The effects of self-help and psychotherapy intervention on child loss: The limits of recovery. *American Journal of Orthopsychiatry, 55*, 70–81.

Weiner, M.F. (1986). Homogeneous groups. In A.I. Frances & R.E. Hales (Eds.), *Psychiatric Update Annual Review* (Vol. 5, pp. 714–728). Washington, DC: American Psychiatric Press.

7

Linkages between the Mental Health and Aging Systems from the Perspective of the Aging Network

Patricia Shane

T he diversity of health and mental health needs presented by elderly people and the marked interdependence of many of their physical and mental health problems make the elderly especially vulnerable to service delivery fragmentation (Blazer & Maddox, 1982; Gurian, 1982; chapters 2, 4, and 5 of this book). The impact of service delivery organizational systems and structural characteristics on underservice and underutilization are only beginning to be studied (Morrissey, Tausig, & Lindsey, 1985). Analysts have recently recommended that future work on these problems focus on systems-level analysis and intervention (Knight, 1986; Sainer, 1983). This chapter presents the results of a survey that examined linkages between state units on aging (SUAs) and state units of mental health (SUMHs) in order to understand how interagency coordination can address the needs of the elderly with mental health problems.

For collaboration to take place among human service organizations, the organizational principals must decide that conditions are favorable and that there are compelling reasons to engage in collaboration. In addition, collaboration requires that organizations acknowledge shared constituencies and complementary goals and adopt common modes of communication.

Historically, health, mental health, and aging systems have been separated by specialization, attitudinal breaches, financial barriers, and functional as well as organizational differences (Burns, Burke, & Ozarin, 1983; Goldman, 1982). The literature indicates that:

> coordination and linkages have a great potential influence on unmet need (Wan, 1976);

This project, conducted at the Institute for Health & Aging, University of California, San Francisco, was jointly funded by the Administration on Aging (AOA Cooperative Agreement No. 90-AP-0003) and the National Institute of Mental Health (NIMH Contract No. 278-84-0017 [SP].) Interpretations and conclusions are those of the author and not of the sponsors.

the service needs of the elderly can be better met if organizational barriers are removed (Alter, 1981; Burns et al., 1983; Michigan State Mental Health & Aging Advisory Group, 1980);

organizational and systems variables are the major predictors in matters of service distribution and equity (Goldman, 1982); and

organization-level variables can make a critical difference in the provision of care (Benson, 1975).

Despite these findings, the literature suggests that established multi-agency programs are limited in number and in scope (Alter, 1981; Burns et al., 1983; Flemming, Rickards, Santos, & West, 1986; Michigan State Mental Health and Aging Advisory Group, 1980).

An estimated 80 percent of older adults requiring mental health services do not have their needs met through existing services (President's Commission on Mental Health, 1978). Many factors have been discussed as critical underlying components of this population's unmet need. In broad categories, the literature has focused on availability of services, lack of awareness of service, lack of acceptability of services, and lack of accessibility (Knight, 1986; Krout, 1983; Ward, Sherman, & LaGory, 1984; Waxman, 1986). Barriers have been variously analyzed as involving client, therapist, and system variables (Gaitz & Varner, 1982; Hagebak & Hagebak, 1980; Hoeper, 1980; Kiesler, 1982; Pardini, Becker, Newcomer, & Sinsheimer, 1983; Platman, 1978; Reisberg & Ferris, 1982; Sainer, 1983; Shapiro et al., 1984).

Survey of State Units on Aging

The information source for the following discussion are data gathered in 1984–1985 through a telephone census of SUAs in the 50 states and the District of Columbia. Project staff conducted 179 telephone conversations with SUA directors or designated respondents. Using a semistructured instrument, interviewers contacted the respondents several times and had one long interview. The SUAs also provided information about area agencies on aging (AAAs) and smaller agencies with which AAAs are linked through the aging network. Analysis of the data was both quantitative and qualitative. The survey data are derived entirely from the aging network, and so reflect its point of view. The National Council of Community Health Directors was simultaneously in the process of surveying its members on linkages with the aging network. Survey results are also reported by the Action Committee to Implement the Mental Health Recommendations of the 1981 White House Conference on Aging (Flemming, Buchanan, Santos, & Rickards, 1984; Flemming et al., 1986). A follow-up study surveying both SUAs and SUMHs was being conducted at the time of this writing and will be presented in Biegel, Shore, and Rogers (in press). Although the SUA survey findings presented in this chapter represent only one side of a two-sided issue, the SUA view is important. Analysis of SUA perceptions of the dynamics of coordination at the state level may foster a process-oriented perspective and enable future policy and research to focus on elements that can support development of coordination between the aging and mental health systems.

Overcoming Organizational Boundaries

In most cases, barriers to interagency linkage appear to be present before linkages are effected. SUAs that have found methods of identifying and minimizing barriers seem most able to effectively use and benefit from coordination strategies.

The primary barriers for most organizations are their own organizational boundaries—organizational missions, scope of authority, and turf issues. Linkages are most enhanced by making organizational boundaries (real or perceived) more permeable. The methods most frequently used for minimizing organizational boundaries and facilitating linkages are the development of multiple points of interagency contact; discretionary power to work with other agencies; high visibility for targeted issues; and special funds or staff assigned to coordination efforts.

Multiple points of contact between agencies are developed through such mechanisms as personal avenues of communication; high staff accessibility (regardless of organizational structure); newsletters or systematic information exchange; and shared representation at meetings, committees, or task forces. In turn, these multiple points of contact serve as a forum for identification of common concerns and a shared constituency; establishment of a common service language to foster joint goal development; negotiation of consensus and methods of attaining shared goals; and promotion of trust and communication.

Decentralization of authority or latitude in discretionary power to work with other agencies is central to overcoming organizational barriers. The opinion generally expressed by survey respondents is that adherence to ideals of separate missions and rigid hierarchical structures are in opposition to an overall systems perspective. The ability to develop a broad, rather than narrow, organizational focus is more likely when the organizational context includes flexibility in staff and resource utilization; a politically neutral setting to compensate for rigid boundaries or sensitive domain; designation of staff liaisons with specific authority to develop interagency coordination; and negotiation employing political bargaining strategies rather than top-down mandated approaches.

Failure to recognize the mental health problems of the elderly as a high priority results in insufficient allocation of fiscal and personnel resources. Broad recognition and high visibility of the problem are enhanced by establishing a coalition with the capacity to serve as advocates; gaining support from existing strong advocacy groups; promoting broadly based community awareness (via education and training for implicated professionals and nonprofessionals) to reduce bias and stigma; and approaching influential people to increase the awareness and commitment of powerful gatekeepers.

Linkages are enhanced if special funds and staff are targeted to coordination efforts. Twenty-eight of the 40 states that specified barriers to linkage development reported resources as a critical factor. Resource limitations include funds, personnel, and staff time. Specific designation of resources for a targeted population serves to create a clearly identifiable point of contact and accountability for issues and services within a system, fosters the development of an informal consultation and technical assistance exchange, and demonstrates an organizational concern and commitment to the identified issue.

Program Activity Issues

Many factors determine the presence, quality, quantity, and nuance of linkage formation. Furthermore, perceptions of these factors appear to be more important than their substantive nature. A factor cited as a barrier in one state might serve as an incentive in another. Thus, two states ostensibly presenting similar organizational or demographic profiles can be at different points in developing linkages between SUAs and SUMHs. The important intervening variables appear to be process arrangements and structural components that impede or facilitate linkages. Such variables are illustrated in the issues raised by the SUA survey. Table 7–1 summarizes some of the questionnaire findings in the 50 states and the District of Columbia. Below are presented findings for four specific program activity areas: training; local planning and implementation; advocacy and public policy; and direct service programs.

Training

There seems to be a greater likelihood that certain program activities will be developed first in coordinative efforts between SUAs and SUMHs. When there is a broadly constituted linkage program, training tends to be one of its initially established components. There appear to be many reasons why training is more easily established than other activities. First, training does not need to be jointly funded or planned. Training enhances communication and understanding between the two systems and needs little administrative or organizational negotiation for implementation. Thus, training appears to have a positive influence on linkage development. Second, training appears to have a greater likelihood than other activities of drawing in outside or collaborative funding support. Additionally, SUA-controlled Older Americans Act Title IV-A funds may be committed to joint training ventures. These resources increase the viability of training as an avenue of exchange.

Table 7–1
SUA/SUMH Linkage Activity by State

State	Liaison	Cooperative activities	Written agreements	Training	Planning and implementation	Advocacy and policy	Local direct services	AAA activity cited
Alabama	X	X	X	X	X	X	X	X
Alaska								0
Arizona								
Arkansas	X					X		X
California	X	X	X	X	X	X	X	X
Colorado		X	X					X
Connecticut								
Delaware	X	X		X			X	0
District of Columbia		X		X			X	0
Florida	X	X	X	X	X	X	X	X
Georgia		X		X	X		X	X
Hawaii	X	X				X		X
Idaho								
Illinois								
Indiana	X	X				X	X	
Iowa	X	X		X	X	X	X	X
Kansas		X	X					X
Kentucky	X	X	X	X	X		X	X
Louisiana		X			X	X		X
Maine	X	X		X	X	X	X	X
Maryland	X	X			X	X	X	X
Massachusetts	X	X	X	X	X	X		X
Michigan	X	X	X		X	X	X	X
Minnesota		X			X	X		
Mississippi	X	X		X				X
Missouri		X	X	X	X			
Montana		X					X	
Nebraska								
Nevada								
New Hampshire		X	X	X				0
New Jersey		X		X				X
New Mexico								
New York	X	X				X		X
North Carolina	X	X	X	X	X			X
North Dakota								0
Ohio	X	X	X	X	X	X	X	X
Oklahoma		X	X	X		X		X
Oregon	X	X	X				X	X
Pennsylvania	X	X	X	X	X	X	X	X
Rhode Island	X	X	X	X	X	X	X	0
South Carolina	X	X	X	X	X	X	X	X
South Dakota		X			X	X	X	0
Tennessee								
Texas	X	X	X			X		X
Utah		X		X			X	X
Vermont	X	X		X			X	
Virginia	X	X	X		X	X		
Washington		X	X	X	X		X	
West Virginia								
Wisconsin	X	X		X	X			X
Wyoming		X		X				0

Note: Code 0 = no AAAs in the state.

Training activities themselves provide latitude and flexibility in meeting diverse needs. For example, many local agencies may be involved in very different stages, phases, and subareas of the collaborative process. The advantage of training activities is that they serve to support groups and activities that are already established as well as to provide information and incentives for joint program development. The appeal of training activities is broadened by the fact that they are often designed with a choice of curriculum tracks. Training activities also provide a politically neutral ground on which agencies may discuss issues such as roles, domain, and responsibilities. Overall, therefore, training creates a forum in which to explore mutual concerns without commitment. Training programs can potentially stimulate broad community interest in joint activities and provide knowledge and understanding of mental health aspects of late life to professionals in both the aging and mental health systems.

Local Planning and Implementation

State-level linkages to facilitate local planning and implementation focus primarily on dissemination of information and the exchange of consultation time. This is often informal and rarely has the benefit of specified resources to underwrite the activity. The backbone for collaborative planning at the state level appears to be the reciprocal review of SUA and SUMH annual plans. Although a reciprocal and usually formalized review process is found in most states, its function is often specified as advisory. Recommendations are discretionary rather than mandated for adoption. Reciprocal review does, however, open avenues of dialogue, exchange of ideas, and possible points of interface. Thus, annual reviews have the potential to overcome identified system problems deriving from mutual SUA and SUMH ignorance of each others' role, structure, function, and limitations. The literature suggests that formalized procedures can support coordinative activities. However, the present SUA survey indicates that organizational commitment of resources may be an additional component necessary for review procedures to be effectively utilized. The findings support evidence from the literature that mandated coordination activities are less effective than those entered into voluntarily.

Respondents were asked to indicate what arrangements are included in their planning and implementation. Table 7–2 shows state linkage activity findings in the area of planning and implementation. It should be noted that procedures for utilizing personnel consultation time are often informal. Internal procedures tend to function as organizational links. They do not reach the status of coordinated activity unless there is also an identified staff liaison with specific responsibilities.

Planning and implementation activities do not constitute the force for linkage development that might be expected. This is because resources are generally not specified for these activities. Furthermore, the formalized process of

Table 7–2
Coordinated Planning and Dissemination

	% of states that include specified activities									
Arrangements	10	20	30	40	50	60	70	80	90	100
Coordinated monitoring of local plans $(N = 19)$[a]	X---------------------------X (53%)									
Procedures to utilize consultation time $(N = 19)$[b]	X---------------------------------------X (74%)									
Coordinated dissemination of information $(N = 19)$[c]	X---X (95%)									

Note: The percentages here represent answers to the following SUA census questions:

[a]Does this arrangement include coordianted monitoring of local plans addressing the mental health needs of the elderly?

[b]Does this arrangement include procedures to utilize consultation time of personnel from state agencies on aging and mental health by local programs?

[c]Does this arrangement include the coordinated dissemination of information?

reciprocal review of annual plans is often limited by constraints on staff time. Joint planning and needs assessment seem essential to the development of a multisystem continuum of services. The findings indicate, however, that formal state and local structures do not tend to support collaboration in the areas of planning, needs assessment, and management information systems. Indeed, working from the state level to implement regional or local coordination appears to be particularly complicated. New boundary and turf barriers may arise, especially when it is necessary to introduce substantive changes to make coordinated local planning and implementation feasible (for example, revamping existing disparate service areas into a unified system).

Advocacy and Public Policy

When the SUA and SUMH have advocacy and public policy linkages, they function as established, boundary-spanning activities. These activities are jointly carried out by separate organizations even though special resources are rarely targeted toward development or continuance. Advocacy and public policy linkages thus appear to hold considerable potential for state agencies that perceive themselves as encumbered by financial or organizational boundary constraints. State-level linkage development in advocacy and public policy can have a strong positive impact on appropriations and program development for this group. However, a necessary requirement for this activity appears to be a designated mental health liaison within the SUA. (See table 7–3).

Both the literature and survey respondents indicate that grass roots advocacy is often lacking for the elderly with mental disorders. SUA respondents also

Table 7–3
Coordinated Advocacy/Public Policy Formulation

	% of states that include specified activities				
Arrangements	10	20	30	40	50
Joint formulation (N = 20)[a]	X--X				
				(45%)	
Coordinated monitoring (N = 20)[b]	X------------------X				
		(25%)			

Note: The percentages here represent answers to the following SUA census questions:

[a]27. Does this arrangement include joint formulation of legislation and/or regulations to address the development of local programs?

[b]28. Does this arrangement include the coordinated monitoring of federal and state legislation and regulations pertaining to the development of local programs for the elderly in need of mental health services?

note that older adults are rarely identified as a mental health target population in state-level mental health policy or program directives; the advocacy role is often fragmented or deemphasized. The lack of mental health and aging policy directives sometimes serves as a rationale at the regional and community mental health levels for not developing appropriate services.

Joint advocacy and public policy formulation seem to be activities that can be developed without special budgetary allocations. Advocacy then serves to encourage a substantial amount of interorganizational reciprocity and leadership. Thus, advocacy appears to be a feasible and perhaps an especially desirable avenue for coordination in states with organizationally separate mental health and aging systems. SUAs with mental health liaisons are most likely to jointly formulate legislation or regulations, which suggests that the more specific the assignment of staff to targeted areas of concern (for example, mental health), the greater the likelihood that relevant products will be completed.

Direct Service Programs

State-level linkages between mental health and aging are highly diverse in direct service programs. Frequently, mental health is only one of several components of these programs. The impetus for coordination is usually an identified statewide service gap. However, when states have developed linkage activities for local service programs, they tend to be part of comprehensive ongoing coordination efforts.

SUAs seldom determine local service program formats. Rather, direct services usually develop from local initiatives at the AAA level. Due in part to funding limitations and to federally mandated priorities, AAAs have focused on developing a core of services for older people rather than on coordination activities. Services are designed principally to meet basic needs and to help maintain maximum independence for elders (for example, nutrition, housing, primary health care, and transportation services).

Linkage would appear to be especially important in developing effective direct service programs. The providers of basic services for the elderly are often called upon for guidance and support for issues such as depression, confusion, loneliness, and loss. Many providers are inadequately prepared to deal with these complex mental health issues. Often there is no clinical back-up to provide needed consultation. There is an overall need for direct service coordination or at least consulting relationships in mental health and aging at the local level.

The importance of designated staff liaison cannot be emphasized too strongly. Having no identified SUA staff member to work with a counterpart in the SUMH leads to insufficient interorganizational groundwork for linkages. One SUA respondent called the function of liaison positions the "lightning rod phenomenon," the dynamic missing when there is no designated person. In most SUAs with no liaison to work with mental health issues, the primary barriers are staff and resource shortages and turf issues.

Prioritizing Programs for Linkage Development

The SUA survey suggests that aging and mental health systems may be able to prioritize and sequence methods for developing linkages and coordination. Initially, both systems might benefit by joint consideration of coordination forms that maximize communication and minimize cost without requiring structural or administrative changes. Training and advocacy appear to be most feasible as initiators of coordination. The linkage activities established may then pull additional resources from outside funding sources. New revenue might then be added. The establishment of linkages adds the capability to target and track the utilization of additional resources for special populations. The linkage activity can then generate substantial reciprocity in support and leadership responsibility.

Issues within Organizational Linkages

Study respondents suggested that linkages are often facilitated or blocked by issues of stigma and bias, organizational legitimacy and structure, and limited resources.

Stigma and Bias

Respondents gave substantial support to statements in the literature on the prevalence of bias and stigma for both aging and mental health issues. Persistent stigma attached to mental illness by the elderly themselves contributes to low utilization of designated mental health services. Planning for the elderly is compromised when the mental health system interprets nonutilization by the elderly as lack of need. Mental health services, packaged as such, are not appealing to many elderly persons, regardless of need. Furthermore, SUA respondents felt that mental health providers do not understand common life-cycle problems and the benefits of mental health treatment for the aged. When problems are related to grief, loss, physical health, and other associates of aging, rather than to designated clinical diagnostic entities, traditional mental health services may be inappropriate and underutilized. SUA respondents saw advocacy and innovative methods of service delivery other than through CMHCs as necessary to break through these biases.

Attitudinal biases seem to persist within both aging and mental health networks as well as in the elderly themselves. Mental health services are often simply not seen as a high priority by many SUAs, especially when priorities are established by the elderly constituency themselves. As one SUA spokesperson said, "If you've never had it (mental health service), it doesn't tend to occur to you as a priority." Some SUA respondents felt that mental health workers often lack sensitivity about the appropriateness of care of the elderly population; that mental health workers view the elderly as "set in their ways" and "having one foot in the grave"; and that state mental health workers are often disinterested in working with the elderly.

In some states, SUAs have almost antagonistic feelings about SUMHs: "your questionnaire seems to imply that coordination with them is desirable." SUA members in these states strongly believe that the mental health system, as presently constituted, is irrelevant to the needs of the elderly. What seems to be involved are different perceptions of appropriate goals for intervention with the elderly.

Essentially, SUA members see themselves as serving the mental health needs of a broadly constituted elderly population, not just those with identified mental illness. Most of these elderly are fundamentally well but suffer from predictable life-change crises or transitions, which, if ignored, can have potentially serious consequences. SUAs wish to see a spectrum of services made available to accurately reflect the continuum of care needs of the elderly. These services should, in their view, be offered in settings where the elderly are routinely found (for example, senior centers, residences, or nursing homes). Because the elderly do not frequently define themselves as mentally ill, services must be planned to accommodate and minimize this bias. For example, some AAAs have attached counseling services to their nutrition programs. Requests for aid come in the context of a nonstigmatized program, and counseling services are provided by trained, but intentionally low-visibility providers.

Another approach is exemplified by an SUMH plan to initiate statewide mobile crisis intervention units capable of going to elders' homes, acknowledging and trying to remedy the bias by elders against clinic utilization. The same state placed its statewide Alzheimer's Resource and Development Office, jointly planned by the state aging and mental health agencies, in the SUA. It was mutually agreed that the service would be more approachable and better utilized if it were housed within the SUA rather than the SUMH.

Organizational Legitimacy

Organizations are reluctant to form relationships with agencies that are not viewed as legitimate. This appears to work both ways in the present study. SUA respondents believe that mental health is seen as more legitimate than aging by state policymakers, commands much larger portions of state budgets, and has superior political clout. Conversely, SUA respondents question the legitimacy of the mental health system's involvement with the elderly because of the system bias toward institutionally based services for psychiatrically diagnosable clients.

Disparate perceptions of appropriate goals for intervention with the elderly jeopardize coordination development and limit the bases for exchange between the aging and mental health systems. Mental health systems generally command much larger portions of state budgets than SUAs. Mental health agency power often derives from this budgetary clout because the legislature is literally "more invested." "Whoever has the money, has the say," states one SUA respondent. Other respondents perceive that this power endows mental health systems with broad latitude to set their own policies and dictate service priorities without interference from outside special-interest groups such as the elderly.

SUA respondents indicate that there are two separate legitimacy issues: one questions the legitimacy of the mental health system's involvement with the elderly; the other focuses on the considerable budgetary edge and superior political clout that SUMHs are perceived to have. This inequality is felt to lessen the legitimacy of the aging network's overtures to the mental health system.

Structural Barriers

SUA respondents assert that often an institutional bias persists in the aging and mental health fields. At least part of the mental health system's legitimacy is seen as a carry-over from the days of big institutions. Several SUA respondents perceive the mental health network as heavily business-oriented. They see the system as uninterested in cooperative strategies unless SUAs can infuse the mental health system with new funds. Despite the disproportionately larger budgets commanded by mental health, SUA respondents acknowledge that SUMHs are operating with successive cutbacks. As a result, mental health programs and services have to be carefully scrutinized for utilization, prioritized for need, and optimized for revenue return. The elderly may not meet the current requirements for funding priority. However, according to the present study, SUAs continue to make overtures and push for the attention of the mental health system to the elderly propulation. The two organizations are more likely to coordinate if they perceive that they have common constituencies. Unfortunately, when the SUMH perceives SUA overtures as a request to add new services to a new population, cooperation is less likely to evolve.

When the SUMH and the SUA are within separate umbrella organizations or one is freestanding and the other is within an umbrella organization, as when the SUA is under the Department of Administration, whereas the Division of Mental Health and Developmental Disabilities is under the Department of Health and Social Services, boundaries are difficult to span. In others, the SUA is freestanding and the SUMH is within a major umbrella agency. Agencies located within a larger umbrella oranization appear to have difficulty pushing their own agenda priorities. For example, one respondent suggests that the SUMH of that state has little autonomy and low visibility because the same agency deals also with welfare, mental retardation, and developmental disabilities. In part because the SUA in that state is a separate, freestanding department, it is said to have more autonomy and control. Such inequity in power and lack of parallel structure makes coordination between SUAs and SUMHs difficult.

Conversely, the location of the SUA within the same umbrella organization as the SUMH produces a likelihood that linkages will be formed. Ease of linkage formation may be attributed to simple proximity, informal avenues of exchange, or the absence of major interorganizational barriers. Proximity clearly enhances accessibility. SUAs under the same umbrella as SUMHs have designated liaisons or found informal linkages so well established that a specified liaison is not deemed necessary. Linkages benefit from accessibility in small states with functionally integrated state structures.

Resource Availability

The most often cited barriers to linkage development are limited resources, including funds, personnel, and staff time. Resources are constrained by limited reimbursement (particularly under Titles XVIII and XIX of the Social Security Act) and constraints in current funding mechanisms. Reimbursement systems encourage inpatient care, providing only limited coverage for ambulatory services, even when they would be more appropriate and less expensive (see chapter 5). Under existing third-party funding mechanisms, consultative, coordinative, and collaborative efforts are often not reimbursable. Consequently, many SUAs and SUMHs perceive themselves to be operating within serious fiscal constraints, which are seen as a major barrier to linkage development.

When there are overall staff reductions, remaining jobs tend to be broad generalist positions with a concomitant inability to focus on special projects or coordinative programming. There are often insufficient staff resources to seek diversified funding or to explore the collaborative ventures that could make coordination a hedge against revenue loss. At the local level, AAAs with the most innovative linkage programs tend to be located in urban areas and to be characterized by their SUAs as having rich resources and access to diverse funding. In rural, economically depressed areas where there are fewer available services and greater distances between them, there is decreased likelihood that effective coordinated networks can be developed, even though the need for coordination may be great. Solutions for overcoming funding barriers vary greatly and are influenced by such factors as urban versus rural location, mix of service availability, and community resources versus community needs. Individual, rather than blanket, approaches need to be tailored for each service area—a difficult assignment in a time of fiscal restraint.

Successful Development Strategies at the State Level

In spite of the many constraints cited above, many states have developed successful solutions and strategies. Some states have built and enhanced the interagency links necessary to address the mental health needs of the elderly. These linkage strategies have been tailored to individual state contexts.

Innovative Methods for Opening Avenues of Coordination

Opening avenues of exchange between aging and mental health systems can be problematic. An initial discussion of areas easily recognized by both as mutually important promotes the identification of a common target population. There is an enhanced view of a shared constituency, and joint advocacy efforts develop around the needs of that population. For example, long term care task forces and Alzheimer's resource centers or programs have the potential to provide such coalescing issues. Vehicles that serve to open avenues of coordination operate at the state level and have joint or multiple representation (see table 7–4).

Innovative Funding Strategies

One state convened a joint Task Force on Mental Health Needs of the Elderly, including both aging and mental health networks. This task force drafted a 2176 Medicaid Waiver proposal, which was funded. The funds provided Medicaid reimbursement for a wide range of mental health services including training, consultation to community-based direct service workers and case managers, and outreach by mental health centers to home-bound elders. The waiver was expected to serve 1,700 clients over 3 years.

Table 7–4
Vehicles of Coordination

Alabama	Mental Health Advisory Council
Arkansas	Task Force for Severe Chronically Mentally Ill; Governor's Advisory Council on Aging, Sub-committee on Mental Health
Colorado	Governor's Advisory Council on Aging, Sub-committee on Mental Health
Delaware	Alzheimer's Resource and Development Office
Hawaii	State Mental Health Advisory Board
Georgia	Alzheimer's Task Force; State Network of Area Planning Development Commissions
Indiana	Interdepartmental Board for Coordination of Human Services; Mental Health and Aging Advisory Group Task Force; Elder Abuse/Adult Protective Services Law
Iowa	Governor's Task Force on Long Term Care; Care Review Boards
Maine	Task Force on Mental Health Service to Elderly Persons
Massachusetts	Governor's Mental Health Action Project; Long Term Care Committee; Mental Retardation Task Force; Governor's State Committee on Alzheimer's; Medicaid Geriatric Task Force
Michigan	Mental Health and Aging Consortium; Mental Health and Aging Advisory Consortium
Minnesota	Legislative Commission on Long Term Care Issues
Mississippi	Proposed SUA/SUMH Task Force
Missouri	Long Term Care Facilities Licensing
New York	Long Term Care Policy Coordinating Council; Sub-Task Force on Mental Health and the Elderly; Governor's Select Committee on Local Mental Health Systems
Ohio	Long Term Care Planning Committee
Oklahoma	Substance Abuse Task Force; Mental Health Task Force
South Carolina	State Coordination Council
Rhode Island	Governor's Council on Mental Health; Elderly Abuse Law Program
Texas	Proposed SUA/SUMH Task Force
Virginia	Long Term Care Council; Local Long Term Care Coordinating Committees
Washington	Mental Health and Aging Systems Coordination Project

Several states stated that cooperative ventures between aging and mental health systems resulted in grant proposals. In one state, a grant obtained from a private foundation was used to develop a community action manual. This manual was designed to help local aging and mental health networks integrate their activities for the mentally impaired elderly through coordinated program planning and dissemination of information. The grant proposal was submitted jointly, and the project was overseen by a joint advisory committee.

In another state, the lack of funds in the aging and mental health service systems was cited as an incentive rather than a barrier for coordinated activity in local planning and implementation. Inadequate resources forced coordination to better utilize dollars. The SUA and SUMH jointly developed informal agreements to assist communities in developing local services. Their emphasis on mental health services in nursing homes was the result of a previous study that indicated that 52 percent of the nursing home population in the state was eligible for Medicaid. For Medicaid-eligible patients, mental health was an allowable expenditure. The result of these coordinated strategies was the development of dual case management; information exchange; multidisciplinary staffings for individual clients; and an interchange between community mental health workers and home health aides to promote outreach, referral, and screening. This venture is particularly interesting because there are no AAAs in the state, so the SUA must carry out regional responsibilities for program development.

In one state, a needs survey for the elderly with mental health problems was jointly developed through SUA–SUMH "brainstorming." Funds were pulled from Older Americans Act allotments and mental health block grants. Although initial efforts were hampered by insufficient funds and an inadequate methodology, a second jointly devised methodology utilized the limited funds available for a smaller sample survey.

As an offshoot idea of the Mental Health and Aging Advisory Group, a state Department of Mental Health funded a Mental Health and Aging Consortium in which the SUA was responsible for providing support services. It was established as a statewide networking project to provide technical assistance and information exchange about mental health and aging issues.

In another state, an interdepartmental cooperative agreement was established for a 3-year period, to be reassessed thereafter. The SUMH and SUA were to jointly overcome differences in case management definition and determinations of departmental responsibility for different clients. They also formalized local agreement requirements. This included a requirement that local linkage agreements be developed and that mental health services to the elderly be established as a target priority. A joint allocation system tied funding to performance. Supplemental mental health funding was to follow for those local mental health programs with improved performance.

Innovative Staffing Patterns

It is not uncommon for SUA respondents to cite staff shortages, or "lack of discretionary staff time," as barriers to network building. These are in some cases the result of hiring freezes in combination with employee attrition; in other instances they result from expanding organizational responsibilities with no corresponding staff expansion. A few states have found noteworthy methods of addressing these needs.

One state legislature funded an aging coordinator in the Department of Mental Health. The position was jointly hired by the state mental health and aging systems via a jointly developed screening and hiring procedure. In another state, it was not feasible to designate an existing SUA staff person to act as liaison with the SUMH. As an alternative, an NIMH training grant was used to support a social work graduate student to serve exclusively in this capacity for 3 days a week. The SUA planned to continue this successful arrangement during the following academic year. In the interval, an ongoing staff person acted as liaison (but at a greatly reduced time commitment).

Another approach was to house an aging specialist in the Department of Mental Health. The staff member's role was to serve as an advocate and catalyst to coordination in the state aging and mental health services. One of the first tasks the specialist undertook was creation of a directory of older adult services, to be distributed statewide. Each service agency was asked to supply the name of a contact person, a process that constituted an effective first step in augmenting the personnel available to develop coordinated efforts.

One SUA established a satellite staff project to focus on recruiting two new staff people and placing them in the state's Department of Mental Health. The SUA requested that these staff additions have a demonstrated familiarity with aging and mental health issues. The SUA initially paid for these positions with AOA discretionary grant money. Subsequently, state-budgeted money was used. The intention of this cross-staffing was to lend the SUMH expertise on aging, to provide liaisons between the two systems, and to promote the negotiation of interagency contacts. These staff people had an on-site supervisor in the SUMH and a supervisor within the SUA. They also retained offices at both agencies. Seven years after initiation, the project is thought to be a definite success. The Department of Mental Health has since appointed an aging coordinator. Many issues originally raised by the SUA are now resurfacing from SUMH sources. Thus, aging services policy is now SUMH policy. As an adjunct to this project, the SUA initiated and now produces the "satellite newsletter," which is credited with opening communication between the two systems in an informative, nonthreatening format. It was widely distributed with over 2,000 people on the mailing list at the time of the survey.

The responsibility for a new Elder Abuse Reporting Law was given to the Department of Health in one state. The statute stipulated that the department was required to establish a reporting system, gather information, and coordinate a service response. Because no money was allocated for these activities, the work had to be accomplished with existing staff. It was determined that the one health department staff person available to work in this area could not be expected to handle all the related duties. An agreement was made by the SUA, the CMHC network, and the Department of Health to assist with an information and service response. All three systems are under the umbrella

Agency of Human Services. A protocol has been developed to specify each agency's role and coordination efforts are in process.

One state Division of Aging is responsible for running State Adult Protective Services. At the time of the survey, the division did not have sufficient staff to carry out service responsibilities. The state, as a cost containment policy, prefers to have the SUA subcontract with other divisions with appropriate personnel already on staff. Each CMHC in the state has a psychiatric social worker. The SUA hopes to formalize an arrangement with the state mental health system by having the Division of Aging subcontract to buy a portion of the CMHC social workers' time to cooperate with the adult protective services team. An advantage to this arrangement is that the CMHC social workers would function with two supervisors, one in aging and one in mental health. Thus, the social workers would maintain access to the mental health system and the expertise of psychiatrists and psychologists.

In one state, the SUA and the SUMH are within the same umbrella organization, the Cabinet for Human Resources. In 1975 an Intra-Cabinet Agreement of Understanding was formulated, updated into its current format in the 1981–1982 fiscal year. In the 1984–1985 fiscal year, the SUA was incorporated into the agreement for the first time. This agreement permitted the purchase of social services between departments. For example, the Social Services Department can negotiate for needed services from the Mental Health–Mental Retardation Department. In turn, the Mental Health–Mental Retardation Department can contract with its 14 regional boards for services with local mental health agencies under them.

Staffing development strategies were also being used in states with few existing linkages. For example, one state program specialist was recently hired by the state Commission on Aging (COA). After the COA identified linkage as an important area, a person with a mental health background was selected to informally explore the possibilities with the SUMH system.

Legislative Incentives

State legislatures can create, either directly or indirectly, the impetus for new linkage activity between SUAs and SUMHs. In some states, the need to push the legislature for change has resulted in the formation of innovative mental health and aging coalitions. In other states, legislative actions have required a coordinated response.

In a state in which the SUA made a large budget request for case management for the frail elderly, no state money was appropriated. Instead, a long term care (LTC) task force was proposed with the primary focus of setting up advisory boards for LTC (to consider long term care in general, rather than the concerns of the aging alone) and to examine methods of cutting health care costs. These considerations included possible legislation on case management.

In a state with no adult protective services statute, the SUMH and the SUA are working closely together in an advocacy role to push for passage of such a statute, and to create a formalized framework for many current informal agreements. This cooperation has formed a powerful coalition to get needed legislation passed.

The planned joint activities of one state using a private foundation grant were underfunded. The SUA and SUMH tried to get state money to complete the project. This failed, but they succeeded in getting mental health and elderly policy accepted as a priority area for consideration in the next fiscal year. The findings of their joint venture were also being used to influence the Governor's Select Committee on the future of the state–local mental health system, although aging was not initially on the committee agenda.

One state legislature created a Legislative Commission on Long-Term Care Issues. In the process of covering these issues, the commission makes requests for reports from various divisions. The Mental Health Gerontology Division was administratively formulated to respond in part to requests being made by this legislative group. This division is placed within the Department of Human Services, which also includes the Division of Mental Health and the Division of Aging Programs. It is significant for crossover activities that staff within the three divisions also see themselves as Department of Human Services staff. The primary joint activity of these three divisions is informal coordination of planning issues. The Mental Health Gerontology Division maintains a good working relationship with the two other divisions and has received help from them in meeting requests from the legislature. The three also worked together on a report that identifies the behavioral characteristics of elders in state-owned hospital and nursing home settings, which keeps them out of community-based nursing homes and in-home care service arrangements. The divisions were planning to do a survey of the mental health service needs of the entire elderly population, but instead decided to develop an aging component in the Mental Health Division's survey of the general community.

A formal committee was established in one state to formulate a legislative and funding proposal for creation of a guardianship program. The initial idea came from the Department of Mental Health and Mental Retardation, because the state was discharging people from institutions to the community without the capability to provide services. As large facilities closed, the need increased. The Department of Mental Health and Mental Retardation was under pressure to "pick up some of the pieces which result from deinstitutionalization." The state mental health–mental retardation, social services, and aging systems were looking at cooperative joint solutions that speak to the issues surrounding public guardianship. The formalization of administrative consent for guardianship was to encompass the elderly, the mentally retarded, and other disabled populations.

In another state, a Health Resources Planning Commission was developing a health plan for the state, which recently added recommendations for geriatric mental health. Both the SUMH and the SUA are to have input and recommendation review roles, but are to function independently rather than collaboratively in these capacities.

Local AAAs have expanded planning responsibilities for adult service as a result of one state legislature's passage of the Community Care and Services Act of 1982. Impetus for this act was an Office of Aging demonstration project, which showed that elderly people experience problems other than physical symptoms. As a result, SUA staff focused on broadening case management services to look at the whole person rather than specific physical problems alone. A state task force was created to develop a solid plan for reshaping service response to elderly needs. AAAs were involved at the beginning to develop strategies, which included changes in the use of Title XIX and Title III monies. This state is unique because most of its AAAs operate under large local planning agencies called "Area Planning Development Commissions." The relationship with a larger planning agency seems helpful to AAAs in taking the lead role for implementation of state mandates, which include the local contracting of case management services. For example, as part of the implementation of the act, local AAAs have CMHC representation on their boards.

Conclusions

In summary, interagency linkages constitute an important mechanism for overcoming systems dysfunction. However, the integration process is complex and has many barriers. SUAs with methods of identifying and minimizing barriers seem most able to effectively use and benefit from coordination strategies. Linkages are enhanced by permeable organizational boundaries.

The methods most frequently cited by SUA respondents for minimizing organizational barriers and facilitating linkages include developing multiple points of interagency contact; discretionary power to work with other agencies; high visibility for targeted issues; and special funds and staff assigned to coordination efforts.

The creation of multiple points of contact between agencies necessitates personal avenues of communication, as opposed to total reliance on formal organizational forums, and on high staff accessibility, regardless of organizational structure. Further contacts are engendered by interaction at meetings, on committees, and on task forces; and they are further defined by shared organizational representation. Newsletters and other systematic information exchange can supplement the personal contacts.

Multiple points of contact are important in that they can lead to the identification of common concerns and a shared constituency. Frequent communication can establish a common service language regarding common interests, and enhance the development of common perspectives and goals. Such contacts can allow the development of trust and willingness to continue communication. All of these elements are important to the negotiation of consensus on common issues and the development of joint strategies for the attainment of shared goals.

Decentralization of authority or latitude in discretionary power to work with other agencies is central to overcoming organizational barriers. Separatist hierarchic organizational views of state agencies do not foster sufficient resource commitment to make linkage development feasible. The latitude to go beyond separate organizations is more likely to be engendered when circumstances in each agency include flexibility in staff–resource utilization; a politically neutral setting to compensate for rigid boundaries or sensitive domain; designation of a staff liaison with specific authority to develop interagency coordination; and negotiation employing political bargaining strategies rather than top-down mandated approaches.

Not recognizing the mental health problems of the elderly as a high priority results in insufficient allocations of fiscal and personnel resources in both aging and mental health agencies. It is important to increase broad recognition of the problem by developing a high visibility for this issue. Recognition and visibility are enhanced by establishing a coalition with the capacity to serve as an advocate, gaining support from existing strong advocacy groups; promoting broadly based community awareness through education and training for professionals and non-professionals in order to reduce bias and stigma; and approaching influential people to increase the awareness and commitment of powerful gatekeepers.

Linkages are enhanced if special funds and staff are targeted to coordination efforts. Twenty-eight of the 40 states that specified barriers to linkage development reported resource availability as a critical factor. These resource limitations include funds, personnel, and staff time. Specific designation of resources for a targeted population serves to create a clearly identifiable point of contact and accountability for issues and service within a system, foster the development of an informal consultation and technical assistance exchange, and demonstrate an organizational concern and commitment to the identified issue.

Overall, this project suggests that coordinated activity has the potential to overcome identified service delivery problems for the mental health needs of the elderly. Some areas, such as training, local level planning and implementation, advocacy and public policy formulation, and to a lesser extent, direct service programming, seemed to lend themselves more readily to joint initiatives. Creation of multiple points of contact between agencies, parallel agency structure and power equity, and decentralization of authority all enhance coordination between SUAs and SUMHs.

Implications for Policy

Coordination between the aging and mental health service delivery systems at the state level can be problematic because of fiscal constraints for both systems;

different mandates, constituencies, and perceptions of mission; different organizations and inequities (or perceived inequities) in power relationships; lack of parallel structure and hindrances in agency autonomy; and disinterest in or even prejudice against, respectively, mental health or aging as a legitimate area for each system. However, linkages between aging and mental health systems have been developed in many states. The best subject areas for coordination at the state level, requiring the least initial commitment of personnel and financial resources, appear to be training and advocacy. Designating a staff person in each agency as a liaison to the other was the next step. (In some small states, or states with one umbrella agency inclusive of both SUA and SUMH, informal, unofficial relationships took the place of formal liaisons.)

The establishment of common activities led to the development of further linkages and joint activities. Often task forces that viewed lack of financial resources as an incentive, rather than a barrier, were successful at getting public monies; or obtained private monies from foundations and used these monies as leverage to get public monies. Actions aimed at influencing the state legislature seemed more common than state legislature initiatives directed toward coordination.

Initial structural barriers and fiscal constraints, rather than initial conceptions of integrated service delivery, were the norm. Nevertheless, many states made ingenious efforts to overcome these barriers and constraints. These were individualized to each situation and are hard to summarize. However, perceptions by key staff in state agencies that barriers should be overcome were essential for any kind of movement to take place.

A major hindrance to integrated service delivery is the differing perception, by aging and mental health service providers, of the mental health needs of the elderly. Are the mental health needs that should be addressed those of the predictable changes accompanying the life cycle, namely the increasing frequency of loss of significant others, grief reactions, changing or declining bodily function, physical illness, or stress due to poor housing and nutrition often associated with low socioeconomic status? Or are the mental health needs of the aged those of clinically diagnosable entities of mental illness meeting DSM or ICD criteria? The public sector aging and mental health systems are not in agreement on these questions (with the possible exception of recent joint initiatives on Alzheimer's and other dementias). Different reimbursement streams (see chapter 5), combined with fiscal constraints, promote adherence to a narrow, less-than-holistic perspective and mitigate against conceptions of a continuum of care and integrated service delivery. It is possible that private-sector mental health providers will eventually serve the elderly with age-associated mental health problems and symptomatology not meeting diagnostic criteria. The evidence cited in the first three chapters of this book, however, suggests that such services are not available at this time. Chapter 8 describes a further example of nonintegration among service systems and the implications for a highly vulnerable population of mentally ill elderly, the homeless.

Thus, mental health services to the elderly continue to be segmented, if not fragmented. Organizational boundaries, funding streams, fiscal constraints, and institutional definitions of need drive services; the elderly must fit (or be fitted) into their Procrustean bed.

References

Alter, C. (1981). *Determinants of case coordination and interorganizational cooperation.* Unpublished research, University of Iowa, Iowa City, IA.

Benson, J.K. (1975). The interorganizational network as a political economy. *Administrative Science Quarterly, 20,* 199–249.

Biegel, D.E., Shore, B.K., & Rogers, R. (in press). *The delivery of mental health services to the elderly: Programmed policy models.* Hawthorne, NY: Aldine.

Blazer, D.G., & Maddox, G. (1982). Using epidemiologic survey data to plan geriatric mental health services. *Hospital and Community Psychiatry, 33,* 42–45.

Burns, B., Burke, J., & Ozarin, L. (1983). Linking health and mental health services in rural areas. *International Journal of Mental Health, 12,* 130–143.

Flemming, A.S., Buchanan, J.G., Santos, J.F., & Rickards, L.D. (1984). *Mental health survices for the elderly: Report on a survey of community mental health centers: Vol. 2.* Washington, DC: Action Committee to Implement the Mental Health Recommendations of the 1981 White House Conference on Aging.

Flemming, A.S., Rickards, L.D., Santos, J.F., & West, P.R. (1986). *Mental health services for the elderly: Report on a survey of community mental health centers: Vol. 3.* Washington, DC: Action Committee to Implement the Mental Health Recommendations of the 1981 White House Conference on Aging.

Gaitz, C., & Varner, R. (1982). Principles of mental health care for elderly inpatients. *Hospital and Community Psychiatry, 33,* 127–133.

Goldman, H.H. (1982). Integrating health and mental health services: Historical obstacles and opportunities. *American Journal of Psychiatry, 139,* 616–220.

Gurian, B. (1982). Mental health outreach and consultation services for the elderly. *Hospital and Community Psychiatry, 33,* 142–147.

Hagebak, J.E., & Hagebak, B.R. (1980). Serving the mental health needs of the elderly: The case for removing barriers and improving service integration. *Community Mental Health Journal, 16,* 263–275.

Hoeper, E.W. (1980). Observations on the impact of psychiatric disorders upon primary medical care. In D.L. Parron & F. Solomon (Eds.), *Mental health services in primary care settings* (DHHS Pub. No. 80-995). Washington, DC: Government Printing Office.

Kiesler, C. (1982). Public and professional myths about mental hospitalization. *American Psychologist, 37,* 1323–1339.

Knight, B. (1986). Management variables as predictors of service utilization by the elderly in mental health. *International Journal of Aging and Human Development, 23,* 141–147.

Krout, J.A. (1983). Knowledge and use of services by the elderly: A critical review of the literature. *International Journal of Aging and Human Development, 17,* 153–167.

Michigan State Mental Health and Aging Advisory Group. (1980). *Are they worth it?* Lansing, MI: Michigan Office of Services to the Aging and Department of Mental Health.

Morrissey, J.P., Tausig, M., & Lindsey, M.L. (1985). Network analysis methods for mental health service system research: A comparison of two community support systems (Mental Health Services System Reports, Series BN, No. 6, DHHS Publication No. [ADM] 85-1383). Rockvile, MD: National Institute of Mental Health.

Pardini, A., Becker, G., Newcomer, R. & Sinsheimer, P. (1983). *Health of older people: A framework for public policy.* San Francisco, CA: Aging Health Policy Center, University of California.

Platman, S.R. (Coordinator). (1978). Report on the task panel on deinstitutionalization, rehabilitation and long-term care (*President's Commission on Mental Health, Vol. 2*). Washington, DC: Government Printing Office.

President's Commission on Mental Health. (1978). *Report to the President.* Washington, DC: Government Printing Office.

Reisberg, B., & Ferris, S.S. (1982). Diagnosis and assessment of the older patient. *Hospital and Community Psychiatry, 33*(2), 104–110.

Sainer, J.S. (1983). Human services constraints at state and local levels. *Gerontologist, 23*, 402–405.

Shapiro, S., Skinner, E.A., Kessler, L.G., Von Korff, M., German, P.S., Tischler, G.L., Leaf, P.J., Benham, L., Cottler, L., & Regier, D.A. (1984). Utilization of health and mental health services: Three epidemiological catchment area sites. *Archives of General Psychiatry, 41*, 971–978.

Wan, T.T. (1976, September). *Organizational analysis of the determinants of unmet service needs for the elderly.* Paper presented at the American Sociological Association Meeting, New York.

Ward, R.A., Sherman, S.R., & LaGory, M. (1984). Informal networks and knowledge of services for older persons. *Journal of Gerontology, 39*, 216–223.

Waxman, H.M. (1986). Community mental health care for the elderly—a look at the obstacles. *Public Health Report. 101*, 294–300.

8
The Homeless, Mentally Ill, and Elderly Population: A Systems Challenge

Joel P. Weeden
Cheryl A. Hall
Maureen Linehan

Homelessness is a disturbing feature of modern U.S. life. Streets, parks, subways, bus terminals, airports, abandoned buildings, and public and private shelters have become the residences of a growing number of the nation's poor. The mentally ill elderly are especially vulnerable in such settings.

Although the needs of the homeless in general, and the elderly and mentally ill in particular, are immediate and extensive, delivery of services has been undertaken without a clear understanding of the composition of these groups and without directives for effective intervention strategies. Programs responding to the crisis have been established within a political climate of fiscal austerity and a professional climate of ambivalence, seen in the philosophical and clinical avoidance of the elderly who are both homeless and mentally ill.

There is little information to date on the aged or the mentally ill among the homeless, so that a synthesis of the literature must rely on the examination of broad issues of homelessness and mental health services. Assumptions must occasionally be made as to how the more general problems and issues affect the homeless mentally ill elderly.

This chapter reviews what is known about being homeless, mentally ill, and elderly. It considers the conceptual and methodological problems of research on the homeless. It examines subpopulations of the homeless mentally ill aged, including the long-term psychiatric client who has grown old, elders impaired by dementia, and elderly victims of life-threatening crises. An expanded look at homelessness and those at risk of becoming homeless is followed by a review of the precipitating socioeconomic factors of homelessness among the elderly and mentally ill. Service delivery systems are viewed from historical and current perspectives in relation to the different paths to homelessness. The chapter concludes with a summary of the issues raised, and a list of options for responding to the special needs of older people who are homeless or at risk of displacement.

Research Limitations

Much has been written about homelessness, but methodological problems unique to the issue limit research knowledge (Levine, 1984). A major difficulty is that the preliminary research tasks of identifying, locating, and counting this population are complicated by the receipt of services outside the traditional systems of health care and social support. Most studies have been undertaken by agencies responding to service delivery needs. These descriptive efforts usually focus on populations within a single site, or at best, multiple sites within a single city. The fact that the aged and the mentally ill are not evenly distributed throughout sites introduces biases.

Studies conducted within the system of traditional service providers may result in further bias because such providers may serve populations that are not representative of such noninstitutional populations as those living on the streets. Seasonal bias may result in studies limited to a short time frame because homelessness may be subject to variations by time of year, date of the month, day of the week, and even time of the day. Ecologic, institutional, and seasonal biases limit the generalizability of the findings; results may be valid for a particular time and place but not for other times and other places.

Many studies also lack statistical power. Sample sizes are too small for statistical tests to detect important differences. This is especially true of differences by age, because the number of aged sample members may be low.

Difficulties in Conceptualization

Research on the homeless is extremely limited, methodologically flawed, and biased (Mowbray, 1985), in part because homelessness is not well defined. Researchers and policymakers have not agreed on a uniform definition (Freeman, 1984; Rousseau, 1981). Variations consequently arise in reports of the number and composition of the homeless population (Anderson, 1985; General Accounting Office [GAO], House of Representatives, 1984, 1985; Levine & Stockdill, 1984). This lack of a uniformity means that definitions and the rates dependent upon them are separately determined in each study (Goldman, Gattozzi, & Taube, 1981). Some researchers use a broad definition of homelessness that includes long-time residents of single-room-occupancy (SRO) hotels (Cohen & Sokolovsky, 1983). Others use narrow definitions that exclude emergency shelter residents (Lipton, Sabatini, & Katz, 1983). Definitions and criteria for measuring mental illness also differ; some investigators use symptomatology, whereas others measure diagnostic categories.

Two dimensions for classifying the homeless are the time duration without housing and the presence or absence of any form of shelter. The homeless mentally ill have also been differentiated by acute psychiatric episodes versus chronic mental illness. It is difficult to separate the interaction of physical and mental illness among the homeless when lack of sleep, inadequate diet, and exposure to the elements are combined with the threat of violence and the daily struggle to survive. Substance abuse and lack of proper medication may also mask or exacerbate existing mental disorders. Based on various descriptions in the literature (Arce, Tadlock, Vergare, & Shapiro, 1983; Coalition for the Homeless, 1984; Doolin, 1985; Farr, 1985; Huth, 1986), the following are three subgroups most likely to include the mentally ill aged:

The *situationally* homeless are those who find themselves without housing due to such external factors as unemployment, loss or delay of benefits, personal or family crisis, or a forced move from affordable housing. They tend to be newly homeless, faced with no place to live for the first time in their lives. In mental health terms, this group shows evidence of situational stress, rather than psychopathology (Arce et al., 1983). This form of homelessness is usually a temporary condition until alternative arrangements can be made. Depending on the availability of informal supports or formal institutional resources, these situational events may develop into episodic or chronic homelessness.

The *episodic* homeless are those who, for extended periods of time, alternate between being domiciled and undomiciled. For example, this may include elderly people living in SRO hotels for part of each month until their benefits run out. The episodic homeless may also include mentally ill people experiencing acute phases of chronic mental disorders. The episodic homeless tend to have diagnoses of personality disorder, affective disorder, or substance abuse (Arce et al., 1983). They may utilize human service or mental health agencies for repeated referral and placement assistance, or they may "fall through the cracks" and drift among SRO hotels, boarding homes, detoxification centers, jails, shelters, and the streets.

The *chronically* homeless are those without shelter who regularly live on the streets for long periods of time. Some of them apparently "choose" this situation, and may actively avoid contact with shelters or other service systems. The chronic mentally ill homeless usually have diagnoses of schizophrenia, substance abuse, or both (Arce et al., 1983). This group may include young adults who are chronically ill and who are avoiding institutionalization or reinstitutionalization. Many cherish their independence, and would rather risk life on the streets than loss of freedom (Baxter & Hopper, 1982). This group is the most difficult to reach or treat.

Both the elderly and younger homeless populations are increasing in all three of these subgroups. The younger population is increasing at a rapid rate, and the proportion (though not the numbers) of older homeless persons is declining (Baxter & Hopper, 1981; New York City Human Resources Administration, 1982; Project FUTURE, 1985). Ladner (1985) believes that the percentage of elderly ending up in a homeless situation would be larger if it were not for the availability of benefits (Social Security and Supplemental Security Income), the ability to "make it" on these benefits due to living in rent-controlled apartments, and the utilization of nursing homes to house the elderly with chronic mental problems.

The conceptual question of how to view the universe of the homeless mentally ill presents further problems in formulating effective service delivery for the various subgroups. Two common approaches have been either to study the prevalence of mental illness among the homeless or to investigate the prevalence of homelessness among the mentally ill. Researchers and policymakers currently use varied age categories, as well as diverse criteria for defining and measuring homelessness and mental illness. Lack of common definitions and measurement criteria has impeded steps to focus on a comprehensive plan for service delivery. New intervention strategies would greatly benefit from consistent empirical data and a preliminary synthesis of the knowledge of the complex and interconnecting problems. Such work can offer a basic understanding of the critical, often controversial, issues from the perspectives of the various disciplines involved with the homeless, the mentally ill, and the elderly.

Highlighted Studies

Many studies have explored the characteristics of the homeless mentally ill. However, few have focused on the homeless elderly. Two studies providing data on the homeless elderly (as well as those at risk of displacement) are highlighted here.

The New York City Human Resources Administration initiated an 18-month research and demonstration project called Project FUTURE (1986) to increase understanding of the characteristics and needs of five target homeless subpopulations and to explore ways of meeting these needs. In the sample, taken from a shelter population, the aged comprised 4.4 percent of the total sample of 8,061 homeless individuals. The aged were less likely, compared to the sample as a whole, to have mental disorders. Among the elderly, 15.1 percent, compared to 22.3 percent of younger sample members, had been hospitalized in an inpatient psychiatric setting. Current psychiatric problems were reported by 13.7 percent of the elderly, compared to 20.2 percent of the total sample. The authors note that the data are based on self-reports, resulting in a possible mental disorder underreporting bias.

In San Francisco, a community-based investigation of elders (60 years of age and older) displaced or at risk of displacement was conducted by the

Coalition of Agencies Serving the Elderly (CASE), in conjunction with the University of California (Weeden & Linehan, 1987). The target population included frail elders who were at risk of becoming, or who had become, displaced due to some traumatic disruption in their lives (that is, abuse, eviction, need for emergency respite). A 1-month sample was taken through service providers who might have contact with this population. The sample consisted of 67 currently displaced individuals and 137 who were considered to be at risk of displacement. Sixteen percent of the survey population faced housing problems due to mental health problems. Thirty-six percent of the currently displaced and 14 percent of those at risk of displacement had been psychiatric hospital inpatients.

Composition of the Subpopulations

Although the chronic mentally ill have received attention as part of the homeless population, other subpopulations relevant to the topics of homelessness and mental illness have not. These include the chronic mentally ill who have grown old, elders cognitively impaired by degenerative diseases, and elders affected by mental decompensation due to acute personal crises.

Chronic Mentally Ill Who Have Aged

The chronic mentally ill are distinguished by the "severity and persistence of disability and dependency of indefinite duration" (Peele & Palmer, 1980, p. 63). The incidence of chronic health problems increases with advanced age, complicating care for those with mental disorders and physical impairments. Bliwise (see chapter 3) notes that relatively little is known about this group, about subpopulations within it, or about effective treatments for these frail elderly. Lurie (see chapter 2) notes a higher prevalence of psychiatric conditions in those with chronic illnesses or disabilities. The restricted use of the state mental health hospital as a facility of last resort makes it less available to care for this group. Families, nursing homes, residential care facilities, and residential hotels must fill the major roles in a fragmented long term care system. The breakdown of these systems makes the chronic mentally ill aged especially vulnerable to homelessness.

Elders Cognitively Impaired by Degenerative Diseases

Older adults with degenerative brain disorders also constitute a significant portion of the homeless mentally ill population. Mental dysfunction may be a consequence of the dementia related to alcoholism and Alzheimer's disease or due to physical impairments magnified by deplorable living conditions.

Alcoholism. Alcoholism as a primary or secondary diagnosis is a major problem for the homeless. Malnutrition and other physical health problems of the homeless are, in many cases, directly related to the disease process of alcoholism. Social deteriorization found in the homeless is also a major symptom of alcoholism (Morgan, Geffner, Kiernan, & Cowles, 1985). Significant rates of schizophrenia combined with alcoholism have been found in several studies of the homeless (Farr, 1985; Lipton et al., 1983; Torry, Bargmann, & Wolfe, 1985).

Cognitive deficits associated with long-term alcohol abuse resemble those of age-related decline and of such degenerative brain disorders as Alzheimer's disease. The incidence of dementia as a complication of alcoholism increases with age and is higher in women than men. Fully one-third of alcoholic women in their seventh decade are demented (Horvath, 1975), prompting some researchers to hypothesize that alcohol accelerates normal age-related declines in cognitive functioning.

In a recent study of the homeless in Los Angeles, approximately half of the 31.2 percent incidence of inpatient psychiatric hospitalization in all age groups is due to alcohol and drug abuse (Ropers & Boyer, in press). In the New York sample, 20.9 percent of the alcoholics have current or past histories of psychiatric disorder, and 23.9 percent in all age groups report inpatient psychiatric hospitalization (Project FUTURE, 1986). Those over 60 show less incidence of alcohol abuse (Project FUTURE, 1986; Ropers & Boyer, in press), but undoubtedly show more negative long-term physical and mental health effects from years of abuse.

Findings from the San Francisco study of both the homeless and at-risk groups show that those with substance abuse problems are slightly more likely to have had contact with a mental health provider. In the displaced sample, 45 percent of those with substance abuse problems have had mental health provider contacts, compared to 39 percent of those without substance abuse problems. In the at-risk sample, 42 percent of those with substance abuse problems have had mental health provider contacts. Those with substance abuse problems also have a greater tendency to inpatient psychiatric hospitalization. This is especially true for those in the at-risk group, 29 percent with and 6 percent without substance abuse problems having had an inpatient psychiatric hospitalization (Weeden & Linehan, 1987).

Alzheimer's Disease and Related Dementias. There are varied patterns in the type, severity, and sequence of changes in mental and neurological functioning that result from Alzheimer's disease. Many other conditions, both physical and psychological, can also mimic Alzheimer's disease at its various stages. The symptoms of this disease are progressive, from difficulty in such specialized activities as balancing a checkbook to wandering and failure to engage in conversation (Lindeman, 1984). Although it is difficult to obtain accurate prevalence statistics for degenerative brain disorders, it is estimated that 1 million people nationwide suffer from severe dementia caused by Alzheimer's disease and related dementias (Max, Lindeman, Segura, & Benjamin, 1986).

Findings from the San Francisco study show that, of the at-risk group, neurological disorders constitute 15.4 percent (the second largest diagnostic category), falling directly behind musculoskeletal problems. The neurological disorders primarily consist of Alzheimer's disease and other related dementias (Weeden & Linehan, 1987).

Physical Impairments and Mental Health. Physical disorders in the older homeless person—acute and chronic arthritis, hypertension, diabetes, and cardiovascular problems, for example—are clearly magnified by deplorable living conditions (Brickner, 1985; Kellogg et al., 1985). Lack of heat and protection from the elements are common problems of the homeless (Thomas, 1985). Psychological impairments decrease the ability to adapt to thermal stresses, resulting in such exposure-related symptoms as hypothermia, frostbite, and heatstroke (Goldfrank, 1985). Additional medical problems documented among the homeless mentally ill elderly population include tuberculosis (McAdam et al., 1985) and trauma, the latter being one of the leading causes of death and disability (Kelley, 1985). Other medical problems common among the homeless include infestations of scabies and lice, and leg ulcers (Brickner, 1985).

Shelter and food are the paramount concerns of homeless persons, thus health needs get little attention. Primarily because of their fear of large institutions, most of the mentally ill homeless do not receive needed health services (Doolin, 1985). Those who seek care usually go to hospital emergency rooms. A major problem in the medical treatment of confused patients for chronic diseases is the inability to comply with complex medication regimens (Cousins, 1983; Filardo, 1985). The homeless mentally ill elderly may end up in nursing homes when their chronic medical problems become severe. Nationwide, communities are currently reorganizing to provide comprehensive and coordinative health services that respond to the special needs of the homeless population (National Health Law Project, 1984).

In a study of the homeless in Los Angeles, Ropers and Boyer found that 45.7 percent of the sample reported a deterioration in health since becoming homeless (Ropers & Boyer, 1986). In the San Francisco study, of those displaced and with a medical impairment, 48 percent had been hospitalized in an inpatient psychiatric setting, and 47 percent had had contact with a mental health provider in the previous year; but among those without medical impairments, 25 percent had been psychiatric hospital inpatients, and 36 percent had had contact with a mental health provider in the last year (Weeden & Linehan, 1987). This finding is congruent with the conclusions from the literature (see chapter 2).

Mental Deterioration of Elders Due to Personal Crises

Personal crises, such as social isolation, malnutrition, or elder abuse may be devastating to the elder's mental health. These conditions may also be implicated in the path to homelessness.

Social Isolation. Researchers have found significant interaction of emotional with physical health in relation to social isolation (Ehrlich, n.d.). Social isolation has been associated with mental disorders such as poor social adjustment and cognitive functioning (Bennett, 1982). Although elders may be isolated in many different settings (for example, while caring for an impaired spouse or while living alone in one's own home), the concern here is the isolation of elders in marginal situations that lead to homelessness. The term "marginal elder" refers to those "on the bordering edge"—the population living on the fringe of community life and presenting one or more of the following characteristics: poverty, atypical lifestyles, or frailty in terms of physical or mental disorders (Ehrlich, 1986).

For marginal elders with health problems, there is also the constant worry about where to obtain the next meal, how to get to the doctor, how to pay the rent, and how to avoid being mugged when benefits checks are received. These elders are under extreme personal stress, which undoubtedly will affect their mental health.

Marginal elders often live alone in SRO hotels, "which are the most affordable and least restrictive form of housing available to those who cannot obtain other forms of housing, whether because of poverty or because they are viewed as undesirable tenants" (Ovrebo, Liljestrand, & Minkler, in press, p. 4). SROs are defined as "partial rooms lacking complete and private kitchen or plumbing facilities and housed within buildings of at least 12 units" (Haley, Pearson, & Hull, 1982). They are often located in undesirable neighborhoods. Bathrooms are typically located down the hall; and there are often steps to be climbed, due to the lack of operating elevators. Findings from the San Francisco survey indicate that 20 percent of elders who live alone and are at risk of housing displacement, compared to 10 percent of those who live with others, have used community mental health services in the last year (Weeden & Linehan, 1987).

Malnutrition-related problems can result in depression, a common symptom in homeless populations (Winnick, 1983). Malnutrition is also a predominant problem for marginal elders. The lack of a kitchen and a refrigerator, limited mobility, social isolation, and a fixed income all contribute to this problem. Chronic malnutrition and dehydration may be associated with paranoid psychosis, memory impairments, delerium, and dementia (Kaufmann, 1984). Lack of social support for marginal elders hinders early intervention that might help alleviate some of these symptoms.

Elder abuse and victimization is the unfortunate consequence of the dependence of physically or mentally impaired elders on their caregivers. The causes of abuse include dependency, the existence of an abuser, and a triggering event such as a crisis or a change in the elder's physical status. It is estimated that 1 in every 25 elders is abused (Quinn & Tomita, 1986). Although there has been much discussion of mental and medical impairments and the role they play in abuse, there is need for greater knowledge concerning the relationship of abuse and subsequent mental health problems and abuse as a potential cause of homelessness.

The Systems Challenge: Underlying Problems

The service systems that come in contact with the homeless mentally ill elderly have had difficulty in working together to provide comprehensive services that could flexibly address highly individualized service needs. The systems with primary responsibility for this population involve mental health, social and health, and housing services. The aging network has a potentially key role. Federal and state agencies are concerned largely with funding, particularly of income maintenance programs. Several problems challenge the service systems in providing quality and accessible comprehensive services to the homeless mentally ill elderly.

Delineation of Financial Responsibilities

Although the homeless are a heterogeneous population with multiple needs, financial responsibilities have not been delineated for such subpopulations as the homeless aged and mentally ill. Emergency shelter networks have served as an important stopgap response to homelessness but can not be expected to meet the special needs of those who are mentally ill or aged. The homeless mentally ill elderly currently do not fit into traditional service delivery systems such as mental health, medical, housing, and other human services. Nor do any of these systems generally consider themselves to have primary responsibility to meet the needs of those individuals characterized as being homeless, mentally ill, and elderly. At the same time, long-term responses to the problems of this population can not be resolved because financial responsibilities have not been clearly specified for the development and maintenance of adequate and appropriate housing resources for populations with special needs.

Factionalism of Service Responses

Existing service systems do not generally work together to address problems of the homeless mentally ill aged such as lack of proper shelter, inadequate diet, physical disorders, and risk of crime victimization. Some emergency shelters have successfully developed gap-filling measures to respond to some of these problems, but difficulties experienced in developing broad-scale comprehensive solutions have resulted in insufficient, fragmented care. The traditional service systems have both the expertise to assist those who are in crisis and access to options that could serve as preventive measures, but these systems have so far not been linked to form a full range of comprehensive services.

Homelessness: Precipitating Mental Health Service Issues

The homeless mentally ill face an inadequate community-based system of care. They do not fit into traditional mental health, medical, or other human service systems, and these systems do not consider themselves to be primarily responsible for the homeless mentally ill. At the same time, fiscal austerity has decreased traditional system resources. Emergency shelters and other alternative systems that have emerged to serve as a stopgap for the homeless also find it nearly impossible to deal with the special needs of the elderly and mentally ill.

Deinstitutionalization

Deinstitutionalization of the mentally ill increased the size and changed the composition of the homeless population. Although less than 15 percent of the homeless elderly are former long-term patients who were deinstitutionalized (Project FUTURE, 1986; Weeden & Linehan, 1987), many either would have been institutionalized under the old system or are currently involved in the "revolving door" between short institutional stays and the street.

A primary motivating force behind deinstitutionalization was financial, in particular the attempt to shift the financing burden from the state to federal and local governments. Although the system of community mental health was expanded, and was to be developed to serve the deinstitutionalized and those who would otherwise have been institutionalized, this system was never adequately funded. Fiscal austerity in the 1980s has led to the decline of those elements of such a community-based system that had been put into place (see chapters 4 and 5 for more detailed discussions of these issues). This decline is exacerbated by problems within the system of community-based care.

Problems in the Traditional System of Community-Based Care

Problems within the community-based system of care that particularly affect the homeless mentally ill elderly include the need for diversified planning, exclusionary policies that serve as barriers to the receipt of appropriate care, and conflicting expectations among providers as to what constitutes appropriate treatment.

Diversified Programming. A major problem in community-based mental health services is the complexity of planning required for an extremely diverse population. Even within subgroups such as the homeless mentally ill elderly there are extensive variations of need. Needs extend beyond institutionally based residential and psychiatric care to such services as assistance to patients in maintaining entitlements, regular physical and mental health monitoring, provision of opportunities for social interaction, and relief for overburdened families (Thurer, 1983). Scarce offerings of community-based services are typically divided among many health and human service agencies in the public and private sectors. As noted in chapter 5, these systems have not been adequately organized or financed to achieve either continuity or comprehensive care (Bachrach, 1984; Segal, Baumohl, & Johnson, 1977; Talbott & Lamb, 1984).

Exclusionary Policies. Programs for the mentally ill are often targeted to the highest functioning members of that population. Bachrach (1984) presents an example of a supervised apartment and group home program for the mentally ill that was available only to those judged capable of being rehabilitated, not for the so-called "hopeless" cases, a label often assigned to the chronic mentally ill homeless. Other programs assist long-time residents of institutions to adapt to life in the community, thereby excluding many chronically or newly homeless people who have never been hospitalized (Segal et al., 1977). Segal et al. note that the lack of a permanent address greatly increases the difficulty of receiving entitlements, because service system routines are often conducted by mail. Another problem is that categorical admission criteria for either mental health or substance abuse programs can serve as access barriers to meeting the needs of homeless mentally ill persons with substance abuse problems, which by all accounts constitute a substantial percentage of the overall homeless mentally ill population (Barrow & Lowell, 1983). Finally, the fact that the "cure" rate for mental illness among the homeless is not demonstrably high makes this group (including the homeless mentally ill elderly) unattractive to service providers who tend to measure their effectiveness in terms of cures (Stern & Minkoff, 1979).

Conflicting Expectations. The inability of many homeless individuals to attain a traditional lifestyle poses special problems for mental health service providers. Traditional services are geared toward rehabilitation. The needs of the homeless are often in conflict with these rehabilitation goals, and are therefore left unmet by the mental health system (Donovan, 1985; Larew, 1980). Some investigators in community psychiatry conclude that there is a great need for residential treatment facilities in which homeless clients can maintain some stability by receiving at least a minimum of attention and by not being exposed to the uncertainties and rigors of street life (Lamb & Grant, 1982, 1983). Such response may conflict with a general concept of the mental health system, that of the "least restrictive alternative" that encourages "freedom" for the mentally ill, based on individual consent to placement in treatment settings (Klein, 1983). Some service providers note that the homeless mentally ill are often unwilling or unable to give consent (Perkins, 1985). The additional physical disorders of old age may further impair the ability of the homeless mentally ill aged to assess their own needs.

Alternative Services Target for the Homeless Mentally Ill

Resources exist in the community through which the homeless mentally ill elderly could receive care and support. The number of Veterans Administration and nonfederal general hospitals with psychiatric units has more than doubled to 1,300 in the past 30 years, and the number of freestanding psychiatric outpatient clinics has also doubled to over 1,000. Community mental health centers received over $213 million in federal funds in 1978 (Thompson, Bass, & Witkin, 1982). However, the fear of involuntary hospitalization prevents many mentally ill homeless persons from accepting any psychiatric services from clearly identified mental health programs (Kellerman, Halper, Hopkins, & Nayowith, 1985). Furthermore, traditional systems wishing to treat the homeless mentally ill experience major service delivery problems when they rely on such approaches as prescribing drugs or requiring regular appointments (Bassuk & Lauriat, 1984). Four basic types of programs have emerged to meet the mental health needs of the episodically or chronically homeless who are mentally ill (Kellerman et al., 1985; Levine, 1984). These include street outreach, drop-in centers, on-site rehabilitation, and psychosocial clubs.

Street Outreach. The experiences of several street outreach programs suggest that homeless people on the streets are older and more disabled than the sheltered population (Baxter & Hopper, 1984). Such individuals are least likely to know where to find agencies, programs, and resources and are most vulnerable to pressures created by too many questions, too many forms, and long waits (Levine, 1984). The flexible approach of some local outreach efforts is important to the homeless mentally ill elderly, and seems to have an impact on serving the hard-to-reach population (Cohen, Putnam, & Sullivan, 1984). Initial steps often include providing concrete services such as food and clothing, and making repeated contacts to establish familiarity and trust (Trotter, 1983).

Drop-In Centers. Drop-in centers require no commitment or formal affiliation for a night's respite from the streets. They are generally small, personal facilities located where street people congregate or have easy access, frequently occupying storefront space (Levine, 1984). Some local programs report success in building an atmosphere of trust with homeless individuals and serving significant proportions of elderly clients (Coalition for the Homeless, 1984). Within these settings, professional staff assess the range of problems experienced by the homeless mentally ill.

On-Site Rehabilitation and Psychosocial Clubs. On-site rehabilitation programs have been established at a number of emergency shelters, community-based residential care facilities, and SRO hotels. Socialization activities are offered in order to reacquaint recently homeless individuals with skills that are an integral part of community life (Kellerman et al., 1985). A similar treatment model is the psychosocial club. Within an informal setting, staff work towards stabilizing psychiatric conditions and encouraging individuals to move from social isolation to social interaction (Kultgen & Habenstein, 1984).

Although these four program types have had reasonable success in meeting the needs of mentally ill homeless people (Wagenfeld, Lemkau, & Justice, 1982), the literature does not address the effectiveness of these treatment programs for specific subgroups such as the elderly. Moreover, relatively few of these alternative programs exist (Levine & Stockdill, 1984). Further, Bassuk (1984) observes that many mental health professionals (unlike the activists within the emergency shelter network) are uncomfortable in assuming the necessary advocacy roles to initiate new programs, particularly when they involve confrontation and political activism, activities that are usually not financially compensated (Bassuk & Lauriat, 1984). Finally, these alternative mental health services may "perpetuate" homelessness, insofar as they provide care that diverts social responsibility and financial commitment from the traditional systems that have been historically and morally charged with caring for the needs of the poor elderly and mentally disabled members of society.

Homelessness: Precipitating Health and Social Service Issues

Recent changes in federal financing policy for both health and social services have resulted in limited access to supportive and preventive services and an increased medical and crisis orientation. These changes place greater stress on individual resources, on caregivers, and on existing community-based systems, resulting in an increased vulnerability of the aged, especially the mentally ill aged, to nursing home placement or homelessness.

Fiscal Constraints

In this era of reduced resources for social services and of health care cost containment efforts, the multifaceted problems experienced by the homeless, the mentally ill, and the elderly often go unaddressed. For example, recent Medicare reimbursement changes have severely limited access to and the duration of general hospital care. The average length of stay for the elderly has been reduced 10 to 20 percent (Wood, Fox, Estes, Lee, & Mahoney, 1986). Reimbursement systems, in particular Medicare DRGs, now restrict how hospitals deal with acute medical problems. These changes result in less hospital flexibility in providing care for individuals with multiple problems, such as the homeless.

With the decreased length of stay, the aged are apparently being discharged from hospitals earlier and in more precarious medical conditions. The effect on community-based programs has been an increased medicalization of services, evidenced by the expansion of the home care and adult day health systems (Wood et al., 1986). The federal focus on medical care gives medical services a more stable source of reimbursement than such supportive social services as senior centers and nutrition programs. Thus the role of the latter programs in the prevention and early detection of medical and social crises is being undermined, and access to services is increasingly dependent upon medical conditions. These changes are especially detrimental for the mentally ill aged. Lack of early access to medical and social services forces the individual to be in a crisis situation before services can be received. Without support for preventive activities, mentally impaired individuals who are barely surviving in the community may be seriously at risk of becoming homeless, due to episodic symptoms of mental illness (Levy & Henley, 1985).

Increased Demand on Fewer Caregivers

Families, especially the female members, have been the traditional providers of care for the aged, serving as important deterrents to placement in nursing homes. Elders who are divorced, separated, or who never married may be as much as 10 times (and widowed elders 5 times) more likely than their married counterparts to be institutionalized (Butler & Newacheck, 1981). Recent trends toward small families, divorce, and geographical dispersal of family members all contribute to a decrease in the available number of family caregivers, in turn placing elders at risk of homelessness, as well as of institutionalization. The scarcity of family caregivers and the increased emphasis on medical care in the home have also placed greater stress on available caregivers. Overburdened caregivers and fiscal constraints on providing services for an expanding aging population have resulted in a greater vulnerability of the aged to crises such as homelessness.

Homelessness: Precipating Housing Issues

The lack of appropriate residential options and the inadequacy of national housing policies have an impact on the ability of the elderly to maintain physical and mental health and to live independently in the community.

Absence of Residential Options

The nationwide deinstitutionalization of state mental hospital patients has resulted in major problems for local communities. The ideology of deinstitutionalization was based on the assumption of discharge to supportive community-based care in a variety of residential settings (Blank, 1978). In actuality, community resistance and the lack of funds prevented the development of special housing facilities and programs in sufficient quantity (Crystal, n.d.), and caused the uneven development of systems for the delivery of mental health services. As a result, obtaining and retaining adequate housing has become a serious problem for the chronically mentally ill who are now diverted from, or never considered for, long-term institutional psychiatric care.

Families of the deinstitutionalized mentally ill were, in some cases, able to care for them. Minkoff (cited in Talbott, 1983) states that in the early days of deinstitutionalization, 65 percent of those discharged returned home, and few lived alone. Crystal (n.d.) notes that others were able to form stable family units and maintain steady employment, thereby achieving a modest standard of living. In other cases, however, the family of origin was unable or unwilling to assume responsibility for sheltering and caring for the deinstitutionalized chronically mentally ill. The issue of family caregiving continues as a problem for those who are diverted from long-term institutional care. Of the estimated 1.7–2.4 million chronically mentally ill in 1977, 800,000 to 1,500,000 lived at home or in a variety of community residences, including board-and-care homes (Goldman et al., 1981).

Nursing homes have become one of the primary "community placements" for many of the chronically mentally ill elderly, replacing the state hospital in the provision of long term care (see chapters 3 and 5). The vast majority of nursing home facility staffs have little or no experience or training in how to work with mentally ill patients.

Residential care facilities (including board-and-care homes) have often been the only community option for supportive care for the mentally ill elderly (Drinan, 1983). The degree and type of care being provided for this population varies. The facilities are at times indifferent (Donahue, 1978), if not hostile (Aviram & Segal, 1973). Although some community-based residential care has proven to be an adequate alternative to institutionally based care, especially when incorporated into an overall community-care strategy for the psychiatric population (Haber, 1983; Hinz, 1983), there appears to be a trend toward reduction in the number of board-and-care beds for the mentally ill.

Public housing has, for the most part, not played a significant role in providing community-based residences for the chronically mentally ill or sheltering the homeless (Department of Housing and Urban Development [DHUD], 1984). Admission criteria usually exclude individuals with a variety of physical and mental health problems that may make them unsuitable for independent living. When elderly persons with chronic psychological impairments are integrated into federally subsidized senior housing, such factors as the pervasiveness of social prejudice against the mentally ill can result in an incompatible environment for mentally impaired elders (Brendenberg, 1983).

SRO housing was affordable and plentiful in the late 1960s and early 1970s, the time of the steepest reductions in state hospital censuses. Had this not been so, the inadequate development of community-based residential facilities would have been apparent much earlier (Crystal, n.d.). Although found in highly stressed, ghettoized parts of urban communities, SRO hotels are suggested by some (Cohen & Sokolovsky, 1983; Erickson & Eckert, 1977) as informal supportive environments for adults with chronic impairments, especially when physical or mental health worsens, causing a need for assistance with activities of daily living. Eckert (1982) found these hotel networks to have minimal involvement and to allow for a high degree of privacy. Unfortunately, the location and style of SROs make occupants visible, vulnerable targets for social control (for example, by police, religious chasteners, or social workers) and displacement caused by urban renewal (Hoch & Cibulskis, 1986).

Clearly, the reality for a great many of the chronically mentally ill, if they were to remain in the community, would be a life of economic hardship, characterized by welfare dependency and limited social resources. In essence, they would have to confront all the problems associated with urban poverty (Crystal, n.d.).

Unresponsive National Housing Policies

The issue of who is responsible for housing the chronically mentally ill has been problematic since deinstitutionalization began gaining momentum in the 1960s, at the same time that the country was undergoing a major urban renewal movement. In its widely accepted social policy to provide adequate housing, the federal government has generally ignored mentally ill and marginal citizens. Government interest in promoting the so-called "private" revitalization of urban America is, unfortunately, threatening to elimate most housing options for the poor and chronically mentally ill elderly. According to literature reviewed by Kasinitz, public sector assistance has included the "aid of municipal planning departments, zoning changes, (historical) landmark designations, federal tax breaks and municipal tax abatements, as well as various governmental grants often funneled through quasi-public local development corporations" (Kasinitz, 1984, p. 9).

The new federalism philosophy of returning housing to the private sector is reflected not only in the promotion of local efforts at downtown revitalization and neighborhood gentrification, but also in the budget cutback or phase-out of many federally sponsored low-income housing programs. That this is intentional policy is evidenced by a statement in the U.S. Presidential Commission on Housing report of 1982: "The Administration places its trust not in subsidies, but in the genius of the private market, freed of the distortion forced by government housing policies and regulations" (cited by Huth, 1986, p. 10). Lacking the economic and political power to resist eviction and displacement, the nation's poor have been unable to protect their dwellings from conversion or demolition for more profitable uses and thus have become at risk of homelessness.

The impact of urban renewal within skid row areas resulted in a net population loss of nearly 40 percent in the 1960s, and 30 percent by the 1970s (Hull, Haley, & Rothman, 1982; Lee, 1978). As the number and affordability of SROs has declined, obtaining SRO housing has become more difficult for the chronically mentally ill. Moreover, the chronically mentally ill with persistent behavioral problems are often no longer tolerated in SRO settings. As the SRO housing supply began to dwindle, these individuals were often displaced by more desirable tenants (Crystal, n.d.). In an SRO resident survey conducted in New York City in late 1985, less than 11 percent of a sample of 505 tenants reported a history of psychiatric hospitalization. This is in sharp contrast to a comparable study conducted 5 years earlier, which found a 23-percent rate of previous psychiatric hospitalization. Crystal explains that much of the SRO housing supply is financially unavailable to the poor, as indicated by the distribution of rent levels found in the survey (Crystal, n.d.). The SSI grant level with state supplementation (SSP) was only $375 per month at the time of the survey, when the median monthly rent for all SRO housing types was $236, and the mean $303. Moreover, these figures underrepresent rental costs, because lower rents are paid by long-term tenants. Twenty-nine percent of the 1985 survey sample were 60 years of age or older.

Further evidence of SRO displacement comes from intake data collected on the homeless using city shelters. In a 1986 study of New York City homeless street people, many chronically mentally ill, brought into shelters through outreach programs, 19 percent had lived in SROs prior to admission to the shelter. Inability to pay the rent was the most common single reason for leaving the prior residence (Goldstein, Levine, & Lipkins, 1986). Lack of SRO housing was an even more frequent reason for homelessness among the elderly in an earlier study by Crystal and Goldstein (1984), which showed that 27 percent of over-60 homeless clients had previously been living in an SRO. The remaining SRO housing stock continues to be threatened by gentrification and downtown revitalization, clearly resulting in fewer options for adults with chronic impairments (Levine & Stockdill, 1984). This growing limitation in residential options compromises the ability of the mentally ill aged to maintain health and achieve a maximum level of functioning (Baxter and Hopper, 1984), and has left many homeless (Bachrach, 1984; Coalition for the Homeless, 1984; Liptzin, 1984; Ovrebo et al., in press).

Homelessness: Precipitating Emergency Shelter Issues

An expanding network of emergency shelters has been developed for the homeless, who are only peripherally, if at all, served by the traditional networks of mental health, social, health, and housing services. For the homeless, these emergency shelters are basically the only alternatives to living on the streets. The rapid increase in the formation of shelters is reflected in the fact that 41 percent of current shelters have been in existence 4 years or less (Stimpson, 1984). This growth is primarily accounted for by the development of the large number of public (municipal) shelters.

Shelters are beginning to take on the image of other institutional settings. Some of the mentally ill homeless are unable to cope with the impersonal nature and regimen associated with shelter facilities, particularly those housing large numbers of people. Many mentally disturbed persons fear the confinement of a shelter facility, after having spent a portion of their lives in institutions (Perkins, 1985). Furthermore, it is generally known that some shelters refuse to serve either the aged or the mentally ill homeless (Levine & Stockdill, 1984). Mentally ill persons who are served by shelters often become long-term users (New York City Human Resources Administration, 1984). Staff resources are often too limited to arrange placement in the even more limited housing market. Staff may also be inexperienced in responding to the special needs of the mentally ill (Flynn, 1985).

Institutional Nature

According to a national shelter survey conductd by the U.S. Department of Housing and Urban Development (Stimpson, 1984), 84 percent of shelters will evict or refuse readmittance to persons who possess alcohol or drugs while in the shelter. Some shelters forbid smoking. Many shelters require client information as part of the intake process. For the chronically homeless mentally ill, sharing such information is antithetical to street sense. It requires a trust in authority that street life discourages (Segal & Baumohl, 1980). Moreover, client identification requirements may conflict with civil liberties. Ironically, large municipal shelters may be required to solicit data on individual clients only for reimbursement purposes, not for care planning (Levine, 1984). The networking of shelters is becoming so formalized that clients now fear being relocated to other shelters outside their own neighborhoods when the site they normally use is full (Coalition for the Homeless, 1984).

Threatening Settings

Many shelters are not appropriate for vulnerable homeless elderly persons. An increasing proportion of younger and stronger men and women is coming into the shelter system. Large numbers of these younger persons are mentally ill and include young male paranoid schizophrenics, many of whom have previously been arrested for assault (Whitmer, 1980). The recently developed large municipal shelters cannot protect the frail, so the homeless elderly increasingly avoid these shelters for fear of the younger homeless (Coalition for the Homeless, 1984; Coleman, 1983).

Difficulty in Meeting Individual Needs

As shelter sizes increase, the facilities become more anonymous, and high client–staff ratios make personalized services exceedingly difficult. Because the larger shelters usually house heterogeneous populations with multiple problems, staff are often unable to establish the one-to-one relationships that are necessary for building trust and support among mentally disturbed persons (Levine, 1984). Several communities are developing programs to meet the specialized needs of homeless individuals. For example, Shasta County in California has developed separate programs for "employable" and "interim assistance" homeless populations with physical and mental disabilities (California Department of Housing and Community Development, 1985). State officials in Florida are in the process of formulating programs to deal with severely dysfunctional mentally ill homeless (J. Noble, personal communication, Aug. 26, 1985).

Preclusive Admissions

The mentally ill are often excluded from emergency shelter programs designed to serve the homeless; and the homeless typically experience difficulty in receiving community-based services designed for the chronically mentally ill. Shelters often lack the funding and staffing capacity to assist the homeless mentally ill (Levine, 1984). This service gap has a direct impact on the revolving-door utilization of local jail facilities by large numbers of the homeless mentally ill. This issue has been extensively covered in daily newspaper articles (Donovan, 1985; Earley, 1983), and the professional literature (Swank & Winer, 1976; Whitmer, 1980). Lamb and Grant (1982, 1983) found in a recent study of the Los Angeles County criminal justice system that more than half of those charged with misdemeanors had been living in cheap hotels, in emergency shelters, or on the street. Of 102 persons selected at random from those referred for psychiatric evaluation, ages ranged from 18 to 79 years; 36 percent of male and 42 percent of female inmates were homeless at the time of arrest.

An Emerging System

Networks of emergency shelters have taken the lead in the development of proposals to ameliorate the problem of homelessness. Recommendations reflect the facts that shelters cannot meet immediate demands and have difficulty in making long-term arrangements, resulting in the persistent need for more low-cost housing. Some emergency shelter advocates also believe the problem of the homeless mentally ill can be solved by the development of such long-term supportive residences as residential hotels with case management services. These new solutions cause concern among some mental health professionals, who believe the development of specialized residential settings for the mentally ill should remain the responsibility of mental health agencies (Bassuk & Lauriat, 1984; Perkins, 1985). Mowbray (1985) contends that as long as government funds are being used to provide mental health services in emergency shelters, it will be difficult to get public support for psychiatric residential treatment facilities.

Another example of shelter-system expansion into related services is the involvement in public assistance programs to help the homeless and others with difficulty in meeting housing costs. Government-funded vouchers allow many of the homeless to temporarily live in hotels or apartments until permanent housing is found. Others, in danger of being evicted, receive government assistance in making rent payments. A variety of additional supportive services are offered, varying considerably by locality (Stimpson, 1984). The provision of these rental payments or vouchers is often targeted to populations with special needs, including families, the physically disabled, the aged, and occasionally the mentally ill (California Department of Housing and Community Development, 1985; Coalition for the Homeless, 1984; DHUD, 1984; United States Conference of Mayors, 1984).

Policy Implications Raised by the Concurrence of Mental Health Problems and Homelessness

This chapter provides an overview of conditions that precipitate homelessness among the mentally ill elderly, and of the consequential challenges to traditional service systems. Much of the multidisciplinary literature on this subject is inconclusive. However, there is an emerging consensus that today's homeless find themselves in need of shelter as a consequence of such precipitating factors as deinstitutionalization; the shrinking supply of low-income housing; the reduction and elimination of entitlements; socioeconomic conditions reflecting changes in the structure of the economy; and fiscal austerity at all levels of government. If present trends continue, such vulnerable groups as the impoverished elderly, mentally ill, socially marginal, and politically powerless populations will remain homeless, and their ranks will be expanded by additional groups currently at risk.

The policy recommendations that follow from the discussion presented in this chapter offer no panacea. An overarching theme is the call for an end to single-issue approaches to ameliorate the complex interrelated conditions that have converged to produce homelessness of a scope unparalleled since the Great Depression. The traditional service delivery systems must work together to formulate a comprehensive approach to service delivery and delineate the focal points of financial responsibility.

A Comprehensive Approach within Traditional Service Systems

Municipalities nationwide want the root causes of homelessness addressed, so that cities do not have to cope with the same emergency situation year after year (United States Conference of Mayors, 1984). Because of current limits on human services funding, public officials will not authorize the creation of new systems to meet unique service needs (Fry, 1983). Emergency solutions currently being developed by several cities incorporate assistance from mental health, medical, social, and housing service systems at various levels of government (House of Representatives, 1984). By not addressing the fundamental causes of homelessness, however, these traditional service systems have substituted one inadequate system for another (Bassuk & Lauriat, 1984). Adjustments need to be made in existing traditional service systems (Fry, 1983), within the context of rising demand and decreases in the growth of government expenditures (Liptzin, 1984).

Responsibility for the nation's mentally ill who are homeless transcends the mental health community. There is growing recognition that comprehensive care for the subpopulations of the homeless mentally ill must involve collaboration across levels of government; across mental health, medical, housing, and human service agencies; and between the public and private sectors. Attention must be paid to addressing both long-term needs and immediate emergency needs of the homeless mentally ill (Levine, 1984).

Components of a comprehensive system of services for the homeless mentally ill elderly could be contributed by existing service systems. Within the mental health system, the experiences of community mental health centers point to the desirability of closer integration between psychiatry and other human services (Musto, 1977). The aging network has extensive experience in the formation of comprehensive service systems involving interagency cooperation, individualized programming, cultural sensitivity, and a flexible format. Additionally, mental health professionals have already proven that psychological care can be effectively provided within senior housing (Cohen, 1983).

The mental health system clearly needs to be actively involved in developing new residential options that promote mental health. Intermediate levels of care are needed to prepare the mentally disabled homeless both to accept existing mental health treatment services and to function independently at their maximum capacity (Cuomo, 1983). Transitional housing programs are needed as an interim step to securing permanent housing and treatment for each resident.

Finally, the development of low-cost housing options in the community is essential to long-range mental health service provision to the homeless (Kellerman et al., 1985). Because an emergency shelter system will always be needed to respond to those who have become homeless due to socioeconomic crises or who choose to remain homeless, the link between the therapeutic and survival imperatives of the homeless must be addressed in this system, as well as in the mental health services system (Baxter & Hopper, 1982).

Financial and Social Responsibility and Jurisdiction for Care

Obstacles to effective service delivery to subgroups of the homeless mentally ill include but are not limited to problem conceptualization and needs assessment. A major issue is whether homelessness leads to mental illness, or vice versa. Agreement on such issues could result in the identification of financial responsibility and jurisdiction of care (Bassuk, Rubin, & Lauriat, 1984).

Development of comprehensive solutions must have political support in order to effect social responsibility. The increasing visibility of homeless people, highlighted by widespread media coverage, has given the issue substantial political value. Public attention to the emergency shelter system has allowed various shelter networks across the country to be successful in obtaining support from elected officials for many gap-filling measures. This direct support for emergency services may negatively affect the ability of some shelter providers to coordinate their services with other systems. At the same time, many mental health experts feel that funds are being deflected from prevention, research, and planning that could minimize the dimensions of the problem (Fry, 1983; Talbott & Lamb, 1984).

Public policy regarding financial responsibility to meet the needs of the homeless mentally ill elderly will likely be created, implemented, and enforced at the state level (Brown & Cousineau, 1984). Such policy could include a plan for a continuum of services, relying on greater public and private sensitivity and financial commitment. Policies such as bans on zoning discrimination against mentally ill persons and reforms of funding mechanisms to ensure utilization of appropriate options are desirable. Regulations, too, must affirm the right to adequate treatment in the least-restrictive setting for both voluntary and involuntary patients and must accommodate cultural differences in services, treatment, and community programs (Hombs & Snyder, 1982).

Integrated, multifaceted responses are required to reverse present trends and begin to reduce the size and meet the needs of the diverse subpopulations among the homeless. Consistent, long-term effort is needed at all levels of government and from organizations located within the public and private sectors. The issues of factionalism and responsibility for the homeless, mentally ill, and elderly population require a response that goes beyond speculation and accusation.

References

Anderson, J. (1985, July 15). Homelessness in America. San Francisco *Chronicle*, p. 49.

Acre, A.A., Tadlock, M., Vergare, M.J., & Shapiro, S.H. (1983). A psychiatric profile of street people admitted to an emergency shelter. *Hospital and Community Psychiatry, 34,* 812–817.

Aviram, U., & Segal, S. (1973). Exlusion of the mentally ill: A reflection on an old problem. *Archives of General Psychiatry, 29,* 126–131.

Bachrach, L.L. (1984). The homeless mentally ill and mental health services: An analytical review of the literature. In H.R. Lamb (Ed.), *The homeless mentally ill* (pp. 11–54). Washington, DC: American Psychiatric Association.

Barrow, S., & Lowell, A.M. (1983). *Evaluation of the referral of outreach clients to mental health services, private proprietary homes for adults, CSS eligibility, and acute day hospitals.* New York: New York State Psychiatric Institute.

Bassuk, E.L. (1984). Homelessness: The need for mental health advocates. *Hospital and Community Psychiatry, 35,* 897.

Bassuk, E.L., & Lauriat, A.S. (1984). The politics of homelessness. In R.H. Lamb (Ed.), *The homeless mentally ill* (pp. 301–313). Washington, DC: American Psychiatric Association.

Bassuk, E.L., Rubin, L., & Lauriat, A. (1984). Is homelessness a mental health problem? *American Journal of Psychiatry, 141,* 1546–1549.

Baxter, E., & Hopper, K. (1981). *Private lives/public spaces: Homeless adults on the streets of New York City.* New York: Community Service Society.

Baxter, E., & Hopper, K. (1982). The new mendicancy: Homeless in New York City. *American Journal of Orthopsychiatry, 52,* 393–408.

Baxter, E., & Hopper, K. (1984). Shelter and housing for the homeless mentally ill. In H.R. Lamb (Ed.), *The homeless mentally ill* (pp. 109–139). Washington, DC: American Psychiatric Association.

Bennett, R. (1982). Socially isolated elders. *Generations, 6*(3), 16–19.

Blank, M.A. (1978). A perspective on de-institutionalization and a proposal for community-based services. *Journal of Gerontological Social Work, 1,* 135–145.

Brendenberg, K. (1983). Residential integration of mentally able and elderly mentally ill patient. *Psychiatric Quarterly, 55,* 192–205.

Brickner, P.W. (1985). Health issues in the care of the homeless. In P.W. Brickner, L.K. Scharer, B., Conanan, S. Elvy, & M. Savarese (Eds.), *Health care of homeless people* (pp. 3–18). New York: Springer.

Brown, E.R., & Cousineau, M.R. (1984). Effectiveness of state mandates to maintain local government health services for the poor. *Journal of Health Politics, Policy and Law, 9,* 223–236.

Butler, L.H., & Newacheck, P.W. (1981). Health and social factors affecting long-term-care policy. In J. Meltzer, F. Farrow, and H. Richman (Eds.), *Policy options in long-term care* (pp. 38–77). Chicago, IL: University of Chicago Press.

California Department of Housing and Community Development. (1985). *A study of the issues and characteristics of the homeless population in California.* Sacramento, CA: Author.

Coalition for the Homeless. (1984). Crowded out: Homelessness and the elderly poor in New York City. In House of Representatives, Select Committee on Aging,

Homeless Older Americans (pp. 119–184). Hearing before the Subcommittee on Housing and Consumer Interests, May 2, 1984. Washington, DC: Government Printing Office.

Cohen, C.I., & Sokolovsky, J. (1983). Toward a concept of homelessness among aged men. *Journal of Gerontology, 38*, 81–89.

Cohen, G.D. (1983). Psychogenic program in a public housing setting. *Psychiatric Quarterly, 55*, 173–181.

Cohen, N.L., Putnam, J.F., & Sullivan, A.M. (1984). The mentally ill homeless: Isolation and adaptation. *Hospital and Community Psychiatry, 35*, 922–924.

Coleman, J.R. (1983, February 21). Diary of a homeless man. *New York Magazine*, pp. 5–14.

Cousins, A. (1983). Profile of homeless men and women using an urban shelter. *Journal of Emergency Nursing, 9*, 133–137.

Crystal, S. (n.d.). *SRO housing and the chronically mentally ill: The hierarchy of housing displacement*. Unpublished manuscript, Department of Community and Family Medicine, University of California, San Diego.

Crystal, S., & Goldstein, M. (1984). *Correlates of shelter utilization: One-day study*. New York: New York City Human Resources Administration.

Cuomo, M.M. (1983, July). *1933–1983—never again*. A report to the National Governors' Association Task Force on the Homeless, Portland, Maine.

Department of Housing and Urban Development (DHUD). (1984). *A report to the secretary on the homeless and emergency shelters*. Washington, DC: Author.

Donahue, W. (1978). What about our responsibility to the troubled elderly? *Gerontologist, 18*, 102–111.

Donovan, J. (1985, July 19). People of the streets. San Francisco *Chronicle*, pp. 28, 30.

Doolin, J. (1985). "America's untouchables": The elderly homeless. *Perspective on Aging, 14*(2), 8–11.

Drinan, R.F. (1983). Who will fend for the chronically mentally ill in the community? *Psychiatric Quarterly, 55*, 208–214.

Earley, P. (1983, June 17). Jails are becoming "dumping grounds," federal advisory panel told. Washington *Post*, p. A12.

Eckert, J.K. (1982). Dislocation and relocation of the urban elderly: Social networks as mediators of relocation stress. *Human Organization, 42*, 39–45.

Ehrlich, P. (1986). Hotels, rooming houses, shared housing, and other housing options for the marginal elderly. In R.J. Newcomer, M.P. Lawton, & T. O. Byerts (Eds.), *Housing an aging society: Issues, alternatives and policy* (pp. 189–199). New York: Van Nostrand.

Ehrlich, P. (n.d.). *Study of the St. Louis "Invisible elderly" needs and characteristics of aged "single room occupancy" downtown hotel residents, Dec. 1974–May 1985: Annotated bibliography*. St. Louis, MO: Institute of Applied Gerontology, St. Louis University.

Erickson, R.J., & Echert, J.K. (1977). The elderly poor in downtown hotels. *Gerontologist, 17*, 440–446.

Farr, R.K. (1985). *The homeless mentally ill and the Los Angeles Skid Row Mental Health Project*. Unpublished manuscript, Los Angeles County Department of Mental Health, Los Angeles.

Filardo, T. (1985). Chronic disease management in the homeless. In P.W. Brickner,

L.K. Scharer, B. Conanan, A. Elvy, & M. Savarese (Eds.), *Health care of homeless people* (pp.19–31). New York: Springer.

Flynn, K. (1985). The toll of deinstitutionalization. In P.W. Brickner, L.K. Scharer, B. Conanan, A. Elvy, & M. Savarese (Eds.), *Health care of homeless people* (pp. 189–203). New York: Springer.

Freeman, P. (1984, April 15). The dispossessed. Los Angeles *Herald* (California Living).

Fry, W.R. (1983). Next steps for the elderly deinstitutionalized patient. *Psychiatric Quarterly, 55,* 214–224.

General Accounting Office (GAO). (1985). *Homelessness: A complex problem and the federal response* (GAO pub. no. HRD-85-50). Washington, DC: Author.

Goldfrank, L. (1985). Exposure: Thermoregulatory disorders in the homeless patient. In P.W. Brickner, L.K. Scharer, B. Conanan, A. Elvy, & M. Savarese (Eds.), *Health care of homeless people* (pp. 57–75). New York: Springer.

Goldman, H.H., Gattozzi, A.A., & Taube, C.A. (1981). Defining and counting the chronically mentally ill. *Hospital and Community Psychiatry, 32,* 21–27.

Goldstein, M., Levine, S., & Lipkins, S. (1986). *Charactristics of shelter users.* New York: New York city Human Resources Administration.

Haber, P.A.L. (1983). The Veterans Administration community care setting. *Psychiatric Quarterly, 55,* 187–191.

Haley, B., Pearson, M., & Hull, D. (1982). *Primary individuals in single room occupancy housing (SROs), 1976 and 1980.* Paper presented at the annual meeting of the American Sociological Association, San Francisco.

Hinz, C.E. (1983). Risk taking in the residential community setting. *Psychiatric Quarterly, 55,* 182–186.

Hoch, C., & Cibulskis, A.M. (1986, August 27–29). *Homelessness in the United States.* Paper presented at the annual meeting of the Society for the Study of Social Problems, New York City.

Hombs, M.E., & Snyder, M. (1982). *Homelessness in America: A forced march to nowhere.* Washington, DC: Community for Creative Non-Violence.

Horvath, T.B. (1975). Clinical spectrum and epidemiological features of alcoholic dementia. In J.G. Rankin (Ed.), *Alcohol, drugs, and brain damage: Proceedings of a symposium, effects of chronic use of alcohol and other psychoactive drugs on cerebral function.* Toronto: Alcoholism and Drug Addiction Research Foundation of Ontario.

House of Representatives. Committee on Government Operations and Committee on Banking, Financing and Urban Affairs. (1984). *HUD report on homelessness.* Joint hearing, May 24 (Serial No. 98-91). Washington, DC: Government Printing Office.

House of Representatives. Committee on Government Operations. (1985). *The federal response to the homeless crisis: Third report* (Serial No. 99-47). Washington, DC: Government Printing Office.

Hull, D.A., Haley, B.S., & Rothman, A.J. (1982). *Single room occupant research study: State-of-the-art report. Vol. 1.* Washington, DC: Department of Housing and Urban Development.

Huth, M. J. (1986). *Homelessness in America: Its nature and extent, victims, contributing factors, and current private and public sector responses.* Paper presented at the annual meeting of the Society for the Study of Social Problems, New York City.

Kasinitz, P. (1984). Gentrification and homelessness: The single room occupant and the inner city revival. *Urban and Social Change Review, 17,* 9–14.

Kaufmann, C. (1984). Implication of biological psychiatry for the severely mentally ill: A highly vulnerable population. In Lamb, H.R. (Ed.), *The homeless mentally ill.* Washington, DC: American Psychological Association.

Kellerman, S.L., Halper, R.S., Hopkins, M., & Nayowith, G.B. (1985). Psychiatry and homelessness: Problems and programs. In P.W. Brickner, L.K. Scharer, B. Conanan, A. Elvy, & M. Savarese (Eds.), *Health care of homeless people* (pp. 179–189). New York: Springer.

Kelley, J.T. (1985). Trauma: With example of San Francisco's shelter programs. In P.W. Brickner, L.K. scharer, B. Conanan, A. Elvy, & M. Savarese (Eds.), *Health care of homeless people* (pp. 77–91). New York: Springer.

Kellogg, F.R. Piantieri, O., Conanan, B., Doherty, P., Vicic, W.J., & Brickner, P.W. (1985). Hypertension: A Screening and treatment program for the homeless. In P.W. Brickner, L.K. Scharer, B. Conanan, A. Elvy, & M. Savarese (Eds.), *Health care for homeless people* (pp. 109–119). New York: Springer.

Klein, J. (1983). The least restrictive alternative: More about less. *Psychiatric Quarterly, 55,* 106–114.

Kultgen, P., & Habenstein, R. (1984). Processes and goals in aftercare programs for deinstitutionalized elderly mental patients. *Gerontologist, 24,* 167–173.

Ladner, S. (1985). Elderly in the New York City shelter system. Paper presented by Project FUTURE: New York City Human Resources Administration at the annual meeting of the National Council on the Aging, San Francisco, CA.

Lamb, H,R,, & Grant, R.W. (1982). The mentally ill in an urban jail. *Archives in General Psychiatry, 39,* 17–22.

Lamb, H.R., & Grant, R.W. (1983). Mentally ill women in a county jail. *Archives in General Psychiatry, 40,* 363–368.

Larew, B.I. (1980, February). Strange strangers: Serving transients. *Social Casework,* 107–113.

Lee, B. (1978, September). *Disappearance of Skidrow: Some ecological evidence.* Paper presented at the annual meeting of the American Sociological Association, San Francisco, CA.

Levine, I.S. (1984, November 12). *Shaping the nation's health agenda for the homeless mentally ill.* Paper presented at the annual meeting of the American Public Health Association, Anaheim, CA.

Levine, I.S., & Stockdill, J.W. (1984). Mentally ill and homeless: A national problem. In B. Jones (Ed.), *Treating the homeless: Urban psychiatry's challenge.* Washington, DC: American Psychiatric Association Press.

Levy, L.T., & Henley, B. (1985). Psychiatric care for the homeless: Human beings or cases? In P.W. Brickner, L.K. Scharer, B. Conanan, S. Elvy, & M. Savarese (Eds.), *Health care of homeless people* (pp. 205–219). New York: Springer.

Lindeman, D. (1984). *Alzheimer's disease handbook.* Washington, DC: Department of Health and Human Services.

Lipton, F.R., Sabatini, A., & Katz, S.E. (1983). Down and out in the city: The homeless mentally ill. *Hospital and Community Psychiatry, 34,* 817–821.

Liptzin, B. (1984). Canadian and U.S. systems of care for the mentally ill elderly. *Gerontologist, 24,* 174–178.

Max, W., Lindeman, D.A., Segura, T.G., & Benjamin, A.E. (1986). *Estimating the utilization and costs of formal and informal care provided to brain-impaired adults.* San Francisco, CA: Institute for Health & Aging, University of California.

McAdam, J., Brickner, P.W., Glicksman, R., Edwards, D., Fallon, B., & Yanowitch, P. (1985). Turberculosis in the SRD/homeless population. In P.W. Brickner, L.K. Scharer, B. Conanan, A. Elvy, & M. Savarese (Eds.), *Health care of homeless people* (pp. 155–175). New York: Springer.

Morgan, R., Geffner, E.I., Kiernan, E., & Cowles, S. (1985). Alcoholism and the homeless. In P.W. Brickner, L.K. Scharer, B. Conanan, A. Elvy, & M. Savarese (Eds.), *Health care of homeless people* (pp. 131–151). New York: Springer.

Mowbray, C.T. (1985). Homelessness in America: Myths and realities. *American Journal of Orthopsychiatry, 55,* 4–8.

Musto, D.F. (1977). Whatever happened to community mental health? *Psychiatric Annals, 7,* 510–522.

National Health Law Project (1984, Summer). A mounting social dilemma—health care for the homeless. *Health Advocate* (141), pp. 1, 7, 8.

New York City Human Resources Administration (1982). New arrivals: First time shelter clients. In House of Representatives, Committee on Banking, Finance, and Urban Affairs, *Homelessness in America* (pp. 272–330). Hearing before the Subcommittee on Housing and Community Development, December 15, 1982 (Serial No. 97-100). Washington, DC: Government Printing Office.

New York City Human Resources Administration (1984). *Correlates of shelter utilization—one-day study.* Unpublished memorandum.

Ovrebo, B., Liljestrand, P., & Minkler, M. (in press). Homelessness and the disappearance of the low-price residential hotel. In R.I. Jahiel (ed.), *Homelessness: A prevention oriented approach.* San Francisco, CA: Jossey-Bass.

Peele, R., & Palmer, R.R. (1980). Patient rights and patient chronocity. *Journal of Psychiatry and Law, 8,* 59–71.

Perkins, J. (1985, February 26). New institutions for the homeless. *The Wall Street Journal,* p. 18.

Project FUTURE. (1985). *Project FUTURE: Shelter client profiles.* New York: New York City Human Resources Administration.

Project FUTURE. (1985). *Project FUTURE: Focusing, understanding, targeting, and utilizing resources for the homeless mentally ill, elderly, youth, substance abusers, and employables.* New York: New York City Human Resources Administration.

Quinn, M.J., & Tomita, S.K. (1986). *Elder abuse and neglect: Causes, diagnosis, and intervention strategies.* New York: Springer.

Ropers, R., & Boyer, R. (1986). *Physical and mental health status among the homeless* (Homeless Research Project Document #1). Cedar City, UT: Department of Behavioral and Social Sciences, Southern Utah State College.

Ropers, R., & Boyer, R. (in press). How are you feeling today? Self-reported physical and mental health among the new urban homeless. *Alcohol, Health and Research World.*

Rousseau, A.M. (1981). *Shopping bag ladies.* New York: Pilgrim Press.

Segal, S.P., & Baumohl, J. (1980). Engaging the disengaged: Proposals on madness and vagrancy. *Social Work, 25,* 358–365.

Segal, S.P., Baumohl, J., & Johnson, E. (1977). Falling through the cracks: Mental disorders and social margin in a young vagrant. *Social Problems, 24,* 387–400.

Stern, R., & Minkoff, K. (1979). Paradoxes in programming for chronic patients in a community clinic. *Hospital Community Psychiatry, 30,* 613–617.

Stimpson, J.W. (1984, November 12). *Policy and research on the homeless.* Paper presented at the annual meeting of the American Public Health Association, Anaheim, CA.

Swank, G.E., & Winer, D. (1976). Occurrence of psychiatric disorder in a county jail population. *American Journal of Psychiatry, 133,* 1331–1333.

Talbott, J.A. (1983). A special population: The elderly deinstitutionalized chronically mentally ill patient. *Psychiatric Quarterly, 55,* 90–105.

Talbott, J.A., & Lamb, H.R. (1984). Summary and recommendations. In H.R. Lamb (Ed.), *The homeless mentally ill* (pp. 1–10). Washington, DC: American Psychiatric Association.

Thomas, E. (1985, February 4) Coming in from the cold. *Time,* pp. 20–21.

Thompson, J.W., Bass, R.D., & Witkin, M.J. (1982). Fifty years of psychiatric services: 1940–1990. *Hospital and Community Psychiatry, 33,* 711–717.

Thurer, S.L. (1983). Deinstitutionalization and women: Where the buck stops. *Hospital and Community Psychiatry, 34,* 1162–1163.

Torrey, E.G., Bargmann, E., & Wolfe, S.M. (1985). *Washington's grate society: Schizophrenics in the shelters and on the street.* Washington, DC: Public Citizen Health Research Group.

Trotter, R. (1983). *Alcohol, drug abuse, and mental health problems of the homeless: Proceedings of a roundtable—March 31 and April 1, 1983.* Rockville, MD: Department of Health and Human Services, Public Health Service, Alcohol, Drug Abuse, and Mental Health Administration.

United States Conference of Mayors. (1984). *Homeless in America's cities.* Washington, DC: Author.

Wagenfeld, M.O., Lemkau, P.V., & Justice, B. (1982). Future directions in public mental health. In M.O. Wagenfeld, P.V. Lemkau, & B. Justice (Eds.), *Public mental health: Perspectives and prospectives.* Beverly Hills, CA: Sage.

Weeden, J.P., & Linehan, M. (1987). *Elders and housing displacement: Community investigation and proposed interventions.* A transitional housing task force report of the Coalition of Agencies Serving the Elderly. San Francisco, CA: Institute for Health & Aging, University of California.

Whitmer, G.E. (1980). From hospitals to jails: The fate of California's deinstitutionalized mentally ill. *American Journal of Orthopsychiatry, 50,* 65–75.

Winnick, M. (1983, October 27–28). *Nutrition.* Paper presented at the United Hospital Fund of New York Conference on Health Issues in Care for the Homeless, New York.

Wood, J.B., Fox, P.J., Estes, C.L., Lee, P.R., & Mahoney, C.W. (1986). *Public policy, the private nonprofit sector and the delivery of community-based long term care services for the elderly: Final report to the Pew Memorial Trust.* San Francisco, CA: Institute for Health & Aging, University of California.

Implications for Research and Service Delivery

James J. Callahan, Jr.

This book presents important research, points out where additional research is needed, and discusses policy implications. It is bound to stimulate the knowledgeable reader to think about specific program interventions that will be responsive to real problems faced by policymakers and practitioners. The choice of interventions, however, is not dictated by the material in this book. The choice will depend on political concerns and levels of understanding, feasibility, and resources. We have identified five choices that we believe are supported by the research findings of this project, cut across a number of important issues, are feasible, and offer the hope of significantly improving the well-being of older persons.

1. The behavioral complications of mental disability present serious problems in the care of older persons both at home and in institutions. Behavioral problems are particularly difficult in the home setting because of the supervision demanded, the disruption caused, and the potential for spilling over into the neighborhood. These problems are an important reason why older persons are placed in nursing homes. Some mental conditions (for example, senile dementia) apparently cannot be cured and suggest a hopeless situation. The research review, however, shows that "effective management of the behavioral complications of senile dementia is possible." This encouraging finding leads to potential program interventions. A state or national center could be established to identify effective treatment techniques, classify them by the type of situation in which they can be most helpful, and experiment with developing additional treatments. The center could develop a dissemination strategy to reach those families and congregate settings dealing with this problem. This strategy would utilize self-help groups, both as management techniques in themselves and as a means of dissemination to caretakers. The self-help material in this book could be used in the design of the groups. Finally, reimbursement strategies will need to be devised to fund programs that manage the behavioral complications of dementia. This will not be a simple task. The research findings, however, show that a better job can be done in managing behavior. There will be a high payoff in patient and family well-being if ways can be found to fund and disseminate these techniques.

2. Elderly people are major users of drug therapy for a variety of ailments including heart disease, arthritis, nervous disorders, digestive problems, and pre- and postsurgical care. Much is unknown about the effect of various types and dosages of drugs on the bodily systems of older persons, yet drugs are prescribed with overconfidence. One of the findings of the research is that medication use and its side effects may produce reversible dementia in 15 percent of persons diagnosed as demented. Obviously, there is the potential of a high human and financial return if something can be done to reduce drug-induced dementia. More clinical research is called for, but more can be done now about managing the problem. For instance, attention can be given to the potential points of effective intervention to reduce side effects by properly diagnosing and correcting them. The potential for successful interventions may increase as more organized systems of medical care grow (for example, HMOs, group practices). The effect of reimbursement on prescribing patterns also needs to be considered by any program aimed at reducing the misuse of medications.

3. A third area for intervention is the overlap between health and mental health services. One of the findings in this book is that mental and physical health problems co-occur to a significant degree. What opportunities does this offer for improving the well-being of older persons? First, there is a need to take a close look at the treatment barriers between the mental and physical health systems. Are these knowledge or structural barriers? What impact do reimbursement systems have on maintaining the separation of health and mental health services? What models have been successful in integrating these two elements? Are some state mental hospitals providing good medical care along with good psychiatric care? Are some community mental health centers using medical resources effectively? To what extent are HMO models using psychiatric resources as a means of reducing the demand on scarce medical services? The answers to these questions should be sought and programmatic implications pursued.

4. Concern with the mental health needs of older persons means a concern with nursing homes. The research finding that "nursing homes are major sites for the care of persons with mental illness but do a poor job" demands action. Little is known about the mental health needs of nursing home residents. More research is required to determine whether the mental illnesses of nursing home patients are organic, medication-induced, or psychological. The needs of nursing home residents have been ignored while press and politician have bewailed conditions in these institutions. Nursing homes face great difficulty in attracting and training staff, obtaining medical care, and maintaining the privacy and dignity of their residents. The time has come for a major national project to examine all aspects of the mental health–nursing home situation. Such an examination would review the following: the role of the nursing home in the system of care for older persons (there are other residential care models that may be better for mentally disabled older persons than nursing homes); the

admission process; the nature of the case mix; types of service required; use of self-help groups; medication practices; training of staff; staffing requirements; delivery of medical care; patient privacy and rights; and the impact of reimbursement policy. Until such a comprehensive review is undertaken, nursing home policy will continue to flounder.

5. The linkages or lack of linkages between the mental health and aging systems are documented in chapter 7. Shane correctly identifies the problems that limit coordination between these systems, and she proposes a set of common activities that may lead to the development of formal linkages and joint activities. Although linkages with departments and mental health are desirable, elder advocates should not make such linkages the exclusive target of their efforts. The well-known difficulties that these official systems experience in serving the elderly, despite good will on the part of participants, raises the question of the extent to which state departments of mental health should be considered as a resource to organizations concerned with the mental well-being of older persons. Although these departments often have large budgets, structural and political factors limit their capacity to respond to the needs of older persons. State departments are reluctant to hospitalize older patients and seek out Medicare-funded beds.

The current public concern for chronically mentally ill persons and the homeless may result in older persons being considered a low priority in an environment of competition for resources. The inadequate record of community mental health centers is well documented. Recent changes in both public and insurance-based reimbursement systems may further limit the capacity of CMHCs to serve older persons.

If our goal is to improve the mental well-being of older persons, it may be wise to accept these limitations and think of new ways of approaching the problem. Funds for mental health services should be added to the budgets of senior citizen centers; medical facilities should add a mental health perspective to services already covered by third parties; self-help groups should be encouraged; and home-health agencies should build a mental health orientation into their covered services. In addition, retiree health benefits and Medi-gap policies need to consider mental health services.

The research findings reported in this book indicate that the linkages between the official mental health and aging systems are not adequate. It may make sense to invest limited time and energy into forging such linkages, but not at the expense of alternatives that may prove more promising.

We have identified five areas of potential intervention on behalf of older persons with mental health needs. These areas, for the most part, cut across the topics covered in this book. They are not the only ideas for intervention and they may not be the best. They do, however, illustrate how the findings of research can be used as a basis for policy and program development. It is our hope that these program ideas will be taken seriously and, to the extent possible, implemented.

Conclusions

Elinore E. Lurie
James H. Swan

T he research and policy implications of efforts to serve the mentally ill elderly emerge from problems and perspectives that cut across all the themes explored in the preceding chapters of this book. Issues of concern span the physical, mental, and psychosocial aspects of mental illness. Synthesis and analysis of the literature concerning the mentally ill elderly suggest research and policy needs and strategies.

Research

There is a need for standard research criteria, particularly in community and epidemiological research and clinical–case studies. Much research suffers from nonsystematic, nonrandom selection of samples; omission of significant subpopulations of the aged; lack of standard, widely accepted definitions and criteria; and disparities in measures. These problems make it hard to cumulate research results. Clinical case studies suffer in particular from lack of standard diagnostic criteria defining "caseness" and from the lack of conversion criteria for studies using earlier diagnostic nomenclature schemes. The absence of accepted definitions makes effective research and intervention difficult (see, for example, chapter 8).

We are not calling here for emphasis on any single research model, such as experimental studies. Indeed, the field needs multiple approaches to mental illness in the elderly. Nor are we calling for the application of clinical diagnostic criteria so rigorous as to rule out symptomatology (of depression and anxiety, for example) not meeting the criteria. We suggest, rather, that for detecting the common problems of the elderly that are amenable to intervention, symptom checklists appear much more on target than does the application of strict diagnostic criteria.

Standards of scientific rigor need to be developed, nevertheless, and consensus obtained on them. Perhaps the National Institute of Mental Health could take the lead in developing such criteria through the use of conferences and the dissemination of conference results.

Conceptually, research on mental illness in the elderly should distinguish genetic factors that appear to predispose toward mental illness at given stages in the life cycle; variables from earlier in the life cycle that appear to be risk factors for mental illness in later life (for example, heavy drinking at midlife); socioeconomic variables (for example, poverty) associated with poor mental health all along the life span; and variables directly associated with poor mental health in old age (for example, physiological changes and illnesses). This research would in turn suggest who is at risk, when intervention should take place, and what types of interventions are most effective.

Research is particularly needed on effective treatment modalities for the elderly. The literature strongly suggests that modification is necessary in traditional psychotherapeutic approaches and pharmacological treatments. More research is needed on behavioral and cognitive therapies and self-help groups, and their adaptation to the needs and habits of the elderly. Much of the research on effectiveness fails to meet scientific criteria.

Two themes cut across the areas of research and policy: (1) whether interventions, services, and service systems should be oriented toward symptomatology, such as depressive symptoms, rather than to clinically diagnosable entities, such as chronic schizophrenia; and (2) whether interventions, services, and service systems should be oriented toward predictable crises of the life cycle, such as widowhood, poor health, declining income, and other losses of old age, rather than to established mental illness. The lack of agreement in these areas contributes greatly to the lack of coherent mental health and aging research and policy.

At least 25 years of research link depression and other forms of mental illness to poverty—directly and indirectly through poor health. This suggests that at least some of the original premises of the community mental health movement were on target. It is time for the pendulum to swing away from a narrow focus on the biological substrate of mental illness, and back toward a middle ground. The studies reviewed here emphasize psychosocial factors causative and predisposing to poor mental health in old age. Ideally, knowledge of predisposing biological factors (for example, genetic or physiological) would form the background rather than the sole focus of research on the causes of mental illness.

Research is needed on the mentally ill elderly as they are encountered in various settings, particularly nursing homes and residential care. Because such care is often supported by state-allocated or -controlled monies (for example, Medicaid) and is typically resistant to penetration by researchers, coordinated research strategies under state auspices, in conjunction with state agencies, would appear to be the key to gaining research access and cooperation.

Additional policy-oriented research is needed, focusing on mental health reimbursement for the aged. Many studies of third-party mental health coverage have included only small samples of the aged or excluded them altogether.

Finally, there remain areas in which good descriptive research would be useful. Some elderly persons remain in state mental hospitals, for example, and the proportions of such elderly patients vary greatly by state. Relatively little is currently known about this subpopulation of the aged mentally ill and about the conditions of their institutionalization, suggesting the need for good descriptive research on this population. The National Association of State Mental Health Directors has begun the task of describing state mental health expenditures. Additional descriptive work is needed, however, to trace particular funding streams and to consider reimbursement and expenditures at levels other than the state. Research is also needed on innovative strategies that integrate funding streams, coordinate the efforts of multiple agencies to provide comprehensive care for the elderly, keep the elderly in the community, support caregivers, and reduce the use of crisis or acute services.

Policy

The research reviewed and presented here suggests the need to train new kinds of professionals who can span disciplines and agencies. These may include psychiatric nurse practioners, general or family-practice physicians and internists with advanced training in geropsychiatry, and psychiatrists trained in internal medicine and neurology, if not geropsychiatry. Because the present generation of elderly do not tend to use mental health professionals, the first two alternatives may fill more immediate needs. It should be remembered, however, that this underutilization may owe much to the attitudes acquired by the present cohort of elderly persons. Future cohorts will have lived in times and places in which psychiatric services are more acceptable and less stigmatized, and thus may be more willing to use such services.

The proposed discipline-spanning professionals could work in community mental health centers, nursing homes, private office practices, and other agencies that treat and serve elderly clients and their families. These professionals would understand physical and mental health needs in the broadest sense, counsel and treat directly, and train others (including nonprofessionals and semiprofessionals, such as aides in nursing homes) who work directly with the elderly.

Both practitioners and service systems need to bridge disciplines for the coordination of service delivery. This may be accomplished in a number of ways: by granting equal scope of authority and autonomy to agencies serving the elderly; by placing such agencies under the same umbrella organization; by designating liaisons across agencies; and by empowering liaison and interagency coordination with the provision of funds. Interagency coordination should include not only departments of mental health and of aging, but also of long term care.

Because mental health has long been considered a state responsibility, most of this coordination should take place at the state level. Moreover, the state departments and directors of mental health, as well as other state mental health policymakers, remain the key persons in establishing and legitimizing adequate, coordinated service delivery that meets the mental health needs of the aged. Thus, although mental health problems are national in scope and may manifest themselves in important ways at the local level (as with the homeless in decayed central city areas), the state appears to be the key level for setting service delivery and reimbursement policy.

Reimbursement and funding constitute perhaps the most important policy area. Counties, cities, and other local governments do not by themselves have the resources to deal with mental health issues. Most mental health funds are generated by the state, although federal funding is also involved, particularly through Medicaid. Even federal Medicaid funding requires equivalent state matching funds, and is defined as involving fairly narrow exceptions to a general state responsibility to fund mental health care. Although other federal funds, especially through Medicare and the Veterans Administration, bypass the state level, such federal participation is itself severely limited. Mental health coverage by Medicare is narrowly focused. The Veterans Administration serves a well-defined (though large) population for which it has a specific mandate.

Changes are necessary in federal reimbursement policy, particularly Medicare and Medicaid, in order to adequately address the mental health needs of the elderly in acute care, ambulatory care, and long term care settings. Proposed improvements include the extension of Medicare and Medicaid coverage for psychiatric care in SNFs and ICFs (at present, Medicaid coverage is a state option only for those facilities designated as institutions for mental disease), greater coverage of SNF and ICF care generally, and permission and reimbursement for SNF-level and subacute care in acute hospital beds (for example, swing-bed arrangements).

Policy at the federal and state levels needs to be developed for reimbursement that reflects the nature of mental illness, its varying severity, and the multiplicity of treatment modalities that may be needed. As DRGs now stand, they do not begin to address the need for matching treatment to illness, nor allowing for individual or age-related variation.

There is need for more public education about mental illness in the aged. Although public education may currently be adequate to destigmatize dementia for lay persons, this statement cannot be made about depression or other common associates of late life. Because community mental health centers faced with fiscal constraints typically first eliminate public education and consultation, and because the National Institute of Mental Health has redefined its mission to eliminate public education as a goal, new approaches need to be adopted. Such public education might be undertaken by the private sector, including medical schools, advocacy groups, and organizations of mental health professionals.

There is, in brief, a need for innovative policy and rigorous scientific research. This would involve more exploration of innovative treatment modalities for the elderly, including self-help groups; intervention and research on common symptoms, known associates, and causes of mental distress in late life. Research, policy, program development, and service delivery strategies must provide an integrated approach to the various elements contributing to the well-being of the elderly. Policies and funding strategies at both federal and state levels must permit adequate care for the mental, physical, and socioeconomic needs of the elderly. The authors hope that this book has documented these needs as the first step toward their fulfillment.

Author Index

Subject Index